The

Reminiscences

of

Rear Admiral Malcolm F. Schoeffel
U. S. Navy (Retired)

U. S. Naval Institute
Annapolis, Maryland

PREFACE

This volume contains the transcript of six taped interviews with Rear Admiral Malcolm F. Schoeffel, USN (Ret.). Admiral Schoeffel lives in Naples, Florida but the interviews were taped in the home of his son, Captain Peter Schoeffel, USN, in Alexandria, Virginia where the Admiral visited in January and May/June of 1979.

Admiral Schoeffel is an early Naval Aviator. He completed the course at Pensacola in 1921. His account of naval aviation prior to World War II is replete with interesting facts and comments for he is a witty, incisive raconteur. Indeed, the entire narrative is most readable and valuable. The apex of his career came when he became Chief of the Bureau of Ordnance in December, 1950. He served there until December, 1954. Other facets of note to the historian are his duty with the Destroyer Force based on Queenstown, Ireland in World War I, his command of the carrier CABOT in the Pacific during World War II, his various tours of duty in the Bureau of Aeronautics, the Bureau of Ordnance and at Dahlgren Proving Grounds.

Admiral Schoeffel has corrected the original transcript. It has been re-typed and indexed for the convenience of the user.

John T. Mason, Jr.
Director of Oral History
September, 1979

REAR ADMIRAL MALCOLM F. SCHOEFFEL
U. S. NAVY, RETIRED

Malcolm Francis Schoeffel was born in Rochester, New York, on April 3, 1898, son of Lieutenant Colonel Francis Henry Schoeffel, USA, Retired, and the late Anna May (Hinds) Schoeffel. He attended public schools in Rochester and Milbrook, New York, and Scranton, Pennsylvania, and entered the U. S. Naval Academy from the Tenth District of Pennsylvania in 1915. As a Midshipman he was a member of the rifle team, won the Class of 1871 Prize (a Navy dress sword and knot awarded annually for proficiency in practical and theoretical ordnance and gunnery), and also received the cup presented annually by the National Society, Daughters of the American Revolution (for excellence in seamanship and international law). Graduated with distinction, first in his class, and commissioned Ensign on June 6, 1918, with the Class of 1919, he subsequently attained the rank of Rear Admiral to date from July 15, 1943. On February 1, 1955 he was transferred to the Retired List of the U. S. Navy.

After graduation from the Naval Academy in 1918, he was assigned duty with Destroyer Force, based on Queenstown, Ireland, during World War I. He served for a brief period in the USS DIXIE, before his transfer to the USS KIMBERLY. He was on board the KIMBERLY when she engaged the German submarine U-91 off Fastnet, Ireland, on October 17, 1918, and later when she rescued part of the crew of the USS SHAW when that destroyer was cut in two by the AQUITANIA in the English Channel. Detached from the KIMBERLY in October 1919, he joined the USS BROOME at her commissioning, October 31, 1919. He continued to serve in the BROOME while she operated with the Destroyer Force, Atlantic Fleet, and later with the U. S. Naval Forces in Europe.

In June 1920 he was transferred to the USS PITTSBURGH, flagship of U. S. Naval Forces in European Waters, and was on board when she grounded off Libau, Latvia, in the fall of 1920. Detached in May 1921, he returned to the United States and in July of that year reported to the Naval Air Station, Pensacola, Florida, for flight training. Designated Naval Aviator on December 20, 1921, he reported in January 1922 to Air Squadrons, Pacific Fleet (later redesignated Aircraft Squadrons, Battle Fleet), and served with Spotting Squadron 4, and Observation Plane Squadron 1, attached to the USS AROOSTOOK, until June 1923.

After instruction in Aeronautical Engineering at the Postgraduate School, Annapolis, Maryland, and the Massachusetts Institute of Technology at Cambridge, he had duty from June to September 1925 in connection with the inauguration of the course in Aviation at the Naval Academy, Annapolis, Maryland. He then served until August 1927 in the Material Division, Bureau of Aeronautics, Navy Department, Washington, DC. He assisted in the organization of Torpedo Squadron 4 of the aircraft carrier LANGLEY, and in October 1927 joined Torpedo Squadron 2, of Aircraft Squadrons, Battle Fleet, based first on the LANGLEY, and later on the carrier SARATOGA.

In September 1929 he was transferred to duty as Gunnery and Tactical Officer on the staff of the Commander Aircraft Squadrons, Battle Fleet, USS SARATOGA, flagship. He was detached in May 1931 for two years' duty with the Aviation Detail at the Naval Proving Ground, Dahlgren, Virginia. Returning to sea, he served as Aviation Officer on the staff of Commander

Battle Force, (USS CALIFORNIA flagship), from May 1933 until June 1934, when he assumed command of Scouting Squadron 1, based on the aircraft carrier RANGER.

From June 1935 until July 1936 he was on duty in the Divison of Fleet Training, Office of the Chief of Naval Operations, Navy Department, Washington, D.C., and the following year transferred to the Aviation Ordnance Section, Bureau of Ordnance, Navy Department. In June 1938 he joined the airfield carrier SARATOGA as Navigator, and in June 1940 again reported to the Office of the Chief of Naval Operations, for duty in the Ships' Movement Division. In March 1941 he was transferred to the Bureau of Ordnance, and served until April 1943 as Assistant Director for Aviation Ordnance in the Research and Development Division, and as Aviation Assistant to the Chief of that Bureau. During that period he served on various coordinating committees dealing with aircraft armament matters affecting the Navy Department, the War Department, and the British Aircraft Commission.

"For Exceptionally meritorious conduct...while serving in the Bureau of Ordnance as Assistant Director for Aviation Ordnance, Research and Development Division, and later as Aviation Assistant to the Chief of the Bureau, from the outbreak of hostilities until April 28, 1943..." he was awarded the Legion of Merit. The citation continues: "Charged with the responsibility of guiding research and development in the entire field of aviation ordnance, Rear Admiral Schoeffel directed the coordination of ordnance developments under his cognizance with aircraft developments undertaken by the Bureau of Aeronautics, thereby assuring continued improvements which have been effective and important in the success of aviation operations of the Fleet. By his untiring efforts, exceptional technical skill and practical judgment, Rear Admiral Schoeffel has contributed materially to the extraordinary record of naval aviation and to the successful prosecution of the war."

Also for meritorious service on the Coordinating Committees, he was awarded the Order of the British Empire (Honorary Officer, Military Division) by the British Government.

After fitting out the USS CABOT, he assumed command upon her commissioning July 24, 1943. Under his command, that aircraft carrier took aboard Air Group 31 and proceeded in November 1943 to Pearl Harbor, T.H., where she joined the Pacific Fleet. Following training exercises, she joined the famous Task Force 58 in January 1944, and took part in the ensuing air strikes on Iwajalein, Roiad and Namur in the Marshalls. On February 16-17 she participated in the initial strike against the Japanese stronghold of Truk. Returning to the Carolines in March, her Air Group assisted in the complete destruction of attacking enemy planes before they could reach the Force. Later that month, she participated in the air attacks on Woleai Island, Palau and Angaur, Hollandia, Wake and the Samar Area, and in the further strike against Truk on April 29-30.

"For distinguished professional excellence in the line of his profession as Commanding Officer of the USS CABOT during the attakcs on the key Japanese base at Truk Atoll in the Caroline Islands on 16-17 February 1944..." he received a Letter of Commendation, with authorization to wear the Commendation Ribbon, from the Commander in Chief, Pacific.

He is also entitled to the Ribbon for, and a facsimile of the Presidential Unit Citation awarded the USS CABOT.

Detached from the CABOT on May 5, 1944, he served briefly as Commander, Carrier Transport Squadrons, Pacific Fleet, before reporting on June 15, 1944 as Assistant Chief of Staff (Operations) to the Commander in Chief, U. S. Fleet. Later that month he was assigned additional duty as a member of the Special Joint Chiefs of Staff Committee on the Reorganization of National Defense. In August 1945, following the capitulation of the Japanese, he was ordered to duty as Deputy Chief of Staff to the Commander in Chief, Pacific Fleet and Pacific Ocean Areas.

On April 1, 1946 he reported as Deputy Chief and Assistant Chief of the Bureau of Ordnance, Navy Department, Washington, DC. On January 3, 1949 he assumed command of Carrier Division 6, and as Commander Task Force 28 of the Atlantic Fleet participated in numerous exercises in the Atlantic and Mediterranean. From May 1950 he was in command of the Naval Air Test Center, Patuxent River, Maryland. On December 27, 1950 he became Chief of the Bureau of Ordnance, the first Naval Aviator to serve as Chief of that Bureau. He was hospitalized from December 1954 until his retirement, effective February 1, 1955.

In addition to the Legion of Merit, the Commendation Ribbon, and the Presidential Unit Citation Ribbon, Rear Admiral Schoeffel has the Victory Medal, Destroyer Clasp; the American Defense Service Medal, Fleet Clasp; Asiatic-Pacific Campaign Medal; American Campaign Medal; World War II Victory Medal; and the National Defense Service Medal. He also has been awarded the Order of the British Empire, Honorary Officer, Military Division.

On August 31, 1925 he and Miss Grace Marcia Briggs were married. They have two daughters and a son. Their present address is 19 Glen Drive, Alexandria, Virginia.

Navy Biographies Section, 01-140
24 August 1955

DECLARATION OF TRUST

The undersigned does hereby appoint and designate as his (her) Trustee herein, the Secretary-Treasurer and Publisher of the United States Naval Institute to perform and discharge the following duties, powers, and privileges in connection with the possession and use of a certain taped interview between the undersigned and the Oral History Department of the United States Naval Institute.

1. Classification of Transcript.

(X)a. If classified <u>OPEN</u>, the transcript(s) may be read or the recording(s) audited by the qualified personnel upon presentation of proper credentials, as determined by the Secretary-Treasurer of the U.S. Naval Institute.

( )b. If classified <u>PERMISSION REQUIRED TO CITE OR QUOTE</u>, the user will be required to obtain permission in writing from the interviewee prior to quoting or citing from either the transcript(s) or the recording(s).

( )c. If classified <u>PERMISSION REQUIRED</u>, permission must be obtained in writing from the interviewee before the transcribed interview(s) can be examined or the tape recording(s) audited.

( )d. If classified <u>CLOSED</u>, the transcribed interview(s) and the tape recording(s) will be sealed until a time specified by the interviewee. This may be until the death of the interviewee or for any specified number of years.

2. It is expressly understood that in giving this authorization, I am in no way precluded from placing such restrictions as I may desire upon use of the interview at any time during my lifetime, nor does this authorization in any way affect my rights to the copyright of my literary expressions that may be contained in the interview.

I hereby classify it "Open".

Witness my hand and seal this 6th day of July 1979

Malcolm F. Schoeffel

I hereby accept and consent to the foregoing Declaration of Trust and the powers therein conferred upon me as Trustee:

R E Bowen Jr

Interview #1 with Rear Admiral Malcolm F. Schoeffel,
U.S. Navy (Retired)

Place: The residence of his son, Captain Peter Schoeffel, U.S. Navy, in Alexandria, Virginia

Date: Friday morning, 5 January 1979

Subject: Biography

By: John T. Mason, Jr.

Q: Admiral, it's delightful to see you. Your name has been on my list for a very long time, so I welcomed the opportunity to talk with your son and learn that you were coming up here. Your career is a very significant one and one that I should like to have covered for our oral-history collection.

Would you begin a talking biography in the proper way, Sir, by telling me the date and place of your birth, something about your family background, which is military, I believe. Then we'll go on to the Naval Academy.

Adm. S.: Certainly. Mrs. Schoeffel said I might show you these which she has just recently put together. This is my grandfather, this is my father, this is myself, and here's my son in his youth. She's going to hang these up somewhere or other.

Q: Quite a lovely family record! Your father was in the Army?

Adm. S.: Yes, and he was retired in 1904, physical disability resulting from a wound received in a savage little jungle fight down in Samar.

Q: In the Philippines?

Adm. S.: Yes. He graduated from West Point in 1891, where he played in the line of the first Army football team and was also catcher of the baseball team. He took part in the expedition to Cuba in 1898 with the Ninth Infantry and then, after that war was over, was sent out to the Philippines and they took part in suppressing the original Philippine Insurrection. Then they went up to China as part of the China Relief Expedition, and at that point, my father got very sick with dysentery and had to be sent home. Upon his recovery, he was ordered to rejoin the regiment in Peking and he took my mother and me with him in the old transport <u>Buford</u>.

I had a sister who did not go along because she got so excessively sick in a railroad car, in railroad cars, they were afraid to take her.

Well, I was about two and a half or three years old at the time -

Q: You had been born where?

Adm. S.: I was born in 1898 in Rochester, New York. As I say, I went along with them, but I was so young I have next to no recollection of any of this - a few very minor vignettes of this and that and the other thing is all I remember.

After some months up there, my father's regiment was pulled out of China and ordered down to Samar, and my mother, who was a very spunky little person, thereupon took me, I don't know just how, whether we went through Manchuria and Korea or not - anyhow, I know we went to Seoul, in Korea. She took me there. Then we went on down to Nagasaki, where we stayed for some months with a very cosmopolitan family. The husband was a Japanese medico, Dr. Saganama. His wife was an American doctor, and they had adopted a Russian boy of about my own age.

Q: Oh, my!

Adm. S.: They were really a mixed group.

I have no recollection of how we got back to the States. When my father was, as I say, eventually retired, about 1904, he went into business in Rochester, New York, then the business got burned out and we moved to eastern New York, to the little village of Millbrook. We were there for three years, and I had a very happy boyhood.

Schoeffel #1 - 4

Q: It's a lovely community.

Adm. S.: Then father went with the Lackawanna Railroad as what they called their chief special agent, which meant their chief of police, and we moved to Scranton. I lived there with my parents for five years, then went to the Naval Academy.

Q: Were you the only child?

Adm. S.: No, I had -

Q: A sister, that's right.

Adm. S.: Yes. She was some five years older than I. She died about ten years ago.

Q: I see.

Adm. S.: To return to my grandfather, he had been a soldier on the Union side in the Civil War. He had actually first enlisted, and this is according to a paper I recently found, in the New York national guard in 1855. By the time the Civil War broke out, he was a captain in command of a company, and, by the time he was mustered out, he was lieutenant colonel of a regiment. He had been wounded in one of the battles in early 1863. I forget which one it was. I remember when I was a small boy, if he was feeling very simpatico toward me, he'd let me sit in his lap and feel his hip and feel the bullet in there!

He had the distinction in the early 1880s of being the first Democrat elected to anything in Monroe County, New York, for a generation, since the formation of the Republican party. He was elected sheriff and, apparently, was a pretty good one. All his life he was influential in the Grand Army of the Republic, the GAR, the Civil War veterans' organization.

Q: I remember them on Memorial Days.

Adm. S.: Yes, that was their great day.
   Well, so much.

Q: How did you happen to become interested in the Naval Academy, with a military background?

Adm. S.: It started so early I don't remember when. I presume it was a result of our voyage around the world. By the way, it's the only time I've ever been around the world. But I know that ever since I was six or seven years old I wanted to go in the navy.

Q: Isn't that interesting? And your father encouraged this ambition?

Schoeffel #1 - 6

Adm. S.: He did, yes, because he said his experience was that the navy lived a hell of a sight better than the army.

Q: And they also got to see the world, to a greater degree, perhaps.

So your early education was in the schools in Scranton?

Adm. S.: Yes, public schools, first in Rochester, then in Millbrook, then in Scranton. And I want to say a word of praise for the Central High School in Scranton as it was in those days. They certainly taught us a lot. There's another retired admiral down in Naples now, Clint Misson, who was about my time, he came along a couple of years afterwards, who also went through Central High School and he speaks as highly of it as I do. And there's another gentleman, a Mr. Evans, down there who went through that high school some years later, and he feels about the same way.

Q: Well, Sir, tell me about the problem of entering the Naval Academy. You got a congressional appointment?

Adm. S.: Yes, I got a congressional appointment from Mr. John R. Farr, who was then the congressman from Scranton. He held a competitive examination for the appointment, and I was fortunate enough to win it.

Q: You got the principal appointment?

Adm. S.: Yes. Then I reported to the Naval Academy in June and was promptly bilged physically because of varicose veins.

Q: In your legs?

Adm. S.: Yes. They required a small operation, which my father arranged for, and I got in sometime in July. I don't remember the exact date of entering there. I remember the heat, however!

Q: Oh, yes, plebe summer in the heat of Annapolis! Quite different from Pennsylvania in the mountains.

Did you take to the navy life immediately? Plebe summer is a pretty drastic thing.

Adm. S.: Well, I expected it to be. I saw no reason why it should be otherwise, and I think that I took to it quite readily. I know I never regretted my decision.

Q: You were prepared for the regimented kind of life that you experienced there.

Adm. S.: Yes.

Q: This was wartime when you entered?

Adm. S.: No, this was in 1915.

Q: I mean war was going on in Europe.

Adm. S.: Yes, World War I was under way at that time, but the United States was not in it, by any means.

In the 1916 election, when Wilson got re-elected on the program that he'd kept us out of war and so forth, and the very next spring he was telling the officers of the Atlantic Fleet, I understand, that we should use "force, force without stint or limit," or words to that effect.

Q: So this was a different attitude that he'd developed within the year?

Adm. S.: Yes.

Q: Was there any reflection of the war situation in Europe in the life at the academy?

Adm. S.: Amazingly little. The only way that it really impinged on our lives was that over Christmas of 1917 I was in the hospital first with mumps and then with German measles, and when I came out of the hospital I discovered that a great change had come over my class in the academy.

Schoeffel #1 - 9

All hands were obeying the regulations most assiduously!

Well, it seems that one of my classmates had a girl who looked with grave disfavor upon the way most of the midshipmen were trying to get away with things. So she bawled her midshipman friend out to such an extent that while I was in the hospital he had called a class meeting and made such a powerful oration that the class took resolutions to be very regulation from then on.

Q: What was the basis of her argument?

Adm. S.: Her argument was that the United States was at war and it behooved us to act differently from the way we had been acting.

Q: And it took a young lady to do this rather than the superintendent of the academy?

Adm. S.: Oh, yes. Well, this reform move lasted about a month, then all things drifted back to their normal state of non-regulation, if you could get away with it.

Q: How large a class was this?

Adm. S.: We entered 270 and I think we graduated 190. The next class, 1920, was the first one of the so-called large classes. They came in with 400 and some.

Schoeffel #1 - 10

Q: Tell me a little about academy life in that period.

Adm. S.: Gee, I don't know what to say.

Q: What about the classes? I mean did you have any electives or was it all required?

Adm. S.: In the studies, no, there were no electives. There were just the various prescribed courses and, after the first year or two, we could all see that they were very sensible and very necessary to the naval profession. None of us had any objections thereto that I know of.

Q: They were all profession-oriented courses? There were very few liberal arts courses, were there not?

Adm. S.: There were very few liberal arts courses, but a naval officer has very little use for the liberal arts.

Q: Except as background.

Adm. S.: Yes.

Q: I mean if he's going to be an ambassador-at-large, so to speak, he had to have some cultural background.

Adm. S.: I don't suppose you ever met the president of my

class, Admiral L. C. Stevens. He's been dead for fifteen or twenty years now.

Q: No.

Adm. S.: His widow lives down in Annapolis. He was probably the closest to a liberal arts man of anybody in our class. It was said that he had given up a Rhodes scholarship to come to the Naval Academy, which most of us thought was rather foolish of him.

Q: As you reflect on the course you received in those years at the academy, what is your estimate of it?

Adm. S.: It could be called narrow. You see, my class only had three years. We were the class of 1919 but we were graduated in the summer of 1918. We only had three years, so that I have the feeling that most of what we got was a little on the smattering side. Certainly the mathematics we got was. I didn't really understand mathematics until I later went to postgraduate school.

I took Spanish at Annapolis and I loved that language. I think it's a great language. It has its rules and it obeys them. Innumerable times since then I've made up my mind that I'm going to study Spanish again, but I never have!

Q: The best way to study it is to be exposed to Spaniards and talk it. There are plenty of them in Florida nowadays! Have the Cubans come over to Naples?

Adm. S.: Oh, some have, and the local cable television runs a channel in Spanish for the Cuban-speaking people, and I cannot understand a word of the Spanish they talk. It's much too fast.

Q: Then, of course, it's kind of a bastardized Spanish, too.

Adm. S.: I suppose so, different from the Castilian they tried to teach us at the Naval Academy.

Q: Yes. What were the facilities like at the Naval Academy? Was Bancroft Hall - ?

Adm. S.: They were quite adequate for those days, certainly up to the level of almost any modest-priced hotel.

Q: What about the athletic program?

Adm. S.: The athletic program was very much to the fore. I was neither big enough nor muscular enough to make any of the normal athletic teams, so the one I could get in on was the rifle team.

Just before an Army game, of course, at 9:30 at night,

we'd get out in the corridors and hold raucous snake dances up and down the place.

Q: What sort of leave program did you have in those days? Were you allowed in town very much?

Adm. S.: Not a great deal, no. Things began to ease up on the subject of leave our plebe year, because we were permitted to have a few days' Christmas leave, and I went home for Christmas. That was something that had been unheard of before.

Q: Indeed.

Adm. S.: As I say, the leave program began to get a little easier than it had been. As far as going out in town, as I recall, if we were not walking the terrace for extra duty, why, we were allowed out Saturday afternoon and Sunday afternoon.

Q: Did you have much of a relationship with townspeople?

Adm. S.: Townspeople? I had none whatever, myself.

Q: You didn't have a young lady there?

Adm. S.: No, I had none whatever myself. There wasn't a

great deal. The townspeople looked upon us as a nuisance and we derisively called them all crabs!

Q: So, it was pretty much an isolated and closed community.

Adm. S.: Yes, except when we would go out to go to the movies and stop at - oh, I don't remember the name of the place, but we got a chocolate sundae for about a nickel or a dime.

Q: Muhlenberg, I think was the name, was it not?

Adm. S.: I don't think it was that name. It was on the corner of Maryland Avenue and, I think, Prince George Street.

Q: What about your summers?

Adm. S.: Well, of course, the summers were cruises. The year before, the annual cruise had gone out to the West Coast and had been considered very fine by the upper classmen. But, with a war on, our cruise, our youngster cruise, was not a very interesting one. We were embarked in three old battleships. I was in the Wisconsin, and then there were the Ohio and the Missouri. We went down to the West Indies and anchored somewhere to the east of Puerto Rico. On the way out the capes of the Chesapeake, we ran into our only violent weather and - well, there were quite a number who were violently seasick. I was fortunate enough not to be among them, but I remember one classmate who was holed up in a hammock netting and suddenly the canvas at the side of thenetting was thrown up and his head appeared and he was as green as that candle over there. The poor fellow, he just retched and then he withdrew. I always remember his face sticking out there.

We went from Puerto Rico down to Guantánamo, which is a wonderful place to spend the 4th of July. Guantánamo, in recent years, has become a lovely spot, but in those days it was the far end of creation. We had the pleasure of coaling ship down there in the heat.

Q: That, indeed, is a pleasure, isn't it?

Adm. S.: Yes! We came up the east coast. I'm not sure where we went first, but I think it was Portland, Maine. We got a little liberty there, then we went to Boston and got some more liberty there, and we re-coaled there. Then as I recall it, we returned to the Naval Academy, so that was no great shakes of a cruise.

Q: Now, let me ask. An experience of that sort was difficult in some sense, did it dissuade some of your classmates from continuing to be sailors?

Adm. S.: I don't think so. I don't know of anybody who

resigned as a result.

The next year, the United States was in World War I and so we did not go off on a midshipmen's cruise. We were sent down to York River, where all the battleships were based at the time, and we were distributed in small groups, comparatively small groups, among the battleships. We spent our three months there. I was in the group on board the Oklahoma, which at that time was one of the newest of our battleships. She was a very impressive vessel, too.

Q: What did she have, 14-inch guns?

Adm. S.: Yes, she had ten 14-inch guns, two three-gun turrets and two two-gun high turrets.

The only time we got to sea was along in August, when the fleet shifted its base from there, from the York River, to Port Jefferson, I think it was, on the north shore of Long Island, and we went out to sea. I didn't get very much on that trip to sea because I was sick in some way or other. I guess I had the 'flu or something like that and was turned in all the time we were at sea.

Then, immediately upon our arrival up there, all the midshipmen were taken off and were embarked in the cruiser San Diego, the one that was later mined off Fire Island. We were all embarked there and sent back to Annapolis to start our September leave. I was still in the sick bay throughout that trip back, and upon arrival off Annapolis,

I got up on deck and I almost fainted, upon getting on deck. I never have at any other time of my life. I went ashore with the rest, and my roommate and I stopped at the old Maryland Hotel and got ourselves a nice, juicy steak. As soon as I had eaten that, I felt all right.

Q: You'd recovered!

Adm. S.: I had recovered.

Q: Does this say something about navy food?

Adm. S.: Well, yes. The navy was having a very difficult time feeding its sailors in those days because it was still held by law to a ration of thirty cents a day. Prices had already gone up a good deal and it was very difficult to feed a crew on any such amount as that, so the mess was pretty poor.

Q: That's why the steak at the Maryland Inn was very welcome!

Adm. S.: Perhaps. At the Naval Academy, of course, we drew our thirty cents a day, but we also chipped in from our pay, so that our ration while we were at the Naval Academy normally ran us about twenty-five dollars a month. In other words, something like eighty cents a day.

Q: You supplemented that from your pay?

Adm. S.: Yes.

Q: What was your pay?

Adm. S.: Our pay was fifty dollars a month and, until our first-class year, fifteen dollars a month of this was withheld to be available upon graduation for the purchase of uniforms. Well, prices had gone up so much that they stopped this withholding so that we were getting our fifty dollars a month plus our thirty cents a day for rations - as I say, it would cost us, perhaps, twenty-five dollars a month for the mess, and then we had to buy our uniforms, our books, and so forth, and have some spending money. As first classmen, we drew - well, as under-classmen we had drawn one dollar a month for spending money. As first classmen, I think we were allowed to draw three dollars a month and a candy ticket worth one dollar.

Q: You couldn't go on very extensive sprees with that kind of income!

Adm. S.: I remember when I got home from my first-class cruise, I think I had something like thirty dollars available for September leave.

Q: Did you supplement that from your father in any sense?

Adm. S.: Well, my father, yes; but there were many midshipmen whose families did not supplement it. Some did, some didn't. They weren't supposed to. My father did on the basis that he would pay me a dollar every time I stood three in any subject for the month, two dollars if I stood two, and three dollars if I stood one in a subject. I was very fortunate in that I had a very strong ability to take examinations, make good marks on examinations, so that I frequently pulled down some money from my father!

Q: Learning there was, in large measure, by rote, was it not?

Adm. S.: No, I won't say that. Of course, some was by rote but, Lord, there were all kinds of original problems that were thrown at you in the various courses.

Q: You came out as number one in your class.

Adm. S.: I did, yes.

Q: That was quite an honor, and with it came awards, didn't they?

Adm. S.: Yes. I got a sword from the class I think of '71,

a very fine sword, which I have now given to my son, and I got a couple of cups and things like that.

Q: Were you a model midshipman, or did you get demerits during the course of your career?

Adm. S.: I am one of the few who was ever put on the report for mutiny.

Q: For mutiny!

Adm. S.: For mutiny.

Q: Tell me about that.

Adm. S.: Shortly before Christmas 1917, I, along with a couple of dozen others, got the mumps. We were all sent over to the Naval Hospital and we were all put into a single big basement room. We were to be there three weeks or four weeks, I forget which. A few of us were really sick all that time and needed all that time to get well, but most of us were all recovered in three or four days and we had lots of high spirits and what were we going to do about it? Well, the result was quite a number of roughhouses, and one night after taps we carried out quite a heavy roughhouse down there. We made considerable noise. Finally, we settled down and returned to our bunks but unfortunately, or, maybe, it was forethought on somebody's part, one bunk was left turned over on its side right across the doorway into this room. All of a sudden, the officer of the day, a doctor, came charging through this door without seeing what was there and he took a marvelous fall. Oh, how wonderful.

Well, he lined us all up and he spat fire and brimstone and all the rest, and I being the senior midshipman, he put me on report for leading a mutiny. Fortunately for me, this was the time when reserve ensigns were having a three-month course, the ninety-day wonders, and one of them was there, too.

So, after I got back to duty, the commandant - oh, gee, I can't think of his name, he was later commander in chief of the Pacific Fleet - well, never mind, he called me in and talked very seriously about this matter for a while, then, finally, he said:

"Well, as you were really not the senior person present, I think we can drop this matter."

Q: What was the punishment for mutiny? Being dismissed, I suppose.

Adm. S.: Oh, it would have been a court-martial and all kinds of things!

Q: Other than that, you were a model midshipman?

Adm. S.: Not exactly. I got demerits, but not very many. I had great difficulty keeping myself adequately clean and I was frequently - not frequently but from time to time - put on report for lint on uniforms, shoes not properly shined, and things like that.

Q: You had great difficulty or lacked inclination to do that, which?

Adm. S.: I have never been able to keep myself really and truly clean! As a small boy, all my friends would go out and play and they would be marvelous to look at when we got through and I would be a mess. All my life, I've never been able to be spruce and "point de vice."

Q: Well, now you came to graduation, which was one of those early graduations.

Adm. S.: Yes, June 1918.

Q: Were you able to state a preference for the kind of assignment you wanted?

Adm. S.: Yes. I, along with many of us, requested destroyer duty and eventually got it. I didn't get it right away. My first assignment was to the then-largest ship in the world, the Leviathan in the Cruiser and Transport Force.

One of my classmates, Schildhauer, also was there. The two of us went to the Leviathan, and we did one round-trip on her from Hoboken to Brest and back, carrying troops.

Q: What were your particular duties in her?

Adm. S.: We stood watches, fire-control watches, and we also stood junior officer of the deck watches. The senior officers of the deck were all quite elderly naval reserve merchant seamen, and they were a delightful bunch. They were old salts from way back. Of course, they were brought up in the tradition that the oncoming officer of the watch - I mean the officer of the watch - stood his watch on the weather wing of the bridge.

Well, the Leviathan was a fast ship. We went bowling across at 24 or 25 knots and the weather was very good. The relative wind was almost dead ahead all the time and it was very difficult to determine which one was the weather wing! The fellow with whom I stood watches, old Mr. Foster, would come up on the bridge and he would look around and sniff the wind. If he concurred with the man he was going to relieve, he'd go right over there and get down to business. But, if he didn't concur, he'd stand there around the wheel and the binnacle and so forth and huff and puff, and the other fellow would stay out on the bridge wing. It was a great big bridge, eighty or ninety feet from one side to the other, and they'd stand there and glare at each other and finally one of them would say:

"Don't you know the customs of the sea?" or words to that effect.

Eventually, they'd get together on mutual territory and there would be a relief and off they'd go. But I got a lot of amusement out of watching these old salts perform.

Q: What kind of wardroom life did you have on board?

Adm. S.: This was very plush, very plush. There had been two dining rooms in the vessel when she was a liner. There had been one on an upper level, which was smaller and much more plush than that on the lower level. All the army officers were assigned to the lower level and all the naval officers were assigned to the upper level.

Q: This wasn't just an accident?

Adm. S.: No, it wasn't just an accident and the army resented it very much.

I found myself sitting up there in our region, which had some very fancy French name - the Ritz. We all sat at small tables, and I was at a table with just two others. One was Captain - I can't think of his name. He was a famous old shellback who went over to France and took command of the navy railroad batteries over there. Do you remember his name?

Q: No.

Adm. S.: He had his aide with him who was Jay Gould, Jr., no less. Well, these two had a great deal to talk about between themselves, nothing to say to me, and I had nothing to add to the conversation, but I listened a lot.

As I say, the meals were very good up there and, as far as my quarters were concerned, I don't know how this came about, but I was assigned to a stateroom under the bridge. It was surely as large as this room here, it had two double beds in it and its own bathroom.

Q: This for an ensign?

Adm. S.: Oh, an ensign, the greenest of ensigns. This room had previously been assigned to the ship's chief carpenter. Well, when they made the ship over into a transport, they ripped out all the fresh-water connections in all the cabins in the ship with the exception of that for the captain, that for the executive officer, and shush, that for the chief carpenter! He, being in charge of this, had fresh water. I fell heir to his room, somehow or other, and I fell heir to his fresh water.

Well, as I say, this was very, very plush. In later years I asked some questions about how much it would have cost to make a one-way trip in that ship when the _Leviathan_ was running as a liner for the United States Line. It was an amazing amount of money. The figure I have in mind, which is probably wrong, is $5,000 for a one-way trip.

Q: I have a friend who was a naval architect and he made several trips across in the Leviathan when she was a troop carrier. His purpose was to rectify the ventilation system, which was very poor, he said.

Adm. S.: I don't recall anything about the ventilation system.

Q: How many troops did you carry over on that trip?

Adm. S.: Something like 10,000. It was a very large number. They were fed only two meals a day, the troops at large. Then, upon arrival in Brest, why, of course, they disembarked as rapidly as possible, and we set to to coal ship. That was a very tough job because, first off, the French brought the coal out in lighters where the coal was down in holds, instead of being on a flag, even top deck. It's vastly easier to dig coal by digging from the side of the pile than it is to dig it by digging down from the top. So that made it hard.

Q: The leverage is different.

Adm. S.: Yes.

She was coaled by putting all this coal in through ports in her side, coaling ports, and, in order to get up to these coal ports, we filled baskets, wicker bushel baskets or, maybe, two-bushel baskets, with the coal. Then we had wooden stagings rigged on the side, and two men on each level would pass the basket up maybe three stages and dump it in there. This coaling went on day and night without cessation for three or four days. No individual was on all that time. It would be eight hours on the coal pile and sixteen hours off.

Q: Eight hours would be pretty strenuous, I would think.

Adm. S.: Yes, it was strenuous, plenty strenuous.

At the end of that time, it was announced that we had put on board some thousands of tons. I don't recall whether it was five or seven thousand tons. The command was very well pleased with the celerity with which the ship had been coaled, et cetera, et cetera. Then we turned round and went back.

When we got back to Hoboken -

Q: What cargo did you take back, if anything?

Adm. S.: Very little. We had perhaps a thousand men on board who were being sent back for one reason or another. Something of that sort, but not very many.

Q: Did she go unescorted?

Adm. S.: She was escorted only in the vicinity of the French coast, because at 24 or 25 knots she was one of the fastest ships in the world in those days, big ships, anyway, and we ran without an escort.

Q: Submarines were certainly not able to keep up with anything like that.

Adm. S.: Yes, nothing like that.

Q: Did you zigzag?

Adm. S.: I don't remember.
 The contrast between coaling at Hoboken and in Brest was breathtaking.

Q: In what sense?

Adm. S.: A bunch of coal barges were brought alongside. Then they were eased up alongside with electrically driven coal hoists. Down in the coal barge there would be one civilian in each barge who would push the coal over to the hoist and up it would come and go down the coal chutes. Well, I suppose the black gang had almost as much work to do in Hoboken as they did in Brest, because this coal had to be evened up in the bunkers. But, as far as the deck force was concerned, there was nothing to it.

Q: This is an example of American ingenuity!

Adm. S.: Yes.

Q: You made only one trip in the Leviathan?

Adm. S.: Made one trip, yes, then hung around New York for a while awaiting orders. Then I was ordered on board the British liner Lapland. There were quite a number of other junior officers, not in the Lapland, but in other ships of the same convoy.

Q: Was the Lapland a troop carrier?

Adm. S.: Yes, she was carrying 3,000 or 4,000 troops, the Wildcat Division from the mountains of Carolina.

I went on board there expecting to have nothing to do and found myself faced with a considerable responsibility because there were 500 completely unorganized, I won't say "disorganized," but completely unorganized sailors on board there. They had been sent in by drafts from quite a number of training stations. There were 500 of them and they had no over-all organization whatever, except that the ship's officers had said that they should be quartered on the promenade deck. Well, that sounds all very lovely, but the promenade deck in days of peace had been glassed in with big glass ports. They had all been removed so the cold and wintery breezes blew right through the promenade deck. They had billet hooks up there for the sailors' hammocks and insisted that all the hammocks be put in certain hammock mannings each morning.

Well, they didn't know what a sailor's hammock was like, because their hammock mannings were about twice the size of this couch.

I found myself the senior U.S. naval officer on board, and these 500 sailors very badly needing somebody to represent them, so I had to turn to on this. In these 500 I found only three or four men who had had any previous military experience whatever. There was one old aviation chief machinist's mate. I remember him with a great deal of respect and gratitude. His name was Rogers. And there was a chief boatswain's mate who, some years before, had done a hitch in the Marines. And there was a Jewish yeoman from New York on duty in the navy. Also there was a blacksmith, but he was about as stupid a man as I've ever run into and was no help whatever.

One of these drafts consisted of about 120 or 130 so-called chief petty officers. They were really watchmakers and had enlisted to be torpedo-upkeep men and given chiefs' ratings, but they didn't know one end of the ship from the other or anything.

I had a terrible time getting control of all these people, but we finally got things organized well enough so that the captain, on his daily inspections of the ship, complimented us upon the cleanliness of our space and so forth, and we eventually got to Liverpool right side up, and I said good-bye to my 500 sailors. I don't know what happened to them after that.

Q: All you men were en route to the UK for assignment, were you?

Adm. S.: Yes.

Q: The Lapland, you say, was in convoy. She didn't have the speed of the Leviathan?

Adm. S.: No. We had a large convoy. The old cruiser Rochester was one of our escorts for a while.

Q: What was the speed of a convoy in that time?

Adm. S.: I don't know.

Q: Very slow, wasn't it?

Adm. S.: It was pretty slow, I suppose around 10 or 12, something like that.

Q: What were the tactics employed by the German submarines? They weren't in packs in those days?

Adm. S.: No, they didn't operate in packs. They were assigned, I believe, areas in which to patrol and look for what they could get.

We went around the north of Ireland to go to Liverpool and, as we went around, with the Irish coast in sight on the starboard hand, it was a beautiful sparkling day. We had a bunch of British destroyers for escort and they were bounding around.

Things were very colorful at sea in that war, with all the ships camouflaged, strange patterns and strange colors and so forth. On a good bright day it was an extremely colorful and elevating sight.

Q: The convoying vessels, were they relieved in mid-ocean, at a mid-ocean point, as they were in World War II, or how was this done?

Adm. S.: I don't know.

Q: Our convoys from New York didn't go all the way across?

Adm. S.: No, I'm pretty sure they didn't. I know that when we started out, as I say, we had the old cruiser _Rochester_ as one of our escorts. I don't know how long she was with us. I know we wound up and came down through St. George's Channel, around the north end of Ireland and we had British destroyers for an escort, but I don't recall whether we had any period without an escort or not. I had nothing to do with that.

Q: No, you were too busy with your 500 men!
What did you do as soon as you got - ?

Adm. S.: As soon as we got to Liverpool, all of us who were bound for Queenstown, Cobh as it is now called, were gotten together. There were a lot of my classmates there who had come over in other ships of the convoy, and they had spent all their time playing bridge or poker while I was trying to keep my sailors out of trouble! We were all put on a small steamer and sent over to Dublin, and we began to run into the horrors of war in Dublin because all they had for us to eat for breakfast was potato and onion pie. Have you ever eaten potato and onion pie?

Q: No.

Adm. S.: Well, I don't recommend it.

Q: I should think it would be very unappetizing for breakfast!

Adm. S.: Then we went by train down to Queenstown. At first, we were all sent over to an old Irish farmhouse on the other side of the bay from the city of Queenstown, called Ballybricken House. Don't ask me how it was spelled, I don't know. This had been taken over first by the British Navy and later by the U.S. Navy and was used as a barracks for people who were awaiting assignments and a lot of enlisted men who were working on torpedo maintenance in the little British navy yard of Haulbowline, which was on an island in the middle of the harbor. Each morning we would all be embarked in boats and go over to Haulbowline, where we junior officers were given instruction in torpedoes, and these men worked on the maintenance of torpedoes.

Then we would be returned to Ballybricken House in the afternoon and spend the night there. From time to time one of our number would be pulled out and assigned to a destroyer. I was there about a month before I got an assignment, and then I went to the destroyer <u>Kimberly</u>, which was No. 80 and one of our then-newest destroyers, one of the first of what were then called the flush-deckers. In World War II the ignorant people we had in the service called them four-pipers. Well, there were lots of high fo'castle four-pipers before the flush-deckers came along.

Q: They had four stacks, anyway!

Adm. S.: Yes.

I went to the Kimberly and she like the others would be sent out to patrol areas or to escort various vessels. One of the most memorable of our escorting jobs was when one time a half-dozen of us were sent out to meet the Acquitania at that time was next to the Leviathan perhaps the largest ship in the world and she was very fast.

We went out to the westward and formed a scouting line in order to contact her and ran into extremely heavy weather, the heaviest weather that I ever saw at sea, though I must say I saw remarkably little heavy weather. This was a real big blow and we had to slow down to 4 or 5 knots. We would pitch back and forth. We'd get down in the trough and the waves would look mountain-high up there and so forth. One poor fellow from another vessel fell overboard and we were not able to recover him.

After this went on for the better part of a day, the Acquitania was sighted and we fell in with her. She was running at about 24 knots. It was very, very difficult for us to keep up in this weather but, fortunately, it was getting better. By midnight, it wasn't bad at all, a big swell running still, though. I stood the mid-watch as junior officer of the deck, and went and turned in. I hadn't been asleep very long when the general alarm sounded. I rushed up on deck and all you could see was darkness and a great mass a flame over in the distance. We didn't know what had happened.

After a while, as day broke, we saw a destroyer, which

we had great difficulty in identifying, minus a bow and heavily on fire up forward. Then there was a bow floating keel up some distance away. There were men in the water and so forth. We stood by and another destroyer, the Jenkins, stood by, while the rest of the escort had gone on with the Acquitania. We put our boats out and cruised around, picked men up, and so forth. The Jenkins went alongside the after part of this burning destroyer. By this time, the fire was pretty well out, and apparently the Jenkins took off all her crew. Our captain was the senior of the two captains present, so he was just considering whether he should torpedo this abandoned wreck and get rid of it or not, when occurred something that was really thrilling. We saw a figure stand up in the after deckhouse of this vessel - she was the Shaw, by the way. He wigwagged over, "Leave me. I am getting under way."

He was the captain of the Shaw and a few men were still on board over there. The after part of the ship was on an even keel, both athwartships and fore and aft, though it was still smoking up around the bridge. She had been cut in two, just forward of the bridge. The bridge was largely smashed, but not entirely so. The bow, as I say, was floating around, keel up.

The captain of the Shaw was a Commander Glassford, who was a rear admiral in World War II.

Q: William Glassford?

Adm. S.: Bill Glassford, yes. He backed that ship about a hundred miles into one of the southern English ports. I don't recall whether it was Portland or Portsmouth, but he backed that ship all that distance, making about 4 or 5 knots, and we and the Jenkins escorting him in.

Q: How did he seal the compartments from the sea?

Adm. S.: I think the forward fire room was flooded but the bulkhead between the forward and after fire rooms held and the engine-room bulkheads held. There were no doors in these bulkheads. To get from one of these compartments to the other you had to go up and over, so as long as that after bulkhead held, the ship just floated as merrily as you pleased.

Q: I understand the Shaw had been cut in two by the Aquitania?

Adm. S.: Yes.

Q: What damage to the Aquitania?

Adm. S.: None, so far as I know. We heard afterwards that practically no one on the Acquitania realized they'd hit anything at all.

The cause of the collision was that the Shaw was in a

position more or less close in on the bow of the Aquitania and was making a turn toward the Aquitania, and was due to turn away when her rudder jammed. Glassford then had to make an immediate decision as to whether he would go ahead full speed and be cut through by the Aquitania or, if he backed down, he would probably ram the Aquitania and possibly cause her to sink with thousands of troops on board. He made the instant decision to go ahead and be rammed himself.

In this collision, the total casualties were not over a dozen or fifteen, something like that. I had two classmates on board the Shaw, both now dead. One was Jeff Metzel and the other one was King Dierdorff. There also was a man who later became my cousin by marriage on board, although this had not yet occurred, a reserve ensign by the name of Ted Briggs. I have a copy of a letter than he wrote shortly afterwards to his parents describing the collision in a very considerable detail. He, having been berthed up in the bow of the Shaw, was the only man who got aft. He heard the collision quarters sound and immediately ran aft and he got through the wardroom to the after part of the ship in time to avoid being cut off.

Metzel and Dierdorff were both asleep in the bow when it was cut off and didn't realize anything had happened until water began coming in from all directions. Then they took mattresses and got away. And down there in Naples there's a fellow who lives about two blocks from me and I found some years ago he'd been a yeoman in the Shaw at the time of this. He also was one of those who got cut off and floated around on a mattress for a while. He says that he was taken on board by the Kimberly and he came on board all slimey with oil and so forth. They cleaned him up and put him in a bunk and gave him a bottle of whiskey (medical reasons) until they got into port!

Q: What season of the year was this?

Adm. S.: This was in October 1918. Very shortly before the armistice.

Q: Well, that indeed was an exciting experience.

Adm. S.: It was an exciting experience, yes, indeed.

Following this, we were sent out once to try to give a welcome reception to a German submarine, which was supposed to make a landfall on one of the points on the Irish coast.

Q: How did we know that?

Adm. S.: The British found this out from German radio transmissions. They were very good at reading German radio by that time.

We went down there. We were one of the few American destroyers at that time that had any listening gear. We had two kinds. One was called the S tube, which was sort of a glorified stethoscope that stuck out of the bottom. We never did get anything from it, although the sub chasers did very well with it. And we had another kind that was called the K tube. Why "K," I don't know, but this consisted of an iron triangle about six or seven feet on the sides with little coils of some sort at each corner. We would stop and lower this thing into the water, then listen on it. Everybody had to stand absolutely still. We insisted that no one speak above a whisper while this was under way. All the machinery was shut down, and we could hold this posture only for a matter of three or four minutes because, at the end of that time, the condensers would start getting so hot that they'd be about to burn out and we'd have to start up the engines again, hoist the K tube, and go somewhere else. But we had pretty darned good luck in hearings things on the K tube.

Well, as I say, we were down here off the Irish coast, we listened, and sure enough, the K tube reported propeller noises and things like that. So we rushed around - this being at night - and shortly we found - well, I guess we had probably dropped some depth charges. Besides going over the stern, we had two of these Y guns aft so that we could make something of a barrage. It was all very exciting, very spectacular, and, after laying one of these barrages, we began to sight garbage and wreckage on the water.

Oh, did we get all pepped up! We rushed around there until, after picking up some of this garbage, we discovered it was bread-wrappings from Queenstown! It was our own garbage and we were chasing our own garbage!

Well, eventually, we lost contact with this fellow but he was never heard of again.

In those days, the British were said to hold that any submarine that wasn't heard of for three or four days was considered to have been lost. So our skipper was very proud of himself and everybody referred to this affair as the Battle of Bull Rock.

Q: Bull Rock!

Adm. S.: Then came the armistice –

Q: Incidentally, to complete that story, in the postwar period was there any record of this submarine being lost?

Adm. S.: I was about to tell you.

Then came the armistice and here in the newspaper was a long list of all the German ships that were surrendered, including all the submarines. We knew the number of our submarine, and the number that sticks in my mind was the U-91, but wasn't the U-91 the one that came into Newport Harbor?

Well, I'm probably wrong about the U-91, but we knew the number of that submarine, and there, sure enough, she was one of those that was turned in. I showed this to my captain and I never saw a man so mad in all my life. He wanted to decapitate me right then and there because I had done away with his submarine!

Q: Yes, you were a real kill-joy, weren't you?

Adm. S.: Yes.

Q: Tell me about the armistice itself, I mean its repercussion on you?

Adm. S.: None whatever. We were in Queenstown Harbor and most of the other ships were in, I guess. We were called up on the forecastle and the captain read off the announcement, then we fell out and I heard the chief boatswain's mate say under his breath, "What are we supposed to do? Cheer?" That's all there was about it!

Q: Pretty blasé, I would say!

Adm. S.: Then we had another submarine experience. We were sent out shortly before the armistice to contact an American submarine, if we could, that had not come in off its patrol.

During World War I we used our submarines off the Irish coast by giving them a patrol area. They would remain submerged all day, listening with the crude gear they had, then they'd come up at night to recharge their batteries. Well, this particular one – they had all been called in – had not come in, so we were sent out to where her patrol area was to try and find her. We went out there and we looked and we listened from daybreak up to about four o'clock in the afternoon. I remember I was down in the wardroom at the time, and all of a sudden a voice blared down the voice tube, "Submarine on the port bow."

Well, we headed over there, hot foot. This was somewhat before the armistice. We headed over there, hot foot, went to general quarters, of course. Shortly the submarine started sending up recognition signals right and left, and we could see somebody up on the conning tower waving an American flag and all kinds of things like this going on over there. They just hadn't gotten the word.

The first thing they said, after we pulled up alongside, was, "Is the war over?" Well, it wasn't quite over. It was just a very few days after that.

Q: Wasn't there a false armistice?

Adm. S.: Yes, but we knew nothing about the false armistice. Shortly before the armistice, all our destroyers, or practically all, were called in and told to prepare for a change of base. That's all I ever knew about just what was meant, although I've done considerable guessing since then, because it is known that there was a strong effort made by the officers of the German High Seas Fleet to go to sea

Schoeffel #1 -44

again. The British evidently knew about this and we were being told to get ready to shift over to Harwich or some such place on the east coast of England.

I've often wondered just how we would have made out if we'd gotten into action in those days.

Q: With the Grand Fleet?

Adm. S.: I'm afraid that we would not have done very well. All these destroyers were really very adept at dropping depth charges and things like that, but we'd had no gunnery exercises and no torpedo exercises for a long, long time, if ever.

On the way back to the United States, we went to the Azores and pulled out all our torpedoes and opened them up, and I'm very much afraid that if we had launched a torpedo against the German it wouldn't have run very far because the water pots had rusted on the inside and there was a lot of rust there in the water. This would almost certainly have resulted in a cold-shot torpedo, which just doesn't go anywhere.

Q: So they were defective in World War I, too?

Adm. S.: Well, they were very different defects.

Q: Yes.

Adm. S.: And we weren't the only country that had defects. The Germans did, the British did, just like ours. I don't know whether the Japanese did or not.

Q: Would you say a little about British ordnance in World War I? You talked about the very primitive sort of sounding gear you had on the *Kimberly*. What did the British have? Did they have anything comparable to their Asdic?

Adm. S.: I have no idea.

Q: You don't?

Adm. S.: No, because we had no contact with the British. They had very, very few ships, none of them destroyers, in Queenstown. It was almost entirely an American base. There were about forty U.S. destroyers based there and about an equal number of sub chasers. Very few British ships, so I have no idea what they had.

Q: What about our communications? You talked about going out and looking for an American submarine and it had not been notified of the fact that hostilities were coming to a close. What about the adequacy of our communications between ships?

Adm. S.: I had no reason to criticize them at the time.

Schoeffel #1 - 46

We had our radio and it seemed to work quite well. We had something that was very new in those days, a radio direction finder. I don't think it worked very well. But as far as the ability to communicate messages, I think everything was pretty good for those days. Of course, we had no voice.

Q: Carrying that a little bit further, in the convoying ships going across, how was communication carried on between them?

Adm. S.: I have no idea. Probably by flags.

When we got to Queenstown, we had to adjust to the British system of flags. They had a distinctly better flag system than the U.S. Navy had used and we adopted theirs. After the war was over, we changed it somewhat, but the flag system tha I knew all during my career in the navy was pretty close to that that the British had evolved by 1918. It wasn't identical, but it was close to it.

Q: Well, hostilities came to a close.

Adm. S.: Yes, and we all started going home. We shoved off for the States, stopped in the Azores for fuel, and north of Bermuda we ran into one day of extremely heavy weather. We had a big sea on the beam. We weren't attempting to do any work. All hands were topside just watching the seas, when we laid over in one of the kind that was called then a bitch-kitty roll.

Q: Bitch kitty, a descriptive term!

Adm. S.: Yes. I had the watch on the bridge at the time and was over on the port bridge wing and went slamming and falling down to leeward, wound up against the starboard bridge wing. Everybody was holding on or doing the same. I found that we had nobody overboard, but our lifeboat had - which was hoisted clear out of the water on the lee side - had been diped in the water and filled with water and broke its back.

Our inclinometer read, after this was all over, 67 degrees of roll. I do not believe that an inclinometer is a very accurate instrument. I think they tend to over-read when you have a really big roll, but that's what this one read, and I have never heard anybody able to better it!

Q: It's a good story. Maybe you made a complete circle!

Adm. S.: I know we looked up questions of stability after this was all over and, according to the ship's data book, we were supposed to be able to roll 95 degrees or something like that and still come back up, but we decided that none of us wanted to try it.

Well, we got back to Boston.

Q: Was there such a great clamor for demobilization as there was in World War II?

Adm. S.: Just the same. I was about to come to that.
    Mr. Daniels -

Q: Josephus?

Adm. S.: Josephus - and the chief of naval operations decided they were going to concentrate a fleet down in Guantánamo that would make the British Grand Fleet look like thirty cents.

Q: What was the motivation for that?

Adm. S.: As far as I know, nothing but pride. I can't imagine any other motivation for it.

So we went down to Guantánamo, and we had quite a number of desertions before going. Most of the men were naval reserve, the war was over, and they felt they ought to be paid off and they weren't going to go off on any damned cruises down in Cuba.

We went down there and every battleship the U.S. Navy had was there. Even the old Oregon was down there. We would go out and perform prodigies in naval tactics offshore, but all I recall about it is that we would go off there and make simulated torpedo attacks on the battleships.

We'd stand in by divisions and make smoke, dash around. It was all very dashing and so forth.

Q: Playing at war!

Adm. S.: Yes.

Then we got back north again and as soon as we got north everybody got paid off, the ones that were to get paid off. So, in practically a day, we found ourselves reduced from a crew of around 120 maybe, to perhaps 20 or 30. Everything else was just like that.

Q: So you couldn't go to sea?

Adm. S.: No, we couldn't go to sea. In fact, a lot of destroyers got ordered down to Charleston to be put in reserve down there. They would run eight hours and then they would anchor for sixteen days, then they'd go ahead again. They got to Charleston in that fashion.

Among those who were fixed as badly as we were was the battleship North Dakota. I had a classmate, Mike Williams, who's still living, down in Texas, there, and Mike was sent out on a recruiting trip throughout New England. Well, if ever a man could talk down Demosthenes it was Mike Williams. He orated to such an extent that he brought in some hundreds of recruits to the North Dakota.

Q: From little villages in New England?

Adm. S.: Yes, all over New England.

We were told to send out recruiting parties and we were sent down to New Haven, to operate from there. Our recruiting party and those of other vessels would go round and see the mayor of the town, and the mayor would say:

"Oh, yes, and do you know Mr. Williams? Well, Mr. Williams has just been here and picked up all the stray young men in this vicinity!"

Mike took some hundreds, I think it was around 700 recruits back to the North Dakota. In recent years, I ran into a fellow who was in the North Dakota in those days and he said they had to go on to Europe very shortly afterwards because they were the only ship that had anything like a full crew in numbers, but he said as far as seagoing knowledge was concerned, this crew was just about the nadir of anything that ever went to sea.

Q: I suppose the economic situation in the States at that time was helpful in recruiting, was it not?

Adm. S.: What?

Q: The economic situation was not too good, so recruits were looking for jobs?

Adm. S.: Well, they seemed to be very anxious to get out of uniform. That's all I can say. We didn't recruit very many, but after a while we were sent down to Philadelphia and we put the <u>Kimberly</u> in reserve down there. Then we took such crews as we had and went and commissioned a brand-new destroyer, the <u>Broome</u>, No. 210. We set to sea in this. She was a better vessel than the <u>Kimberly</u>. She carried a good deal more oil so we could steam both faster and farther.

We went up to Newport to get our torpedoes and while we were there both our captain and our exec received notice that their resignations had been accepted. This sort of skimmed off the top!

Q: So the third man had to take over?

Adm. S.: Yes. Almost immediately a lieutenant commander came on board with orders as the executive officer. I'll tell you the name of this infamous character. What the devil was his name? I'll think of it later. He took charge and we were due to go on a shakedown cruise to the West Indies, to Guantánamo. Well, he decided that the way to get from Newport to Guantánamo was by way of 96th Street, New York, because he was engaged to the actress, Fay Bainter, at the time and -

Q: Fay Bainter!

Adm. S.: Yes - and he wanted to see her before he shoved off.

This character in earlier months had commanded a destroyer which, with several others, ran up and down the Hudson River and they would run races out there in the river and their wakes just raised hell with the beach. Everybody got into a lot of trouble, but everybody got out of it.

So, we were going to go to the West Indies by way of 96th Street and, since his date with Fay was fairly early in the evening, we ran at full power from the time we got outside of Newport Harbor until we got to Hellgate. We were making 36 and 37 knots all the way down the Sound. I don't believe we did any damage with that, but when we got to Hellgate, Reggie Venable - that was his name - slowed down to 20 knots and we went through there whistling and down the East River at the same speed. We got right off the Brooklyn Navy Yard, I happened to be in the wardroom, sitting at the table with Webster's Dictionary on the table in front of me, when, all of a sudden, wham, wham, wham, and the ship started going up and down like this. The dictionary jumped that far off the table -

Q: Was this an unabridged one?

Adm. S.: Yes! Things quieted down shortly and it turned out that we had fouled some submerged wreckage, and we couldn't run the starboard engine, the steering gear was out of whack, and there was a lot of water coming in to the steering engine room. Of course, tugs promptly came out from the Navy Yard and put us in alongside the dock.

Venable got a taxi and went up town. Oh, he was a character that fellow, he didn't give a damn.

Q: Did he eventually marry Fay?

Adm. S.: No.

They got us in dry dock and found that the starboard propeller strut was broken right in two, a chunk that big gone out of it, and there was a lot of heavy steel cable wound around the starboard propeller, which was all sort of wilted like a wilted daisy, and there were various other difficulties. So they turned to to fix this ship up.

Q: Did there have to be a court of inquiry in the thing?

Adm. S.: Oh, yes, and people came in with large bills for damage done by our wake in the East River and so forth.

Q: Twenty knots was quite a speed in the East River, wasn't it?

Adm. S.: Oh, I should hope to shout!

Venable didn't seem to be at all concerned about all this. I know he appeared before the court of inquiry but somehow or other he seemed to have a good deal of pull with Mr. Daniels. I don't have the faintest idea what it was, but it's true that he was shortly relieved from command of the Broome by Captain Austin, who was a most careful old lady. Two more different people, you can't imagine than those two.

Venable made the newspapers not long afterwards. I'll be darned if he wasn't given command of another destroyer. Meanwhile, Fay Bainter had been over in England and she was returning on a liner. He took his ship to sea without anybody's by your leave, went alongside the liner, took Fay off, and took her in to port. Well, this caused a great ruckus. We in the poor old Broome didn't have anything to do with this, but all the hierarchy of the navy down in Washington wanted to hang, draw, and quarter this young man, but Mr. Daniels thought this was very spirited -

Q: Very dashing!

Adm. S.: Very dashing, very spirited. There were certain members of the State Department who didn't think much of this, either, because there were a couple of ex-ambassadors returning to the United States on board the liner when the destroyer came alongside. They thought it had been sent out to take them off, and their noses were very out of joint!

Q: They thought they outranked Fay!

Adm. S.: Yes! I never saw Venable after he left the Broome, but in later years he was in command of the Hannibal, which was a survey ship. Then I don't know what happened to him. I don't know whether he's still alive or not.

It took months to get that ship fixed, but we'd get her apparently all fixed, we'd have dock trials, and everything seemed to be hunky-dory with her starboard engine. We'd go out to sea and as soon as we get up to 20 knots, down in the engine room it sounded as though people were wielding sledge hammers on the starboard reduction gear. Such knocks you never did hear. After about three trys at fixing all this in the navy yard, the reduction gear was taken out and sent back to the manufacturer to be retooled and then it worked all right.

Eventually, we got under way to head for Europe and the Asiatic. I was all full of beans about going out to the Asiatic. Well, I had a sort of a falling-out with the captain. When we arrived at Gibraltar, the old cruiser Pittsburgh, which was then the flagship of U.S. Naval Forces in European Waters, wanted another junior lieutenant to stand watch, so I was taken out of the Broome, where I was enjoying myself thoroughly and went over to the Pittsburgh, where I was a fish out of water for a long time.

Q: What did you do to incur the wrath of the skipper?

Adm. S.: We were up in the North River and word came that the Board of Inspection and Survey was going to come out and visit the ship. Captain Austin took it for granted that they were going to make a most meticulous inspection of everything on board the ship, and he insisted upon all the bright work being most highly polished. Well, most of the bright work was brand new, and brand-new bright work won't take much of a polish. I had the duty that morning and we were not getting things polished to his satisfaction, so he relieved me and sent me below with contumely and so forth.

Q: He liked a patina on things!

Adm. S.: So I went over to the old Pittsburgh at Gibraltar. I was given one of the quarterdeck divisions, stood watch, and so forth. We went up to Cherbourg, then we went up into the Baltic, to Danzig.

Q: What was the purpose of that?

Adm. S.: At that time, the Poles and the Bolsheviks were having a war. First, the Poles had chased the Bolsheviks way back into the Ukraine, and then the Bolsheviks turned around and started chasing the Poles back very rapidly. I don't know what the real purpose of our visit was but it was supposed to be to help bolster the Polish government in some way or another. That's what we were given to understand.

Q: The State Department was back of this?

Adm. S.: I suppose so.

About this time the French sent a marshal who had been Foch's righthand man in World War I over to advise the Poles, and as soon as he took charge, why, the Poles chased the Bolsheviks right back.

After about a week in Danzig and having coaled ship there, we were suddenly ordered to get up to Finland, Helsingfors, as quickly as possible. We set out, and at that time - well, during World War I the Russians had laid a lot of minefields off the Baltic coast and they were thought to extend in to about five miles off the coast. So we were running along close to the coast. Our gyro compass was out of whack. We were running on magnetic compasses. There were a lot of forest fires ashore so that visibility was not at all good. After a short period at sea, I had the second dog watch, I think it was, I was relieved and hadn't been below more than about an hour when, all of a sudden, things seemed to feel a little strange. Bells began to ring, boatswain's mates' whistles tootled, and so forth, and we were hard and fast aground.

We didn't know just where we were, but at break of day we found ourselves aground right off the middle breakwater of the harbor of Libau. This is a place where numerous other ships, apparently, had gone aground, too.

Q: There was no lighthouse there or anything?

Adm. S.: No, there was no lighthouse there at the time.
   We had pretty well scraped our double bottom off, our outer bottom, but the inner bottom held so we weren't in any particular danger. Then we started to throw overboard all this coal that we had just put on board, and I'm going to tell you uncoaling a ship in harder than putting it in.

Q: Well, it's a rare thing, isn't it, to uncoal a ship?

Adm. S.: Yes. We worked and worked. A couple of destroyers arrived and then the cruiser St. Louis arrived. A lot of weight was taken off the ship and eventually we got off and proceeded very gingerly down to Sheerness, at the mouth of the Thames River, where we went in to the royal dockyard at Chatham. We were there for quite a number of months, in which time they put a brand-new outer bottom on the ship.

Q: What happened to the skipper of the Pittsburgh?

Adm. S.: First they had a court of inquiry for him. It was headed by a famous old sundowner by the name of Andrews — I don't remember his first name.

Q: Adolphus Andrews?

Adm. S.: No, not Adolphus. I knew Adolphus quite well. He was a fine gentleman. This was quite a different Andrews.

I was called in to testify, naturally, and I went in there feeling as free of guilt as a jay bird, and I came out of there feeling that the whole reason for the ship going aground was my fault. That's the way I felt. However, I was not called to any further account, but the captain, the exec, and the poor officer of the deck, one Johnnie Walker, who was standing his very first top watch.

Q: Just an hour after you!

Adm. S.: Yes - they were naturally brought to trial. Various expert witnesses appeared and testified that there was no reason why we were running so close to the beach. One said that the Russian minefields were notoriously inefficient (as we found out <u>otherwise</u> in later years). The Russians are really very efficient at mining and have been ever since the Crimean War, but this fellow said that they were notoriously inefficient and, anyhow, they'd all been swept up.

He was just about ready to sit down when an orderly came in and handed the president of the court a dispatch saying that one of our destroyers had been fooling around about thirty miles from where we had run aground and had hit a mine which had blown her stern off and she lost thirty or forth men! Well, this word came out at just the psychological moment.

Q: It certainly did.

Adm. S.: The upshot of it was that Captain David Worcester Todd was fully acquitted. I don't think they went so far as to say "fully and honorably," I think he was fully acquitted. Anyway, he kept the ship. The navigator was acquitted and I think the officer of the deck was acquitted, too.

Q: A timely dispatch!

Adm. S.: Well, we went to Chatham then. We all became very British in our months there. Eventually we got out from there and went down to the Mediterranean, into the Gulf of Gabes, where we fired target practices and so forth. I was told it was the first time that our guns had been fired in practice since 1917 or 1918. By this time it was 1921.

Q: The reason for that was just conservation - ?

Adm. S.: The ship had been running around on diplomatic missions all the time.

Q: But neglecting readiness?

Adm. S.: Yes. We were not a good warship at all. We were a very poor warship, not only due to the faults of the original design, a 15,000-ton ship with four 8-inch guns and twelve 6-inch, and that was all the battery we had. Then, a very poor crew, no chance to exercise at real readiness. But we got our target practices off and then we returned to nothern European waters by way of Nice and Villefranche and so forth.

There I was detached and sent home on board the old Chattanooga. Upon our arrival in Boston, we decoaled the Chattanooga.

Q: Why?

Adm. S.: She was going out of commission.

Then I caught the train for Pensacola.

Q: How did you happen to make arrangements to go to Pensacola?

Adm. S.: I had applied for aviation duty some months before, for avaition training.

Q: Incidentally, during the time that you were at the academy, there was no introduction to aviation at all?

Adm. S.: No, none at all, at that time. I got my first

flight in the summer of 1919 up at Newport. There were a number of navy seaplanes in there, the large twin-engine flying boats the F-5Ls, and I went over and got a flight in one of them.

Q: When you made application for Pensacola, was there any attempt to dissuade you from doing so?

Adm. S.: None whatever.

Q: Aviation was not a very popular part of the navy at that point, was it?

Adm. S.: No, not among the old shellbacks. I know that there were people who either were dissuaded or whom others attempted to dissuade, but that was not so in my case. Another officer, Lieutenant Campman, from the Pittsburgh went at the same time and we were in the same class at Pensacola. And a fellow by the name of Dillon, known as Gotch Dillon, was in the next class. He came from the Pittsburgh also.

Interview #2 with Rear Admiral Malcolm F. Schoeffel,
U.S. Navy (Retired)

Place: His son's residence in Alexandria, Virginia

Date: Tuesday afternoon, 9 January 1979

Subject: Biography

By: John T. Mason, Jr.

Q: It was in July of 1921 that you reported to Pensacola to take a course in training as a pilot.

Adm. S.: Yes. Our class, as I remember it, numbered forty-eight at the start, and I think we eventually graduated thirty-two. The greater number of classmates of mine, this being the first time my class had had an opportunity to take flight training - let's see, there was Admiral Greer, Jimmy Lowery, who died many years ago, Tom Jeter, who's still living in Coronado, Sid Wildman lives now in northern Florida. I won't name them all, I couldn't, anyway. The senior student was Commander Jimmy Berg.

In those days, all our training was in seaplanes. There wasn't a land plane in that part of Florida. There wasn't a land plane closer than the army station up at Maxwell Field, 200 or 300 miles away. We started off in small, two-seater seaplanes known as N-9s, with Hispano-Suiza engines. We were, in general, required to be checked out for solo after not more than ten hours of dual instruction, although occasionally somebody got extended as far as thirteen hours.

Q: Didn't you have some ground indoctrination first?

Adm. S.: Yes, we had about a month of ground school first, before we started flying.

I got checked out for solo after about nine and a half hours of dual, the normal figure. I was checked out by Wu Duncan, who later became vice chief of naval operations. I remember in the course of that flight he made a landing with the airplane and I was certainly struck with the smoothness with which he went on the water.

After the N-9s we had quite a period in a horrible airplane known as the HS-2L, the L standing for Liberty engine. It was a small boat-seaplane carrying three, pilot and the copilot side by side and a navigator-radio-gunner-bomber in the bow. The engine was mounted - a single engine was mounted high up behind the pilot, so that if one of these things should spin, why, the engine would come loose and make a perfect bull's eye out of all the crew. Very few people survived crashes in that airplane.

Q: You didn't have parachutes, anyway, did you?

Adm. S.: No, and they were very tricky to fly. You flew around at the tremendous speed of about 50 knots and, if you were going to make a turn, you nosed the airplane down and picked up another 5 knots to make sure that you didn't stall or go in.

We only had one crash in an HS-2 while we were down there. My classmate, Peet Thurston, spun in in one, but survived, which was very unusual.

Following that, we were graduated to the twin-engine flying boats, quite large airplanes for those days, with a span of perhaps 100 feet and twin Liberty engines. They were either H-16s or LF-5Ls, and they looked so much alike it was hard to tell them apart. They could carry quite a crew and they were rather pleasant to fly. In them we made death-defying navigational hops as far west as the mouth of Mobile Bay and as far east as the eastern end of Santa Rosa Island. We bombed and we shot gunnery and so forth.

By the middle of December, we were finished with the course and received our qualifications as naval aviators. Let me see. I think we had by that time an average of about 120 hours of flying time, something like that.

Q: How many had been lost from the class?

Adm. S.: Nobody had been killed, but about a third of the class fell out for one reason or another.

Schoeffel #2 - 66

Q: You mean they had been flunked, some of them?

Adm. S.: Yes, they flunked in some fashion or another.

Q: You must have been a bunch of fatalists, were you not?

Adm. S.: Fatalists?

Q: Yes.

Adm. S.: I don't think anybody had any philosophy in him!

Q: Well, I mean, flying these HS-2Ls, you must have been fatalists in order to have the fortitude to do it!

Adm. S.: Most of us applied for duty in the Pacific aircraft squadrons.

Q: Before you do that, Sir, you might tell me in more general terms, you might give me a picture of Pensacola in that time.

Adm. S.: Pensacola was a small city, and the naval air station was seven or eight miles south. The only well-paved road in all west Florida ran from the middle of Pensacola down to the naval air station. It was a concrete road. The main street of the town was Palafox Street and it was paved with wooden Belgian blocks, and whenever it rained very hard, which it did from time to time, these blocks would all float up! Palafox Street would be impassable for a while.

Of course, this was long before the days of air-conditioning and it was very hot down there.

Q: What were the living accommodations at the air station?

Adm. S.: Well, there was a sizeable hotel in town called the San Carlos, but it was too expensive for most of us. The first month there, Harry Campman and I, being unable to get quarters on the station, roomed with a widow who had two sons named Pickett and - who was Pickett's number two man in the charge at Gettysburg? Armistead! So, you can see where their sympathies had been.

Q: Yes, indeed!

Adm. S.: Pensacola has since become a huge splurge of living all over the place. In those days it was a small city of, perhaps, 20,000.

Q: How many cadets were training at one time there?

Adm. S.: Well, as I say, our class entered, I think, forty-eight. That was as many as there were.

Q: That was the total?

Adm. S.: That was the total, yes, because at that time there was one class after another at six-month intervals.

Q: I see.

Adm. S.: Pensacola, I don't think, looked upon us with too much - well, they didn't think too much of us. The local police were likely to gather us in if we drove a little too fast, because we all acquired ourselves automobiles, most of us for the first time. I can remember Harold Martin, later a vice admiral, driving along at night on the way down to the air station, and he unfortunately ran into the rear end of a poor but honest bootlegger who was just taking his stuff down the road, spreading everything all over, and it certainly made a stink.

Q: Did you fellows deserve the reputation you seem to have in the eyes of the townspeople?

Adm. S.: Well, we were not exactly a pious and quiet bunch! Like a group of young men anywhere, whether it be in Oxford, England, or Pensacola, Florida, the townspeople and the students look at each other somewhat askance. However, quite a number of the local girls got married to young naval officers in those days and, as I say, still live down there.

Q: Would you say something about the requirements, the physical qualifications?

Adm. S.: Yes. We had to be in first-class physical shape. They gave us quite a comprehensive and strict physical examination on first reporting there. It contained a number of things that were thought essential but are no longer done. For instance, one was the spinning chair. They put you in something like a barber's chair, then spun you around like mad. You were supposed to get dizzy, but the question was how did you snap out of the dizziness, and, if to the satisfaction of the doctor, you snapped out properly that was okay. Then there was another thing known as the - well it was like a miniature gasometer. You had clips on your nose and a tube up your mouth and you breathed in and out as long as you could from the initial amount of air that was in this thing and, at the point where you suddenly fell over from lack of oxygen, as everybody eventually did, they deduced how high you could go without oxygen.

Q: A homespun test!

Adm. S.: I remember that you went along and you didn't feel the least bit of distress in any way and thought that everything was fine and, all of a sudden, you fell over in the doctor's arms.

And they had another test known as the Snyder Index and that stayed with us for a long time. First, you were laid out flat on your back for about five minutes and they took your pulse rate and your blood pressure and made certain marks on an arbitrary scale. Then they had you stand up for a couple of minutes, and then they took your pulse rate and your blood pressure and made some more marks on an arbitrary scale. Then you put one foot on the seat of a chair and you raised yourself up onto the seat of the chair, oh, half a dozen times, and they took the same things and gave you another mark.

As I recall it, a mark of twenty-one was perfect, and a mark of eight or nine was passing. I myself generally ran ten to twelve, on the low side. The trouble was that my blood pressure was generally too low, which in some ways in these days is considered to be a good thing to have.

Q: Yes.

Adm. S.: The Snyder Index was useful in various ways because many years later a couple of my shipmates came around to my house one Sunday afternoon - they were fellows from the squadron I was in, of which I was exec - and they told me that they were very much afraid that another one of our people had gone off his chump and that he was getting ready to beat up or maybe kill his wife. Something had to be done about this.

We went around to this fellow's house and found him and his wife, apparently quite amiable and amicable. But I knew that this chap had been under very heavy strain for the previous month, so I felt that the thing to do was to get him on a long leave. But you couldn't just call a man in and say, "I think you're going crazy. You'd better take some leave." So I arranged with a flight surgeon to send for three of our pilots the next morning, including that fellow, and just say, "We're giving surprise Snyder indices."

We got them down there. I haven't the faintest notion what kind of a Snyder he had, but they pulled long faces and said, "You've got to go on a long sick leave." So he did and everything turned out all right.

Q: So that was a very constructive test under different applications. Did you have any of what would correspond to modern-day aptitude tests?

Adm. S.: No. At least, I don't remember any such.

Well, we finished by late December and most of us wanted to go to Pacific air squadrons because the Pacific Fleet was scheduled to get the Langley, which was being converted in those days, whereas the Atlantic air squadrons just flew up and down the coast in F5-L seaplanes.

Q: Largely on reconnaissance, observation?

Adm. S.: Yes, that sort of thing.

We were all ordered to embark in the old transport Château Thierry at Charleston, South Carolina, I think about the end of January, which we did. We went down through the canal and up the west coast and arrived in San Diego on a foggy morning, which it generally is out there in the winter, and we found ourselves all assigned to the USS Aroostook. Before World War I she had been one of the New York-Boston passenger vessels. She was taken over during World War I and converted into a minelayer. By the time we arrived out there, which was early 1922, she was a tender for the aircraft squadron, Pacific, which at that time consisted, on paper, of two fighter squadrons of land planes, two observation squadrons of land planes, and two squadrons of big-boat seaplanes.

Q: You make a distinction. You say this was on paper?

Adm. S.: Yes.

Q: In actuality, what existed?

Adm. S.: In actuality, what existed was - they could either man two squadrons of fighters or they could transfer over pilots to the observation squadrons and man two squadrons of observation planes. The fighters were the little Vought VE-7, and, oh, what a sweet little airplane those things were. They were terrific.

Q: In what sense?

Adm. S.: Just sweet to fly. They weren't particularly fast. I guess you could probably get 115 miles an hour in one of them or something like that, but they climbed well, they were very easy on the controls, they maneuvered well, they stunted well, and all the rest of it.

The observation squadrons were equipped with the DH4-B, which was for those days quite sizeable, a two-seater biplane, which was intended during World War I to be the main day bomber airplane in the army air force. They were good airplanes to fly, too. For the next eight or ten years, you couldn't say much better of an airplane than "it flies just like a DH."

Well, we arrived out there, none of us ever having flown a land plane -

Q: This was all based on North Island, was it?

Adm. S.: Yes, all based on North Island.

None of us had ever flown a land plane and the activity at that time was spotting for the gunfire of the battleships, all of which were based up at Long Beach. The aircraft squadrons had already begun to make a name for themselves as very, very good observers of battleship gunfire, but we were told at first just to go out on the line in the morning and hang around and soak up all the atmosphere we could.

I don't remember who was Commander, Aircraft, at that time, but the chief men out of the line were Mitscher and George Murray, both of whom amounted to a great deal in World War II. But, after a few days of that, which was becoming very boresome, we were all informed that we would be turned over to the naval air station for instruction in land planes and we would by flying the famous JN-4. Well, except that the Jenny had wheels, it was almost identical with the N-9, so we weren't lost, by any means.

The chief instructor was from the Naval Academy class of 1918 who had gone through Pensacola six months ahead of us, generally known as Injun Joe Tomlinson. He's still living, by the way -

Q: Doesn't he live in Arizona?

Adm. S.: I think he lives in Oregon, but I'm not sure.

I believe he is largely Seneca Indian. Joe was not exactly a naval officer but he was - I do not believe the navy ever had a better throttle jockey than Joe Tomlinson. In other words, a man who could get the last ounce out of an airplane. He could fly an airplane to the queen's taste, into anything, out of anything. Like those Indians, he just didn't know the meaning of the word "fear." I won't say he never got upset because I saw him really upset a couple of times at mistakes that Greer and I made; but he was a splendid pilot and a very good instructor.

We flew around, got checked out in the Jennys, and he took us out on cross-country hops, over death-defying distances, as far as Los Angeles and places like that. I remember our very first one when Greer and I were sent off together, on the very first cross-country hop, and the very first place to land was a place called Rosedale Farm. I guess it's all built up like San Diego by this time, but in those days it was up on the Mission Valley mesa, and there was an abandoned farm completely surrounded by high eucalyptus trees, but there was one place where there were a couple of gaps in the eucalyptus. We'd slide in there, get through the gap, then we'd do a side slip with the airplane to get it down to the ground, and when you had it down just above the ground you'd kill your speed by fish-tailing it and then put her on.

Well, we went in there for our first landing. Greer had the controls. I was just a passenger that time. He sort of overshot and there was a shallow ditch at the other side of the farm. We went into that and the landing gear came off. There we were, flat on our bellies. Tomlinson was not too critical of this. He didn't like it, but he said he'd send somebody back to the air station to bring some help out, and he would go on with the rest of them, leaving us there. No food, no water, hot as billy be damned, and by midafternoon nothing had arrived. So we went out and walked down the road - it shouldn't be called a road, it was nothing but a trail that led up to this place - and, sure enough, we found a navy truck with half a dozen sailors in it, stuck in the sand. We turned to and we exercised ourselves mightily and, by golly, we made a four-wheel drive out of that truck by taking lines and tying them on the spokes of the rear wheels, up over the hub of the front wheels, tied to the spokes, and then we would go ahead half a turn. We had a four-wheel drive and we would gain half a turn of the wheel each time.

Eventually, we got free and got over to our airplane. By this time, it was dark, and we got some wood and built a fire, took the airplane apart and loaded it on the truck. We were very careful when we loaded it on the truck but we managed to knock off an oil cooler on the bottom of the fuselage.

Well, we had been hearing stories over at the BOQ about how somebody went out and cracked up and if he'd had any sense he'd have put a match to it. We didn't think very, very strongly about the preservation of material. We had a hard time getting down this sandy road, but eventually we got down to the ferry leaving from San Diego, for North Island, just in time to catch the last ferry. Nobody had had anything to eat nor anything to drink in the meantime. If we missed that ferry, we would have to drive clear around San Diego Bay and up to North Island, a matter of thirty or forty miles.

Well, we started to take it on the ferry and discovered that the tail stuck up far enough so that the top of the stabilizer would not pass under a lattice affair across the entrance to the ferry. So I said, "To hell with it. Bust it," and we took it on board. We got back to North Island very late, excessively tired, and thought no more about it for a while. Then, a couple of days later, lot of things broke loose.

The captain of the air station had been down among the shops and he saw a busted Jenny fuselage on a truck - no, it was the engine, I guess, on a truck. The truck went around a corner a little too fast and the engine slid and fell off the truck. Well, where did that come from and so forth. Then the story all came out and the next thing we knew there was a board of investigation. I was particularly under fire since I was the senior man present. The upshot of it was that I got a letter of discommendation - I forget what they called it - and that was about all.

Greer and I were put back into dual instruction.

Q: You didn't know it all at that point, did you?

Adm. S.: No. After a while we were deemed adequate to go forth with Joe on another one of his cross-country expeditions. This time, the first place to land was going to be the old oil-well field up on Soledad Mountain. Someone had cut a long swath of bushes up there on the mountain and had tried to dig an oil well and, I guess, had gotten no oil. It was a very small swath in the bushes and over on the east side there was quite a cliff going down to railroad tracks, steep and high. Over on the left side there was a rather easy slope down toward the lowlands.

In order to land in this place you had to come in and then you had to land in an unusual way because it wasn't level. You had to put the left wing down. I was at the controls this time and made a most excellent approach, but at the last moment didn't get the left wing down far enough and the first thing that hit the ground was the right wing, and around we spun.

Q: At what speed was this happening?

Adm. S.: Oh, about forty miles an hour.

At this point, I remember Joe jumping up and down, hands clenched over his head, and shouting:

"As a pair of birdmen, you two parrots ought to be kept in a cage"!

We looked over the airplane and it really wasn't hurt very much. There seemed to be some cracks in some of the wing spars and things like that, so Joe said:

"I think it'll fly, so you two take it back to North Island and the rest of us will go on."

So, we took it back to North Island and it flew all right.

Many years later, in World War II, Joe said to me, "I've often thought since then of the chance I took with the lives of two rear admirals."

Flying was a lot of fun in those days. Every time you went out anywhere you had an adventure.

We eventually got through the course. I don't recall where Greer was assigned. I was assigned to one of the observation squadrons and started flying DHs.

Q: This was observation plane squadron No. 1, was it?

Adm. S.: Yes.

Q: Still attached to the Aroostook?

Adm. S.: Yes.
Then, having gotten into VO-1 there, we went on a terrific expedition. Twelve DHs we flew off to San Francisco for I guess it was Armistice Day or something like that.

Q: But independent of any ships?

Adm. S.: Yes. This was terrific stuff for us in those days. We got up there to San Francisco and put up at little old Chrissy Field, out from the Presidio, and came the day when we were supposed to fly in formation over the city and then head south again.

Q: You were, in a sense, forerunner of the Blue Angels, were you?

Adm. S.: Oh, no!

Q: Well, you were on exhibit, weren't you?

Adm. S.: We were putting on an exhibit, but - well, we didn't get twelve airplanes in the air because one of them had its engines conk out on takeoff and landed in the bay. Both people swam ashore unhurt.

Q: Was this a commonplace thing with planes in those days?

Adm. S.: Oh, quite, You might say flying was an adventure in those days!

Well, we flew our eleven - I think it was eleven - over San Francisco and headed south. We were going to stop at Bakersfield for gas en route. About halfway to Bakersfield, the weather began to get bad. Low clouds set in and they pressed us down and down. Finally, we got into a canyon, flying along by this time in no vee, just one after the other, and it was so narrow that I doubt we could have turned around if the weather had closed in on us. But we got through the vee at the top and came out into a big, big, open valley, I'm not sure just where it was. We began to get together and only ten turned up. One was missing, but the ten of us went on to Bakersfield and landed somewhere out there near a gas station, called in town, and gas trucks were sent out. The eleventh airplane finally turned up. They had had a real scarey one because they had pulled up into the clouds, and in those days the only instruments you had in an airplane were a magnetic compass, altimeter, airspeed meter, and a couple of ancient instruments, tachometer and a thermometer, and, flying in clouds was esteemed to be very dangerous.

We'd heard stories about pilots who could tie sacks over their heads and fly the airplanes blind for a half an hour, but that was a lot of lies. Nobody could ever do that, then or now.

Well, these people pulled up into the clouds. The magnetic compass suffers from an inert difficulty - my wife would remember the name of that but I don't. Anyway, under certain conditions, when you turn to the right actually the compass will indicate that you're turning to the left. This will confuse the pilot completely.

Q: That's related to the earth's magnetism, is it?

Adm. S.: Yes. Well, these people climbed and climbed. Then, all of a sudden, everything seemed to go haywire with them. They didn't know what was going on, but the air speed built up to a very high figure for those days. Suddenly, they broke out of the clouds and there was just room enough to get the airplane under control and come on over. Those two fellows came as close to being killed as anybody I ever knew of who didn't get killed.

Q: What kind of maps were you equipped with?

Adm. S.: Maps? We had no maps except Rand-McNally road maps. There were no airplane maps in those days. Speaking of that, the Rand-McNally map showed down at the southern end of the San Joaquim Valley nice great big Lake Tulare. Well, when we flew by there we looked for Lake Tulare and we couldn't find any lake, because Lake Tulare had been -

Q: Prehistoric, wasn't it?

Adm. S.: Not quite, but it had been all drained. But, if you looked very carefully, you could see the outline where the lake had been; there were farms.

Well, along in the thirties I was flying over that country and, by gum, there was Lake Tulare back again, all full of water. I got down low to take a look at things and here were all these farmhouses with just their roofs sticking up. You could see where all the roads were by the telephone poles sticking up out of the water. So Lake Tulare comes back from time to time!

That was a big expedition.

Q: Did you carry binoculars, too?

Adm. S.: No.

Q: I would think to use in conjunction with the road maps?

Adm. S.: No, we didn't. It was generally considered that if you got yourself lost the thing to do was find a railroad, then go down and fly around the railroad station until you could read the name on the station. Then you knew where you were and what to do. This persisted until after Lindbergh's day because - oh, who was the old fellow who used to spin a rope for Flo Ziegfeld?

Q: Will Rogers.

Adm. S.: Will Rogers! He flew across the continent a couple of times. Then he announced he was sick and tired of this business of reading railroad station signs and he'd give $1,000, or something like that, to any town that would put out a big arrow on the ground somewhere, indicating north and in very large letters giving the name of the place. I think a lot of towns took him up, too. That was quite a bit later.

After we'd been out there a year, I was picked up from VO-1 and was put on the staff as the so-called flag secretary.

Q: Before that, let me ask a question about VO-1. Did you do any spotting for the battleships?

Adm. S.: Not while I was in it. The gunnery season for the battleships was over before we new blood were assigned to the squadron. The older pilots had done it, but we of the new blood had not done any as of that time.

I was assigned as flag secretary. Captain Henry Vernon Butler was commander of the air squadrons at that time.

Q: And you were on his staff?

Adm. S.: Yes. Admiral Forrest Sherman was also a member of that staff. He was tactical officer, I think.

Well, nothing in particular happened in that year that I can think of.

Q: Did Forrest Sherman show the intellectual prowess that he did later?

Adm. S.: Yes, very much so.

Following that, I was detached in the summer of '23 and went to PG school in Annapolis to take aeronautical engineering. There was one other man taking that course, Red Townsend.

Q: This was a routine assignment, was it?

Adm. S.: Yes.

Q: Had you been married by that time?

Adm. S.: Not yet. I hadn't met my wife yet.

While we were there in Annapolis that year we maintained our flight status by going once or twice a month up to Anacostia, getting an airplane there, and going out and flying around.

I lived with three classmates in half of a very nice old colonial-days house on King George Street, with Dave Clark, who was later chief of the Bureau of Ships, with Jack Redmond, who was later director of naval communications, and with Jeff Metzel, who died very shortly after World War II. One of the professors lived next door and he had two daughters who were known to midshipmen as the Helium Twins, lighter than air! Clark, in particular, was a great ladies' man and extremely handsome. Well, when they saw him walking in next door, they really cast eyes at him, but I recall his putting one of them over his knee and giving her a good s spanking and sending her home. So they eventually gave us up as a bunch of old fogies.

The instruction there at the postgraduate school was excellent, and I think we all learned a great deal.

Q: It was pretty rigorous, too, was it not?

Adm. S.: Oh, it was tough, yes, really tough.

Along in the course of that fall there was a big football game up in Baltimore with Princeton. We all went up to the game. When we got back my three housemates all had girls there, they were beau-ing around. I was a red mike myself and feeling sorry for myself, when I got a telephone call from a Mr. Briggs, who was a great friend of my father, and he and his niece, Marcia, were over at Carvel Hall, and would I come over and have dinner with them. I most certainly went over there and I took Marcia to the dance that evening and about ten or eleven months later we were married, and I was the first one of the four to get married, in spite of the fact that I was a red mike and they were all the beau brummels.

Q: Surprising, the turn of fate!

Adm. S.: Yes.

Q: How did you manage to court the young lady and carry on your studies at the same time?

Adm. S.: Well, it was difficult, but it went on! I got some leave. She and her uncle were living just outside of Rochester, New York, and I went up there on Christmas leave and so forth.

At the end of that year, Townsend and I went up to MIT

Schoeffel #2 - 87

in Boston.

Q: This was predicated on your record there at Annapolis, was it?

Adm. S.: Well, it was the regular aeronautical engineering course at that time. It was a two-year course. The first year was at Annapolis - and all of the PG courses at that time were either two or three - I think a few of them were three-year courses, but most of them were two. The first year in Annapolis, the second at a civilian university, getting the rest of the specialty you were in.

Q: Did you get a degree with it, too?

Adm. S.: I did not get a degree. I could have, but I'll come to that later. There was a master of science degree open to us.

As I say, Townsend and I went up to MIT and we found there for flying that there was a little reserve flying facility over on South Boston Bay with a couple of small seaplanes, and over at the Boston airport was a wrecked Jenny belonging to the navy. It had been wrecked by no less a person than Felix Stump, who had been in the previous year's class at MIT.

Well, it was in a hanger there with the landing gear off and the wings off and the engine out and lots of holes in the fabric of the wings and the fuselage, and it had a broken longeron in the fuselage. Oh, it was a mess. But Townsend was a man of his hands. He liked nothing better than to get a few monkey wrenches and so forth round his waist and go to work. He was of the class of 1918 at the Naval Academy and, therefore, the senior man, and he was all for our turning to and fixing that Jenny, which we did in the summer when we were up there.

We had a terrible time scrounging materials for it, but we did get the navy yard to build us a steel brace to put around the cracked place in the longeron. There were lots of other cracked-up Jennys lying around there, so we'd go over to one of them and cut out a piece of fabric and go back and paste it on our airplane.

Eventually, we got it all put together, all lined up, and ready for our first hop.

Q: It was a relatively simple process in that day, wasn't it?

Adm. S.: A hell of a lot of hard work!

Q: Yes, but compared to the modern plane.

Adm. S.: Yes. Now we discovered to our horror that in spite of all our care the horizontal stabilizer was in line with the right wing and quite a bit down as far as the left wing was concerned. We checked everything over again and we couldn't find the fault, so eventually we thought we were taking our lives in our hands but we decided we'd give her a try, and she flew just as well as any other Jenny! So we had our little Jenny to fly all the rest of the year. It was our airplane. We didn't have to go and beg anybody for it.

Q: The navy supplied the fuel?

Adm. S.: Yes, we worked out an arrangement whereby we could get fuel and oil and so forth.

During that summer we had a rather strange schedule. Five mornings in one week we would have classes and then, if I recall correctly, three or four mornings the next week. Well we had just two classes, one in aerodynamics and the other one - this is a very, very fancy name, advanced calculus. Both of these classes were taught by the same instructor and, oh, he was terrific. His name was Dinty Moore, a great big man, the most knock-kneed man I've ever seen in my life, and he was darned near blind. He would wear two and three pairs of glasses so he could see what we wrote on the blackboard. But he had a great way of instructing.

In each one of these classes we had a third man with us, in each case a civilian. One of them was a son of Dr. Hovgaard, who was the well-known naval architect and very eminent in those days, and the other was a very nice chap from Providence whose name escapes me for the moment. Well, the instructor would send one of us to the board each morning and say, "Now, expound the lesson for today," and he re-required us to justify every statement we made. I think he would have accepted two plus two equals four, but only if we said "equals four when added linearly. Nothing else! You had to give your authority for everything.

So we went along and I think we learned a lot from him.

Q: Did you have any direct supervision from the navy at that point?

Adm. S.: No.

At the end of the summer, I got a month's leave and went down to Rochester, Marcia and I got married, went off and had our honeymoon and so forth, and we returned to Boston, where we got ourselves an apartment overlooking the Fenway. Then we started the winter class, which was under the direction of Professor Eddie P. Warner, and he was a genius if there ever was one. He knew aerodynamics and airplane design, as it was known in those days, to the nth degree. He was absolutely abreast of all the latest developments.

A third navy man joined us at that time, George Chapline. He had started out on the previous PG course but had been in an automobile accident and had to spend a lot of time in the hospital, so he joined us. There were several army people there. The only one whose name I can now remember was the redoubtable Jimmy Doolittle. Jimmy was in his second year at MIT and he was quite the fair-haired boy there because, at the end of his first year, he had gone out to the old army McCook Field at Dayton and by conducting various rather hair-raising flights had confirmed a theory on the subject of the relationship between the angle of attack of a wing and the lift of a wing.

Well, we had a very fine year there. Along in March Chapline said that a friend of his who was skipper of a submarine, which had just finished overhaul in the Boston navy yard, was about to take her out for a post-overhaul dive, would any of us care to go along. So Chapline, Doolittle, and I went along. We went out somewhat beyond Boston lightship and went down to 200 feet, rested on the bottom, and couldn't see anything, then came up again and started in to the navy yard. I got in a conversation with Doolittle about what he was trying to do then. He was trying to write a thesis on the subject of either proving or disproving the old much-held belief that an airplane would climb better if you took off upwind than if you took off downwind. All theory said that, in reality, you climbed just the same, it was simply that you covered more ground going downwind and therefore you had the impression that you hadn't climbed as well as if you'd taken off upwind. He was trying to prove this, and he said he was trying to fly around Boston Harbor but it was so bumpy that he couldn't get any data.

Q: The air was so bumpy?

Adm. S.: Yes, and I said rather facetiously, "Why don't you come out here by the lightship? It's pretty smooth out here," and I thought no more of it. Well, we got in, and then Jimmy turned to me and said: "Red, let's go over to the airport and get in an airplane and fly a little."

Okay.

So I went over with him. He broke out a Jenny and, just as he was about to taxi out, he leaned over and called to a soldier on the line:

"Oh, I'm going out by the light ship. If we're not back in about two hours, send a boat out to look for us."

Well, I grabbed him and said:

"Hey, Jimmy, that water is damned cold out there. At least let us get some life preservers."

He growled about that but we got a couple of kapok life preservers, and we went out there. He had me taking data for him from back in the back seat. He'd get this airplane down about ten feet off the water, then he would ease the throttle back and ease the throttle back, try to keep it in the air, then just as it was about to settle, he'd slam on the throttle.

Now, here's the difference between an honest-to-god throttle-jockey pilot like Jimmy Doolittle was and a poor benighted one like me. I would have been half a second behind Jimmy and I would have been in the drink and would have been drowned. He avoided it.

However, after a little while, I said to him:

"Look, Jimmy, you're doing this all down on the leeward side of the lightship, and the nearest land is over there at Cape Ann, about twenty miles down there. Why don't you start from the lightship and do it up that way, so if we go in the drink, they'll see us and pick us up?"

Well, he agreed to that. After a while he had all the data he wanted, gave me the controls, and, believe me, I got that airplane up in the air and headed back to Boston and climbed out. I bawled the life out of him for being such an idiot as to go out there. I said to him:

"Look, man, you're the fair-haired boy of the army air forces. You can get anything you want, and the place for you to do stuff like this is at Aberdeen, on the Chesapeake." They had a good flight facility there.

Jimmy took it okay.

Q: He was flying a navy plane up in Boston?

Adm. S.: No, he was flying one of the army's Jennys. They had a lot of Jennys.

Q: Oh, they had Jennys, too?

Adm. S.: Oh, yes, they had all kinds of Jennys. The Jenny was really an army airplane.

While we were up there, the round-the-world flyers came back from their long expedition.

Q: Wiley Post?

Adm. S.: No, I've forgotten the names of them, but before Wiley Post, they went out for a round-the-world flight. The army got together a group of about a dozen pilots and I think they had six airplanes. They were Douglas airplanes alternately either on pontoons or wheels, and they flew from somewhere in the United States to Alaska and made their way with a great deal of difficulty through all the foggy regions up there to Japan -

Q: They went down to the Kuriles?

Adm. S.: Yes, and they got around the world. They came in while we were up there, and there was a big celebration for them, of course.

Referring now to the question of an academic degree, along in the latter part of the winter, Professor Warner got hold of us and said:

"Well, now if you're going to get a degree you've got to write a thesis, and here are some subjects for theses."

I looked them over and I didn't find any of them that

interested me in the least, so I said, well, I think I'll probably do better for the navy if I just do a little more studying on my own on these other subjects rather than try to write a thesis and get a degree.

Q: Why weren't you tempted to think of another subject on your own?

Adm. S.: I couldn't think of any.

Unfortunately for me, about three weeks or a month before we left there when it was much too late to start, another subject did come up that would have interested me very greatly. But it was too late to do anything about it, so I never did write a thesis and I never did take a degree.

Q: Did Jimmy Doolittle get his degree?

Adm. S.: Oh, yes, he got a degree. I think he got a doctor of science because he'd gotten a master's the year before.

Q: I see.

Adm. S.: Whereas Chapline and Townsend went in together on writing a thesis and doing some flying around that I thought was rather picayune. I think they got degrees.

Then I found myself ordered down to the Naval Academy

to do some instructing in this first year of instruction in flying for midshipmen.

Q: Had this been organized or was it in the process of being organized?

Adm. S.: It was just starting. I got down there and I found myself assigned as the instructor in aerodynamics, which I was very well qualified to do at the time, just having spent a year of aerodynamics under Professor Warner, who was a splendid instructor. I instructed in aerodynamics and I was also given the job of instructing the midshipmen in aerial gunnery. We didn't do any bombing. It was just machine guns and so forth, which I did over at the rifle range.

Q: What kind of planes did you use?

Adm. S.: For the aerial gunnery?

Q: Yes.

Adm. S.: I'm not sure whether we did any shooting in the air. It was more ground instruction in the machine gun which, at that time, was the old Lewis gun. I rigged up various targets to illustrate the use of the sights used in the air. I suppose we did shoot a little in the air but I don't remember that for sure.

My wife and I lived in a wing of old Carvel Hall that year. I've never seen so many tables in my life as there were in that little building. I think we counted something like sixty-seven tables in the small living room.

Q: You mean for diners?

Adm. S.: Well, they were nested, here, there, and everywhere.

Q: Oh, I see.

Adm. S.: Then I was ordered to the Bureau of Aeronautics.

Q: Tell me a little more about setting up this course.

Adm. S.: About the only thing I can think of is one day I was over in the old Dahlgren Hall there, marking midshipmen's papers on aerodynamics just outside the office where Captain Anderson, later Admiral Anderson -

Q: Was this Walter Anderson?

Adm. S.: Walter Anderson, yes.

Q: He lives in Washington now.

Adm. S.: I thought he just died.

Well, Walter was in a tantrum. He was shouting - who the devil was with him? Another navy character was in there with him, trying to calm him down. Oh, Walter was shouting that the midshipmen who couldn't qualify on the rifle range would have to lose their September leave. I didn't think very much of this idea but I had nothing to say in the matter until I was called in and was asked. I replied to him that I thought that the midshipmen who couldn't qualify on the rifle range in just the ordinary sense of the word didn't lose any leave over it and I didn't see why these midshipmen who were taking this aeronautical course should lose any leave, at which point he was completely deflated!

I think I saved someone a lot of trouble.

There's not a great deal more to tell about it.

We had a number of F-5Ls and some small float seaplanes set up there at Annapolis. There was a group of pilots who took the midshipmen out flying around. I was entirely in the ground end of it. I did no instruction in the air. The midshipmen were not instructed in flying, they were just shown what it was like.

Q: Did they evince a great deal of interest in naval aviation?

Adm. S.: Yes, a good deal.

Q: Was Walter Diehl around there, by any chance?

Adm. S.: No, he was up in BuAir. I met him later that year up in BuAir.

After the summer was over, I was ordered to the Bureau of Aeronautics and was assigned to the aircraft instruments desk there. I had one civilian assistant, practically no funds, and we had a very difficult time scraping up instruments to put in the navy's airplanes.

Q: They weren't so very plentiful, either, were they?

Adm. S.: Well, they were much more plentiful than our instruments were!

Q: What was the array of instruments?

Adm. S.: Oh, there was a compass and there was an airspeed meter, an altimeter, there was a tachometer, there was an oil-pressure gauge, an oil-temperature gauge, and a water-temperature gauge. I think that was about the sum total. Oh, and a fuel gauge, a gas gauge, and a bubble inclinometer. That was the sum total.

Q: What kind of research was being done in this area, aerial instruments?

Adm. S.: We had a strong contact with the Bureau of Standards through my civilian assistant, Clarence Seward, who had come to this job in the Bureau of Aeronautics from the Bureau of Standards, from their instruments section, which was headed by a Dr. Brumbacker. He remained in charge of it for many years, and they did our research, such as it was, but they were primarily involved in testing instruments for us that had been delivered by contractors, giving them the necessary acceptance test.

Q: Was Ford in business, on Long Island? Ford Instruments?

Adm. S.: Yes, but they were devoted entirely to fire-control instruments.

Q: I see.

Adm. S.: The Taylor Instrument Company in Rochester, New York, had made a lot of air-speed meters and altimeters during World War I, and they were one of our sources of supply, but they were not at all forward-looking about aircraft instruments.

Then there was an outfit in Brooklyn, Pioneer Instrument Company, that was quite forward-looking on aircraft instruments, but most of their stuff was too expensive for our small amount of money. They were working primarily for the army out at McCook Field.

One day, three Russians came into the office, a Mr. Reichel was the one who spoke the best English and was the most voluable, and he became a very dear friend of mine as the years went on, and there were a couple of doctors. They had a small contract with the navy which had been let by my predecessor on this desk for a form of so-called earth-inductor compass, which was just becoming known. They came in to see us because -

Q: They were stationed in the U.S.?

Adm. S.: Yes, they had a shop in Philadelphia. When I say "Russians," they were all of Russian birth and upbringing but had become American citizens. They had a small contract and their money was running out. The poor old boss doctor explained the situation and I never saw a man who was more upset in all my life. Sweat stood out on his forehead in globules as big as my thumbnail.

By the time they came in there'd been a new fiscal year and we had gotten more money, and Seward and I were slightly in the chips, so we were able to assure them that we could modify the contract because it was apparent that the contract had been drawn at a time when very little was known on this subject. It just didn't apply and we had to put more knowledge into it. We could modify the contract and give them some more money.

I remember the poor old doctor pulling out a handkerchief

the size of a bath towel and if he didn't wipe his brow! They went off feeling distinctly better.

Shortly after that, we put out an order for one or two hundred air-speed meters. This was big stuff in those days, for us, anyway, and Reichel came in with an air-speed meter in his hand that did not conform to certain of our specifications and which we had just copied from McCook Field, those aspects of it, and he said:

"If you will consider this air-speed meter, we can give them to you for thirty-some dollars a piece," whereas the ones that we had been thinking in terms of were one hundred dollars apiece.

We took his air-speed meter, sent it out to the Bureau of Standards, they tested it, and it passed every test with flying colors. It was much better than anything we'd ever had before. So the upshot of it was we recalled our previous request for bids, made the specifications over so that Reichel could get his air-speed meter under the wire, and gave them a job.

Well, in no time at all, he was coming down every few weeks with some other new instrument, all of them better than the ones we had and less expensive. Their shop was a rented work bench in a loft somewhere in Philadelphia. The three of them did all the work themselves with their own hands. They had no employees, and they got started.

In later years, they merged - Reichel broke off from the other two, I don't know what became of the other two, but they merged with the Pioneer Instrument Company up in Brooklyn and took it over. That became quite successful. By the time of World War II, Pioneer had been absorbed by Bendix and Reichel worked on aircraft instruments for Bendix for many years. He became quite an authority on the subject of gyros and he introduced a good many gyroscopic instruments of one kind or another.

Q: He must have been quite prosperous, too?

Adm. S.: Oh, yes, he wound up quite prosperous. Yes, indeed.

Q: That's quite a success story.

Adm. S.: Yes.

Q: In this earlier period there, when you were in the bureau, what about the status of instruments in the Royal Navy? Were they in advance of us?

Adm. S.: I have no idea.

Q: We had no knowledge of it, we had no interchange or anything?

Adm. S.: I have not the least idea. My only knowledge of what was going on in British aviation in those days was

Schoeffel #2 - 104

reading C. C. Grey's articles in the magazine, Aeroplane, which we all read with a great deal of delight.

Q: Well, that was an interesting assignment there. What else took place?

Adm. S.: Oh, our first two children were born while we were there. Marcia's dear old uncle, who had first introduced me to her, died.

Q: Who was head of the bureau?

Adm. S.: Of the Bureau of Aeronautics at that time, Admiral Moffett.

Q: Tell me about him and your relationship with him.

Adm. S.: I had next to no relationship with him. I would see him once a week when he had a morning conference to which a lot of people were pulled in. I would see Admiral Moffett at that time. I had a considerably closer relationship with Commander Rogers, who was the assistant chief of the bureau.

Rogers came to the Bureau of Aeronautics from Hawaii and out there he had become extremely interested in the subject of the application of celestial navigation to airplanes. He came in and I had found myself, more or less by default, the supposed navigator of the Bureau of Aeronautics because Seward and I used to go out to the Naval Observatory, and they had a few of the old Byrd sextants out there, and they were purchasing a couple of bubble octants intended for the use of airplanes -

Q: Bubble what?

Adm. S.: Octants, not sextants.

Well, Brumbacker, out at the Bureau of Standards, had devised a bubble sextant for use in aircraft which later, during World War II and for a while afterwards, had a great deal of use, particularly in the army air force.

As I say, Rogers came to the Bureau of Aeronautics, and he was very much upset to find that the Bureau of Aeronautics was doing very, very little, if anything, about aerial celestial navigation. To begin with, there were no navigation tables at that time that were at all easy to use in an airplane. They were huge, voluminous things. It was about that time that Weems -

Q: Mammy Weems!

Adm. S.: Mammy Weems got interested in the subject and saw a formula composed by a Japanese that he thought could be used, and he brought out a little book of tables, which was very, very far in advance of anything else for use in the air at that time. In fact, during World War II he ran a school primarily for army air force navigators, and I guess he graduated a great many of them.

Weems tried out all the various forms of sextants and octants and he went for the Bureau of Standards type, which he liked very well. I guess it probably was the best and the handiest. He wrote a book on navigation, in which he very kindly gave me some credit, on which I drew royalties of about a dollar and a quarter a year for some years!

Q: I have a copy of that book.

Adm. S.: You do!

About that time a form of Dutton's Navigation was put out, in which I contributed a chapter on aerial navigation. I didn't have much to say about celestial navigation in there. Mainly, it was just to find your way from here to there. I can remember many years later, as a flag officer at sea, I was haunting the flag plot and one of the quartermasters came up to me with a Dutton's in his hand and said:

"Admiral, by any chance, are you the man who wrote this chapter?" I said yes. Well, my prestige with the quartermaster's group went up 100 per cent that morning!

Q: When you were there in the bureau, do you remember a very beautiful, relatively young lady, Joy Bright Hancock?

Adm. S.: Yes, but I don't believe I met her until later.

Q: I see. She was there, in the bureau.

Adm. S.: Yes, she was there.

I got my first lighter-than-air hop in those days. What was the name of the lighter-than-air designer in BuAir? He was a Bostonian, a very, very Boston name and very, very Boston accent, and a lot of fun to be around. He took me up to Lakehurst and he installed some strain gauges on the Shenandoah, which was moored to the high mooring mast. Getting on and off those big gas bags was quite an affair. You got up to the top of the mooring mast, about 150 or 160 feet up, and there was a narrow walkway into the nose of the ship. Then you requested permission to come on board. This was no mere matter of formality, the way it is on board a ship. They wanted to know how much you weighed, where did you want to go, how long were you going to be there, and quite a bit of information. Then they did some things, I think, on a slide rule and after a while, they told you you could either come on board or you would have to wait.

Eventually, we got on board and he installed his strain gauges. Then the ship took off and made a short flight. We came back, and they were going to put her in the hangar. Well, they lined all us passengers up and, as she went into the hangar, it being a sunny day, the nose got into shadow and the gas up in the nose started to cool and to contract, so the nose would be losing lift and the tail would still have as much lift as before. Well, they had us all aft there and, at the proper time, the word would be passed, "Two passengers jump off," so we would jump off. We only jumped down maybe so far, and we'd get on the ground in that fashion!

Q: Was Ralph Barnaby around?

Adm. S.: Yes, Ralph was there.

Q: He was interested in gliders at the time.

Adm. S.: Yes. I don't think he got to be a big glider man until later years, but Ralph was there.

Q: Gene Wilson was there, too, wasn't he?

Adm. S.: I think Gene had already resigned.

Q: No, he didn't resign until 1931, I believe.

Adm. S.: Oh. Yes, you're quite right. I don't remember whether he was there. Henry Mullinnix was there and it was said of him that the engine section did not have to spend any money on long-distance calls because Henry just put his head out of the window and shouted!

During that period, I had one interesting little adventure. I got down to the office one day and I found that the two people at the next desk, who were the radio wizards of BuAir, Piggy Price -

Q: Is that Admiral Price?

Adm. S.: No, this fellow died quite a while before that - and the other one was the fellow who had been radio operator, radio officer, on the NC-4 - I can't think of his name.

Q: Lavender?

Adm. S.: No.

Q: Was Captain Lavender around, too?

Adm. S.: Oh, yes, Captain Lavender was around. I never knew him at all well, just very slightly.

Well, these two were taking an F5-L down to Norfolk and I wanted to try a little something in the navigational line, so I asked if I could go with them. I climbed up in the bow and we went to Norfolk without any incident, but on the way back we hadn't gotten very far when the bay began to fog over. It was blowing strongly out of the southwest, but the fog was beginning over on the eastern side of the bay and advancing across the bay against the wind. Price was doing the flying and he put her down. We hadn't been on the surface any length of time before we were enveloped in fog. Okay. They turned to me, "Where are we?" I had the maps, and I tried to estimate as well as I could where we were, so they decided to taxi back to Norfolk.

Well, one of them was at the controls and he got the plane up on the step. We must have been making about 50 knots. We were going along like mad, I was up in the bow, and fish stakes were going by right and left, scaring me to death, when, all of a sudden, whammo. This airplane practically stood on its nose and then settled back.

We were hard and fast aground on a sandbar.

Well, where was this sandbar? We didn't exactly know. I thought it was probably off the mouth of the Back River, down by Langley Field.

Q: Celestial navigation is not as easy from the water, is it?

Adm. S.: In a fog! A thick fog.

They cranked up their radios on the skidfin antenna, which ran across the top of the upper wing and in no time at all they had communication with Norfolk and were just about to tell Norfolk about our plight and please notify our families, when apparently somebody pulled a switch on the electric switchboard and there was no more communication. We never could raise them!

There were seven or eight of us in this airplane, including the pigeon man from the Bureau of Aeronautics, and he had a crateful of pigeons. We took stock of our food and water. We had no water but there was plenty coming down out of the air, nice and cold, and as far as food was concerned there was one mech who had four of five little sandwiches and that was all.

I made the suggestion that we might cook up some of the pigeons . Well, as far as the pigeon man was concerned, forget it.

Q: Government property, wasn't it?

Adm. S.: Yes, but we were government property, too! I might just as well have suggested that we cook and eat his children, because he grabbed his basket of pigeons and quietly retired to the uttermost limits of the stern of the fuselage of the airplane. He got himself two Very pistols on the way back and he sat there with the Very pistols loaded and cocked!

So we did nothing about eating pigeons.

The tide ebbed and we got out and walked around the sandbar, and it was an island. There was a duck blind on it, that was all. Then, along in the middle of the night the tide flooded and we got off the island and went out and anchored. I spent the night in the region immediately behind the pilot's seat, a nice trickle of water leaking through, wet and cold, expecting to wake up with pneumonia of the worst variety, but I woke up the next morning and I never felt better in my life, and all the rest of us about the same.

We got under way and decided to taxi again, still thick fog. Eventually we saw something that looked like Willoughby Spit. We were very much afraid of getting too far to the left and going out to sea, so we headed in for this land. It was not Willoughby Spit, but it was a small island that no longer exists down there, and it was off Back River. There was a bunch of fishermen out there. They took us in and they fed us royally, but they had no communications. They had no telephone or radio.

Along in the afternoon the weather began to clear up, so we got out in the plane and started off, got in the air, the radio working fine, except we couldn't raise Norfolk, couldn't raise anybody. We kept on going. We got up the mouth of the Potomac and, just as we started up the Potomac, fog began to form again, so we landed at a little bit of a fishing village called Lewissetta, on the Northern Neck. Lewissetta was really a place that was out of this world. They had a telephone there and they had had it for about three months, the first they had ever had and they were very proud of it.

So we got on the telephone and told Anacostia where we

were, that we were all okay, and so forth.

These people told us that in the hard winter of 1917 and 1918, they had darned near starved to death until finally a steamer managed to break the ice and get some way up the river and they went out over the ice about half or three-quarters of a mile and got provisions. That was all that kept them from starving. Roads down in that region were almost nonexistent in those days.

The squire put us all up for the night. He had a big house, pretty ramshackle. Dinner was corn on the cob and oysters. Breakfast was corn on the cob and oysters. Very good, all of it. Then we tried to offer them some money and had a terrible time getting them to take anything, but he finally accepted, I think, fifty cents apiece, or some such amount, and thought he was being very unpatriotic for doing it.

Then we got out to the airplane and one engine got started. We cranked up the other one and it didn't start, and the mech said, "Well, there's only one dog left on the starter." I don't remember very much about the starter. It was a hand-crank affair they had on the old Liberty engine, but there were three dogs on this starter and these starter dogs frequently broke. Well, as long as you had one there was still some hope you could get the engine started. So we hoped, and it started, and home we came.

My wife always kidded me thereafter, "You called up and said you'd be late for dinner. Yes, you were late for dinner!"

This was just another one of the little adventures we had in those days. As I told my son, the fun all went out of flying when they started flying above 10,000 feet!

Interview #3 with Rear Admiral Malcolm F. Schoeffel,
                                    U.S. Navy (Retired)
Place: The residence of his son, Captain Peter Schoeffel,
    in Alexandria, Virginia
Date: Friday morning, 12 January 1979
Subject: Biography
By: John T. Mason, Jr.

Q: As we broke off, Admiral, last time, you were talking about your tour of duty in the Bureau of Aeronautics in the years 1925 to 1927, and, unless you have some things to add to that chapter, I think you're ready to depart from the Bureau of Aeronautics and go out to the Langley.

Adm. S.: I do have a couple of things to add.

Q: All right, Sir.

Adm. S.: While I was there, I gave his first airplane flight to a young brother-in-law who was then a cadet at West Point and is now a retired lieutenant general of the U.S. Air Force, James E. Briggs, my wife's younger brother. I flew him down to Dahlgren, a long flight! - in a DH.
    Before I get away from that, also, I'd like to speak

of something that has nothing to do with the Bureau of Aeronautics. It goes back to the old Pittsburgh. I wrote some years ago to Peter that I had seen an article, really just a yarn, in the back of the Naval Institute about the armored cruiser squadron in the early years of this century, and I attached a picture for the article showing the Colorado in all the splendor of the old white and buff paint. They also did other things than paint differently in those days, for although she is obviously at anchor, I do not see the jack flying from her jackstaff.

The author of the article wonders just what purpose the armored cruisers were supposed to perform in case of war, and he quotes a part of the old song,

Why the hell did Uncle Sam

Build these ten ships not worth a dam?

It must be they're to fight Japan

In the armored cruiser squadron

Which was frequently sung the "harmless boozer squadron."

I have often independently wondered the same and have believed on no authority that they were thought to embody the lessons of the Chinese-Japanese War, our Spanish war, and the Russo-Japanese War. In those conflicts few, if any, hits were made by the 12- or 13-inch guns of the battleships, and most of the damage was done by 6-inch or even smaller guns. At the Yalu, the Japanese had no battleships but the armored cruisers successfully took on the Chinese battleships. At Tsushima, Togo commanded his little force of battleships, while Kamamura handled independently a squadron of six or eight armored cruisers. These battles seemed to indicate the armored cruiser was a pretty effective weapon in action.

On the other hand, at Santiago our battleships completely destroyed four Spanish armored cruisers, but this was largely due to the fact that the Spaniards had such bad coal they couldn't come anywhere near their legend speeds of 21 knots. The only ships we had there that could have kept pace with them were our two armored cruisers, the Brooklyn and New York, also 21-knotters. The New York, having taken Sampson to Siboney for a conference with General Shafter, never got into action at all. Our fastest battleship was the Iowa, rated at 17 knots, with three Oregons at 16 and the Texas only 14.

We started building our armored cruisers before the Russo-Japanese War, and built six of 13,500 tons at 22 knots, the Colorado, California, Pennsylvania, Maryland, West Virginia, and North Carolina. Each carried only four 8-inch guns and fourteen 6-inch, and a number of 3-inch. They were followed with four more 13,500-ton, 22 knot-, four 10-inch guns and so forth, the Washington, Tennessee, Montana, and South Dakota. Going back to the rhyme -

The Washington and Tennessee,

The finest ships to sail the sea.

They rounded Cape Horn just to be

In the armored cruiser squadron.

And the "finest ships" is also sung at times as the "damnedest ships."

The armored cruiser squadron was based on the West Coast and was our Pacific Fleet in those days.

Commander C. G. Davie, class of 1907, was my World War I skipper in the Kimberley. He had been in the Colorado, I think, and he used to regale our wardroom with stories of its glories. According to him, they had a truly wonderful esprit de corps and could steam, shoot, or race rings around any battleship anywhere. This was implicit in another song of which I know only one couplet -

Sixteen battleships all in line

Down at Guantánamo look mighty fine.

I authorize you, Peter, to go into a perfect frenzy and fill this out, extolling the glories of the armored cruiser squadron. As to their steaming ability, I know it firsthand. I was an observer in 1920 on board the Pittsburgh, ex-Pennsylvania, for a twenty-four-hour, full-power run, and her reciprocating engines still did the full 22 knots. Also, she won the engineering red "E" three years in a row. As to their shooting ability, quoting again -

The Maryland boys can shoot 6-inch,

Gee, but the battleships are a cinch

For the armored cruiser squadron.

In support of this last, I depose as follows:

Our exec in the Pittsburgh was Commander E. D. McWhorter, later rear admiral, class of 1907, who had been in the

Maryland. In the spring of 1921, we in the Pittsburgh went to the Gulf of Gabes, off Africa, to fire target practices. All during World War I the Pittsburgh and some of her sisters were stationed on the east coast of South America, where they wined and dined like mad and fired nothing but their saluting batteries. In fact, the scuttlebutt said they had shot nothing else since 1917, four years before, and all hands fully expected the guns to burst. For these 1921 firings, I was plotting-room officer, very much, as the French say, faute de mieux, not because I knew much about it, but because I knew more than anybody else. Being able to work a plotting board and to adjust our only fire-control instrument, a baby Ford range-keeper.

Before the firings, McWhorter asked me what it took to get a 6-inch "E on short-range battle practice, and I quoted the book, as I remember it, "four hits per gun per minute." McWhorter was very contemptuous of this figure and declared that a gun of his battery on the Maryland had made twelve hits per minute in her night practice. I disrespectfully hooted at this figure and challenged him to prove it. This he did by breaking out a letter of commendation he had, fully supporting his statement. He did admit that they had violated every safety rule to do it, but twelve shots per minute from a hand-loaded, 6-inch gun, firing 105-pound shells and using about sixty-pound cartridge cases was really almost unbelievable.

I never heard anything else like it until the late

thirties when the new Brooklyn-class, 6-inch cruisers were reputed to be able to fire ten shots per gun per minute from their twelve-gun battery.

As to the esprit de corps of the armored cruiser squadron, I remember a couple of other verses of the song, but never mind about them. They have nothing much to do with it, but I did want to get in that about McWhorter's statement of what the Maryland had done in the old days.

Q: That's taken from a letter you wrote to Peter?

Adm. S.: Yes.

Q: When did you write that?

Adm. S.: In '75.

Q: Very interesting.

Adm. S.: In the summer of 1927 -

Q: That's right, August 1927.

Adm. S.: Marcia and I and our two little girls departed the Washington area for California, where Marcia had never been. We got out there and rented a house in Coronado. I reported ostensibly to VT Squadron 4. Well, as it turned out, there never was a VT-4 until years later, but after some time this VT-4 business was canceled and my orders were changed to VT-2, where I became Flight Officer.

At that time, the squadron was operating SC planes either on twin floats or on wheels as torpedo planes. All the pilots were qualified on board the Langley, which was the only carrier we had, but we did not take the SCs, which were large aeroplanes for those days, on board the Langley. All the qualification had been done on smaller planes. The technique of torpedo-dropping was to fly very low and very slow just as you were about to let the torpedo drop, and if I made a rhyme I didn't mean to do it!

Q: Very slow, how many knots?

Adm. S.: Just above stalling speed, so that if you misjudged things a little, there was a real danger of going in the drink.

Q: You also were a very good target, were you not?

Adm. S.: Yes, but what did they have to shoot at us with? Practically nothing. We were elementary, but so was anti-aircraft in those days. They talked a good deal in the battle wagons about putting up splash barrages, but I am willing to bet nobody knew how to fire a splash barrage.

Well, they'd have these monthly Battle Force tactical

exercises. The battleships would come steaming down from San Diego - I don't know where all the destroyers were at that time - but the battleships were generally surrounded by a big circle of submarines on the surface as their outer screen and they had a few cruisers with them. We would go out and simulate a bombing and a torpedo attack on them.

Q: Their progress must have been very slow with submarines as escort?

Adm. S.: I suppose they steamed at about 12, something of that sort. In Admiral King's later words, it was probably a case of doing the best you could with what you had.

I remember one time, returning from one of these exercises, looking back toward the battleships, a number of them in column, not far from the Coronado Islands, and I saw three or four submerged submarines lined up on the near side of these battleships and apparently just about to go in for an attack. I knew that the big submarines, the V boats, as they were called, 3,000-tonners, big for those days, were trying to develop tactics of submarine attack, not necessarily in formation but in concert. But, as they had practically no means of underwater communication, it was a pretty darned dangerous thing for them to try. Here were these several submarines, and it's one of the few times I've ever seen a submerged submarine, but I could see them very plainly.

Q: Q: This was an early concept of the German wolfpack, was it?

Adm. S.: Yes.

In those days, the navy talked a good deal about fleet submarines. I don't know just what they expected a fleet submarine would be likely to do, but this business of trying to operate in concert was certainly a part of it, and in all probability, the idea was to try to get the submarines acting in concert into an enemy fleet in the course of a battleship action, because in those days everything was expected to hinge upon battleship action and, truly, had there been a war at that time, I'm sure it would have, because none of the other weapons were sufficiently advanced to have very much effect on anything. Certainly, aircraft were not in those days.

After some months, we were reequipped with newer airplanes, the T3-Ms, which for those days were very large biplanes, entirely land planes, and were very hard to fly.

Q: Who turned them out?

Adm. S.: The Martin Company.

We were moved upto the big land-plane hangar in the middle of North Island and operated from there. At that time none of the surface of North Island was paved in any way and the landing area became just a deep desert of dust.

Any time an airplane took off or landed, the amount of dust thrown up was just unbelievable.

Q: That must have been very difficult.

Adm. S.: It was very unpleasant.

These airplanes were equipped with very large engines for those days, Packard, I think, 1A 2500, or some such - the 2500 is correct. They were 750 horsepower engines, which were very powerful for those days.

In the meantime, the fighter squadrons were working away at the development of dive-bombing. It was something quite brand new. In fact, very shortly after I arrived there, they put on a special test of dive-bombing on a towed target at sea, and I was told off to be the chief observer for this thing. Of course, they had no bombs of any size but they were quite accurate and I turned in a voluminous report on this subject, which I think set forth the advantages of dive-bombing reasonably well.

Q: Was this concept employed by any other navy in the world?

Adm. S.: Not at that time. Now, it is true that many years later Forrest Sherman had an argument with the Air Force or Air Corps and dug up a statement in the official history of the Royal Air Force in World War I, in which it speaks of dive-bombing the zeppelin hangars up in north Germany. But I'm very dubious as to whether the British really dove on them. They probably just went in in a moderate glide.

One of the most successful dive-bombers in those days, early days of it, was Injun Joe Tomlinson. He was in one of the fighter squadrons and it was reputed that he would climb to 19,000 feet, put his airplane into a 90-degree dive, and really come down, let his bomb go at about 1,000 feet, then pull out and level with the sage bushes.

Although we were a bombing squadron, we had no really worthwhile bombsights. Nobody did in those days. We had something called the Mark 3 bombsight, and all it would indicate to you was that now was a good time to release your bombs for altitudes up to maybe a couple of thousand feet, but I don't think it was worth a hoot at any higher altitude. You had to take a preset wind and set it and it was stabilized by some bubbles and by a magnetic compass. It was a very elementary affair.

Q: But at least they were thinking in these terms and felt the need for a bombsight.

Adm. S.: Oh, yes, we had bombsights way back as far as World War I.

As far as qualification on board the Langley was concerned, I will now tell you the sad, sad tale of my shipmate,

Logan Ramsey.

As I say, we were hangared in the big balloon hangar and one afternoon I was up there in the office, going through the paper work, and Logan came in. Well, he was never what I would call point de vice, he was never snappy in his clothing, but he looked particularly rough. He looked as though he had been dunked in water and only partially dried out, there was a big rent in his breeches. He went up to the mail box, pulled out a letter, and sat down and started to read it. Then he let out a low moan. I turned to him and said:

"Logan, what's the matter?" And he said:

"Listen to my day. Larry and I went out on the Langley to qualify. He made ten landings and qualified. I had made seven or eight, then the hook stuck and it would wouldn't come down. They made a lot of motions at me."

Oh, I missed something. On the way out he got into a wardroom bridge game and they took about three dollars from him. In those days, three dollars was a lot of money. Then he got up on deck and he had made about seven landings, when the hook stuck. They made all kinds of motions with flags and things at him, and he zoomed his airplane but it apparently wouldn't come down. Eventually, they put up the green flag, which meant come in and land. Well, as he came in, he noticed they did not have the landing gear rigged. He remembered that the year before an experimental fighter plane known as the Tin TS had landed on board the Langley without any arresting gear and that people had run out and grabbed her wing tips. It had been quite successful, so he thought that this was what they were going to do with him.

So he came in and put her down on the deck and he rolled up the deck and he said: "To my utter amazement nobody came out to grab my wing tips and the first thing I knew I went over the bow." The plane guard was the little old minesweeper, the Gannet, the one that we always called the Me Too. She picked him up, hauled him on board, and, he said, "The ship's dog bit me, and that's how I tore my pants. Then," he said, "I get back here and I receive this letter. All our household goods were being shipped around from Baltimore by steamer, commercial steamer, and this steamer got as far as Descanso Point, about thirty miles south of here, when it runs itself aground and I am now informed that her cargo was mainly marble and that under the law of general average I have to pay fifty percent of the value of my household goods to get them released."

That was Logan's day!

Q: Quite a series of tragedies.

Adm. S.: Then in 1929 we were very happy to get rid of the T3-Ms. They were replaced with another Martin airplane called the T4-M, which was an excellent airplane, very easy to fly. It had an air-cooled engine, one of the early Pratt and Whitney Hornets, and was really a major step forward. Along in the fall, the Saratoga and the Lexington came around from the East Coast. They had a small contingent of airplanes on board and had done a little operating but not very much.

Q: They were almost brand new, weren't they?

Adm. S.: They were brand new. We went out and qualified in them with the T4-Ms and everything went very well.

That winter we went south to Panama with the fleet on a big cruise and it was the first time that the U.S. Navy had really had carriers to operate with it. The rivalry between the two ships was very intense. The fleet problem that year envisioned an attack upon the canal by the Saratoga, with the Lexington being on the defending side. Admiral Reeves was Commander, Aircraft, at the time and he took the Saratoga way down south, just off the Galápagos Islands. We went over the equator and all us pollywogs got wet down and so forth. Then we turned around and started back at full speed.

The night of the final run-in, we were dogged for several hours by a cruiser of the other side. She had all her searchlights playing all round, trying to bring in her friends. I don't know what ever became of her, whether her engines went phooey or whether we were supposed to have beaten her off with our after 8-inch guns. Of course, if we'd fired those 8-inch guns, we'd have smashed a lot of our airplanes, but I guess nobody paid any attention to that sort of thing. Well, along about ten o'clock at night, Reeves called a meeting of all the pilots in the wardroom. He addressed us and said he was getting ready to send us off when he got in the proper position, and I remember him winding up by saying, "And we'll beat that <u>Lexington</u> if I have to keep all of you up all night," at which point we all cheered and hollered and so forth.

Flight quarters was sounded very early in the morning, maybe at three o'clock or something of that sort. We got up there for Reeves, after much consultation with his staff, had decided on doing a very bold thing, really quite a rash one. He was going to launch the whole air group in complete darkness and fly them to hit the canal at about the break of dawn. At that time none of us had ever done any night flying to speak of. Down at Pensacola I know I myself had participated in two night landings with an instructor at the controls. That was the sum total of my night experience and I think of about everybody else, and just how we were going to get off in the dark and get together and so forth, none of us had any good idea.

Q: Did Admiral Reeves?

Adm. S.: He just said he thought his pilots could do anything! I think that was about as far as the staff thinking went.

Finally, we manned our planes and I was in No. 2-T-10, I was the exec of VT-2 at that time, way back near the stern. I thought I heard the word passed "Stand by to start engines," so I primed up the engine and had my mech ready to start her, we had inertia starters. He turned up the starter, just waited to throw it in, but no call came to start engines. After about ten or fiften minutes, again "Stand by to start engines," and this time my engine wouldn't start. It wouldn't start. We had about ninety airplanes on board there, and eighty-nine of them left, took off, and went to Panama, and one didn't. That one was I. I was left on the deck. All the talent of the ship was turned loose on my engine but it wasn't until about nine o'clock in the morning that we could get the damned thing to run. After that it ran beautifully. I felt very, very low indeed and I was very much afraid I was going to be accused of being yellow. Fortunately, we had another operation a day or two later and I was able to do my stuff!

Q: Did the eighty-nine get off and proceed?

Adm. S.: Oh, yes, they proceeded to Panama. They were met by a few army fighters, but our fighters had much better performance at that time, air-cooled fighters, than the army's water-cooled ones, so we brushed their fighters aside and bombed and strafed and so forth. It's perfectly true that, as of 1929, if we had made an actual carrier attack at that time, we had neither the sighting equipment nor the bombs to do really very much damage. We couldn't have hurt that canal very much, but it was very hot stuff just the same. One of the Lexington airplanes appeared over the Saratoga along about eight o'clock but we didn't pay much attention to them. We were all full of beans, of course.

Then, a few days later, we had another night operation. This time the battleships were going to bombard some of the forts, and our squadron, VT-2, was told off to lay a smoke-screen for them. We were launched in the dark again, got out there, and all I could see was some lights ahead. We didn't do much getting together, but I was able to head over toward the proper area and, upon arrival there, three or four of VT-2's airplanes joined up with me. The squadron commander was nowhere to be seen. We were supposed to lay this smokescreen at a certain time, so we went out and laid the smokescreen and we got a good smokescreen. Then we proceeded back to the ship.

The squadron commander was Commander Harry Bogusch, who would have been quite an effective officer in World War II, I'm sure, if he had not unfortunately died of a heart attack a few years later. I can remember Harry bustling into the ready room and he was so lavish in his praise of me that I was very much embarrassed. He said he couldn't find his way to the right place and get there at the right time and he thought everything was all shot to bits, and he said:

"Suddenly, right on the dot, I saw the smokescreen begin, and I knew my boys had been sufficiently indoctrinated to go and do it."

Later on on that cruise I had - this is a lot of "I" but - I had another opportunity to make myself known. The cruise was going to wind up with a great big operation, the whole U.S. Fleet against a simulated enemy fleet down there in the Gulf of Panama. The simulated enemy fleet was composed of some train ships, a couple of storeships, tankers, and things like that. To my utter amazement, I received a secret letter from the commander in chief of the U.S. Fleet, not signed by him but -

Q: Who was it, by the way?

Adm. S.: I don't remember who he was at the time, 1929.

Q: Wiley?

Adm. S.: May have been. Yes, I'm sure it was Admiral Wiley because I remember he came on board the Saratoga on the way north.

This secret letter established "Force Fox", which was to consist of four airplanes from VT-2 commanded by me, by name, to lay a smokescreen for the enemy fleet. We were to join the enemy! and lay a smokescreen for them. I went over and saw the enemy fleet commander, who was a very pleasant captain whose name I don't remember, and we agreed quite quickly that all we could do was find him and then fly around until he made a certain flag signal, at which point we would fly out and lay our smokescreen.

This operation got under way and about 180 airplanes came from the Saratoga and the Lexington. They came over and dusted us all off. Then eighty or ninety destroyers came bustling in and torpedoed us right and left. Then the signal went up to lay smoke, so we headed for the battle wagons, which we could see over in the distance, there were ten or twelve of them, and we split. We started laying our smoke, two of us went to the left and two of us went to the right. When our smoke ran out, I looked back and I saw that we had left a holiday right at the start, a small hole. We really didn't have any smoke left but we bustled back there and tried to plug it but were not successful.

Then we returned to our ships. Some days later, after the critique, I heard that the fleet brains decided that the enemy fleet had invented a marvelous new tactic, holes in smokescreens, because it so turned out that my side could look through this hole and see a number of battleships and concentrate on them, whereas the other side couldn't see much of anything through this hole! So the enemy fleet was supposed to have invented a great new tactic. In fact, the commander in chief sent a "well done" to my fleet commander and the fleet commander most politely passed it down to me. His letter said he thought that really the commander in chief's "well done" was primarily based on the smokescreen. So I got a lot of kudos out of that one, for no good reason.

By this time it was 1931, and I found myself picked up out of VT-2 and taken on the staff as gunnery and tactical officer, so-called, really as assistant operations to Lieutenant Commander Art Davis, later a vice admiral.

Q: This was on the Saratoga?

Adm. S.: From the Saratoga. We shifted over to the staff.

Q: The date should be 1929.

Adm. S.: Yes. Admiral Butler was again Commander, Aircraft, and, oh, what the devil was the name of his chief of staff, a fellow who out in the Philippines many years before had gotten out of a submarine by going out through a torpedo tube, just to prove that it could be done. He had been quite a boxer at the Naval Academy in his day. Kenneth Whiting!

Well, between us, Admiral Butler was a very nice gentleman but he wasn't really much of an admiral, and the chief of staff was a lot of fun to be shipmates with but he wasn't much of a chief of staff, and Art Davis really ran the outfit. I was in those days extremely conscientious about my work. Oh, how I labored. I wrote reams and reams and reams that nobody else ever read. All of a sudden, it was decided that all the destroyers, practically all of them, had some grave defect in them, either bad boilers or they were top-heavy or something of that sort, and they practically all had to stay north and couldn't go on the cruise. So the Pacific Fleet had only about half a dozen destroyers to take with it. It wasn't Admiral Wiley and I've forgotten who it was by this time who had the Pacific Fleet, but he called upon us to be prepared to do screening for the fleet with aircraft, and it was turned over to me to devise the ways and means. In this, we were much hampered by our desire for safety because we didn't want our airplanes to be farther away than twenty-five miles from a destroyer at any time, just in case somebody went in the drink.

I eventually wrote up a lot of stuff that got approved, but it was horrible. It was really horrible - quite unworkable in practice.

However, in the course of that year I had one very pleasant duty to perform. C. R. Brown, Cat Brown, later four-star, came into my office one day and asked if he could go out in town and buy some gold leaf and put a gold "E" on his airplane because he had just made sixty hits out of sixty shots at Individual Battle Practice, Machine Guns. So far as I know, he is the only man who ever made sixty hits out of sixty shots on that practice. If I recall correctly, something like twelve got you an "E" so I had the pleasure of being able to tell Cat to go and do it.

Another funny thing with him. One of our squadrons went out to fire a gunnery exercise offshore and they violated one of our safety rules that was firing over clouds when they couldn't see what was underneath. The upshot of it was that they rained 50-caliber bullets all over La Jolla. Nobody got hurt but quite a number of people got scared. I know some of their bullets fell around the doorway of a school just as school was letting out. I said nobody got hurt, but some of the kids burned their fingers by picking up the bullets while they were still hot, but those were the only casualties.

We tried to pin this thing down. We had all these bullets and we had read a lot about forensic ballistics. Cat was made the recorder of a board of investigation and he was told off to take all the guns from this particular squadron that was suspect and fire bullets through them and recover the bullets. This sounds very easy. He went out to the sandbank at the edge of North Island, fired into the bank, and when he did manage to dig a bullet out it was so deformed he couldn't tell a thing. Well, we tried this, that, and the other thing and eventually Cat devised a scheme. He got some metal sewer pipe and had it cut in two longitudinally to make a sort of a trough out of it. He plugged up one end, I guess with clay, and the other end he plugged with very heavy grease. Then he put water in between. He took as much powder out of the cartridges as he could and still have them fire, and he fired through the grease into the water. Well, there was grease all over that part of North Island!

Q: But at least the shell wasn't deformed?

Adm. S.: Yes. Then all of these bullets were very carefully put into little boxes and sent in to the Navy Department along with a report - I don't believe I ever saw the report - and in the Navy Department somebody put the boxes down on his desk, picked the bullets up, then he put the bullets down, and he didn't put them back in the right boxes, so when it was all through nobody knew which bullet belonged in which box, so nothing could be done about it! Oh, oh!

Well, we went off south on that cruise. Admiral Butler was in command.

Q: South of the Panama Canal, you mean?

Adm. S.: What?

Q: Toward the Panama Canal again?

Adm. S.: Yes, the same sort of thing, and Captain King had the <u>Lexington</u> that year. Well, the <u>Lexington</u> was smearing us right and left that year. We got up to Guantánamo and in the final climactic battle of the fleet problem we were put out of action very thoroughly by the Lex. I came down from the bridge feeling very, very badly about this, and as I stood on the flight deck I looked down into the water and, for the second time in my life, I saw a completely submerged submarine, absolutely clear, off our starboard side.

Q: At what depth?

Adm. S.: She must have been forty of fifty feet down. There wasn't a ripple on the surface, not an indication. This submarine's paint job was not in very good shape. I remember seeing red-lead rust blotches on her. But she was absolutely clear down there. It was amazing. However, we were already out of action, so any attack she may have made on us didn't count. It was also that day that I saw the only water spouts I've ever seen in my life. It was a beautiful clear day and then along came a long, narrow cloud running from southeast to northwest, not very high, but from it there depended three water spouts. They weren't very big and they didn't pass near us and we didn't hear any noise or anything of the sort. The only ones I've ever seen.

I don't know why I had gotten this particular yen for my next duty. I was due to be detached end of '31, I mean of '29 -

Q: No, '31 this time.

Adm. S.: I was due to be detached in the summer of '30 and I was very anxious to go to duty at Dahlgren, second choice Hawaii. The aviator on duty at Dahlgren at that time was John Ballentine and he got a further year there, so Dahlgren was out. Admiral Butler was a very kindly gentleman and he arranged for me to get my orders quite early so that we could get our household goods gathered up and shipped out to Hawaii, so that they would be there when we arrived. The household goods were packed and shipped. Then Admiral Reeves relieved Admiral Butler, and Admiral Reeves asked for me to stay on with Art Davis. I don't suppose he asked for me because he didn't know anything about me.

Q: It was probably Davis who asked?

Adm. S.: Yes. Captain A. B. Cook was chief of staff and a greater difference in the command you cannot imagine than the Reeves-Cook pair versus the Butler-Whiting.

Q: Savvy Cook?

Adm. S.: No, not Savvy Cook. This was Arthur Byron Cook. This pair was great and we had a most successful year. Upon the completion of it, I did get my orders to Dahlgren. Meanwhile, all our furniture had been out in Hawaii, on the dock, for about six months, and it eventually caught up with us in Dahlgren.

Q: What did the family do in the interim?

Adm. S.: They'd gone into an apartment.

And that Dahlgren duty was great. Oh, how we did enjoy that down there. It was a very small community at the time and it was truthfully said that Dahlgren was ninety miles from a streetcar and thirty-five miles from a haircut, meaning thirty-five miles from Fredericksburg.

I had the aviation detail, which had twenty or twenty-five enlisted men. Those were practically the only enlisted men at the Proving Ground at that time, because practically all the other employees were civil. I had half a dozen airplanes, a couple of seaplanes, three or four land planes, bombers, fighters, and so forth. I practically did my own scheduling. Once in a while the station called upon me to do something or other, but most of the time I was absolutely my own boss.

The chief job was evaluation of the Norden Mark 15 bomb sight. Two prototype models had been delivered a month or so before I got there, and the Norden Company charged the U.S. government a total of only $15,000 for these two prototypes. That was all, for the development and manufacture, and those two prototypes were practically as good as the Norden bomb sight was throughout World War II. I state this price in contrast to the present day when even a study of the bombing problem would cost many times that.

myself. Well, it was an extremely bumpy day. I was down in the bombing compartment when we hit one lollapaloosa of a bump and I was thrown up against the bomb-release handle. I wasn't sure whether it had been actuated or not. We had a little port in the side of the bombers compartment so I could look out and see the bombs and, sure enough, one of them had gone. Where had it gone? I looked down. Nothing but swampy woods. Think no more of it. So we went on and did our stuff.

Q: From what height were you bombing?

Adm. S.: In general from about 5,000 to 7,000 feet because we had conducted quite a series of tests indicating that if we expressed the error in terms of an angle which we did as mills. of the altitude, the error in those terms was practically constant in terms of altitude. In other words, we could bomb at a reasonably low altitude that didn't take all day to climb to and get a figure which, in mils., was good for any other.

Next morning, the leading chief came in, Percival Huntington Ford, always called Henry Ford, a little bit of a chap but, gee, he was great. He came in and he said:

"Mr. Schoeffel, about that bomb that fell off the airplane yesterday."

"Yes."

"Well, I think that maybe there's some trouble because

Schoeffel #3 - 143

the mills man told me that the people who live up here on the ridge to the westward say that something came down in their yard and scared their grandfather almost to death."

I went rushing up to Captain Schuyler and we agreed that the thing we'd better do was for me to go out there right away and see these people. So, I went out and here was this old fellow sitting on the front porch of this little country house. He had a wooden leg and his good leg was up on the porch railing. I made myself known and that I was there to apologize and take care of any damage done. He said:

"It did no damage. You can see the hole it made out there in the front yard."

It was a hole about two feet wide and a foot deep. That's about what they did, these water-filled bombs. He said:

"It took the tail off a chicken and we had a lot of chicken feathers around here. It made a big noise. I had a carpenter up fixing the roof and I thought he'd fallen off the roof, but found he hadn't. Then we began to find pieces of metal around and about."

We got into a little conversation and it seemed that he had been on the Confederate side at the Battle of Fredericksburgh and had lost his leg there. Then I told him that he might have been shooting at my grandfather who was trying to climb these heights for the Union side at the Battle of Fredericksburg. So we became very simpatico and shortly he went out in the kitchen and came back with a jug and a couple of glasses and we had a perfectly lovely time!

Q: I would think that impetus of that sort of not necessarily bombs, but shells, would have disturbed some of the residents round about frequently.

Adm. S.: Occasionally, yes. I don't recall any shells going in the wrong place around there, except for some smoke shells that got in the wrong place. Most of the people around there knew that Dahlgren was their bread and butter, so they were not prone to complain. One of the reasons that Dahlgren had been established after World War I was because of an incident of this kind with a shell up at Indian Head. Schuyler used to talk about it, and I think it was a 14-incher when they were first proving them that ricocheted and went into some old lady's house way down the line. Then they decided that they just had to pick up and go somewhere else, and they moved down to Dahlgren.

We had a great time there.

Q: Did you have any missions other than the Norden bomb sight?

Adm. S.: Not a great deal. I'd go out occasionally and spot shot for them and things like that.

Schoeffel #3 - 145

Q: Why was it taking so long with the Norden bomb sight? I remember Ballentine worked on that, too.

Adm. S.: He worked with the Mark 11. This was the Mark 15.

Q: I see.

Adm. S.: At the end of a year, I had a voluminous report - a little over a year - prepared and sent that in to the Bureau of Ordnance.

Then, in the spring of '31, it was announced that the navy was going to conduct bombing tests on the old cruiser Pittsburgh. The bombing team was going to be composed of absolutely service personnel, and P. D. Stroop got told off to do the bombing job.

Q: This was in the Atlantic?

Adm. S.: Yes. The air force, air corps then, had just tried to sink an old merchantman off the Virginia Capes and had had a perfectly terrible time. They achieved no results and eventually the old vessel was sunk by gunfire from a Coast Guard vessel. So they sent a couple of their extremely hot-shot people to observe the navy's efforts on the Pittsburgh.

Stroop came up to Dahlgren and I spent a week or so instructing him in the use of the Mark 15, and I had all my tables of probability worked out and so forth. I figured that he would probably make about 10 or 15 percent of hits. Well, he went off and he couldn't do a thing wrong. Practically every bomb he dropped was a hit, leaving these army observers absolutely open-mouthed. They went charging back to Washington saying, "We've got to get this bomb sight. We've just got to get this bomb sight." I think Arnold was one of the two observers.

Q: Hap Arnold?

Adm. S.: Yes, but I'm not sure of that. Stroop did an outstanding job. I must say I think that my tables of probability were closer to the general average than his performance was, but it got to the point where they would say "put the next one on the port side of the fo'c'sle," which he would proceed to do!

These were not explosive bombs that were dropped. The navy was then trying to develop bombs having a great deal of explosive in a very thin shell, and they were trying to see what sort of a shell would be needed. Then about that time BuOrd erected a big metal bombing target on the Proving Ground itself. It was about forty feet square, two decks high, and made of the same metal that ships' decks are made of. I was sent out to bomb that from time to time. The object was to develop fuses that would function with a slight delay after the bomb got through the first deck but

Schoeffel #3 - 147

before it would hit the armored deck, which would bust up the bomb. They rigged the bombs that were used for this with no explosive but with fuses that would fire off a gunpowder charge and make a lot of smoke, and we got some very spectacular pictures of these bombs going off in various places and so forth.

I was very anxious to get a third year there just as Ballentine had and was promised that I would. Then suddenly a telegram came in saying Admiral Reeves, who was about to take command of the Battle Force, wanted me on his staff. I tried to protest and was told to pipe down, if Commander, Battle Force, wanted me on his staff I just had to go.

Q: It was really your fault for making an impression on him!

Adm. S.: Yes.

In the meantime, I had a great bit of luck. I took my exams for lieutenant commander that spring. This was the year that they were going to dock everybody's pay 15 per cent on the 1st of July. Well, I was informed that I had passed my exams, then I got a telephone call from my classmate Tex Settle back in Washington, saying:

"You'd better get up here tomorrow, the 30th of June, and get your commission, then get back to Dahlgren and get sworn in, because if you do it's true you'll get docked 15 per cent but it will be on a lieutenant commander's pay and not a lieutenant's pay."

I got up there and I got my commission, rushed back, and got sworn in. Well, in the upshot, three or four of my classmates had as good luck as I did. Settle did, Tom Jeter did, I think, but the rest of the poor chaps just had 15 per cent taken off what they'd been making before, whereas I had 15 per cent taken off of an up salary.

Q: The living quarters at Dahlgren must have been pleasant?

Adm. S.: Yes. We had a very nice bungalow there and our son Peter was born there. Mrs. Schoeffel said it looked to her as though the wives of the aviation detachment knew that Peter was coming before she did! They were very kind and helpful.

I've spoken of Henry Ford, the leading chief, and I want to tell you a little story about him.

One afternoon he said to me something about one of the other enlisted men, "That fellow is insanely jealous of his wife." I didn't know anything more about it than that, but a night or two later, Mrs. Schoeffel and I were about to turn in when our doorbell rang. I went to the door and there was a young woman, bare-footed, no stockings, and obviously with just a dress on and nothing under it, and she said:

"Isn't there anything anybody can do to save a poor woman's life?"

"What's up?"

Well, her husband had threatened to drive an icepick into her brain. She was the wife of the fellow whom Ford had said was insanely jealous, so, of course, I took her in, and Mrs. Schoeffel got her calmed down, put her to bed, and so forth. Then I went around and reported to the exec, who broke out the small Marine detachment we had there and we went looking for her husband. He wasn't home but we eventually found him driving around in a truck. He shouted:

"Where's my wife? Where's my wife?"

I told him she was all right. That didn't satisfy him at all and finally I said:

"She's over at my house and Mrs. Schoeffel is looking out for her."

Well, he was absolutely amazed but everything apparently was now okay. He just stopped being frantic at that point, but the exec saw fit to put him in the brig for safekeeping, which was done.

The next morning was a Saturday and I had made arrangements to go up to Washington for something or other and I called the exec and asked if, under the circumstances, I should stay or go ahead. He said go ahead. Well, as Mrs. Schoeffel and I were driving back that afternoon, we were passed by a Dahlgren car with Ford at the wheel and a first class aviation machinist's mate by the name of Orem with him. Ford was small and wiry, Orem big and very muscular, and the thing that struck me was that they were both in dungarees. This was just not done, to be off the station in dungarees. How did this come about, I wondered.

They went on ahead of us and when we got home, Ford was there and said that all had been well with our man who was so jealous, except that our junior doctor had gone around to talk with him and the junior doctor fancied himself as a psychiatrist, and he just got this man so maddened again that the fellow went for the doctor. At that point it was decided that he should be transferred to the hospital in Washington. He wanted to go home and they took him around to his quarters so he could pick up some of his personal effects, and he and the Marine sergeant, who was a great big proper figure of a man at arms, went into this little house, and the next thing they knew the Marine sergeant came out without waiting to open the screen door. He just went right through the screen and this other fellow after him with an ice pick in one hand and a big carving knife in the other!

What to do about this? Well, he stood out in front and dared them all to come on. He'd cut their lights and livers out. Some bright soul sent for the fire department. They came there and still nobody knew what to do. Finally, Ford said to the exec:

"Mr. Hunter, you can catch more flies with honey than you can with vinegar. Let me try."

So he walked up to this fellow who was in a maniacal rage and just talked to him for a little while. Eventually, the fellow turned over his weapons to Ford and went off to the hospital.

So you can see that's one of the reasons I had a very warm spot in my heart for Henry Ford, now long deceased. He was a lieutenant in World War II and retired as such.

The aviation detail took up a collection for the poor little wife and she went home to Mississippi, where she and her husband had been boyhood and girlhood sweethearts. Then this chap was given a medical discharge and he came down to Dahlgren and thanked me for what I'd done for him and for his family. Well, he had other people to thank much more than me, but that touched me very deeply, his coming down there.

We went back out to the West Coast. This time I was to be in the California with Admiral Reeves, so we didn't go to Coronado, we settled in San Pedro. We eventually got a house way up on the mountainside, at just above the fog level. We could look out of that house and look out of that house and look down on the fog almost every morning.

Adolphus Andrews, then a captain, was chief of staff. Bill Glassford was operations officer. Savvy Saunders was the fleet construction officer. A little fellow whose name I don't remember was the personnel officer because Commander, Battle Force, handled a great deal in regard to personnel functions. Then Joe Rochefort was somewhere - I don't know just what his job was.

Q: He was an intelligence officer.

Adm. S.: Yes.

Q: And Rivero was there, too.

Adm. S.: Yes, but he was –

Q: He was very junior.

Adm. S.: Yes, and he was not actually a member of the staff. He was a member of the communications department. The communicators were all ex officio members of the staff but they were attached to the ship.

A fellow by the name of Forster was the staff communications officer, and my classmate Tommy Atkins was flag lieutenant. Who was flag secretary, a most delightful guy, later a vice admiral – Francis Dennebrink.

Q: That was quite a crew!

Adm. S.: Yes. We had a very successful year. I enjoyed it thoroughly and made myself obnoxious to a number of people. I remember once going on board the Langley and being met by the captain who said:

"What trouble have you come over here to make now?"

Q: Why had you gained that reputation?

Adm. S.: Oh, because I was doing a great deal of writing that Admiral Reeves was signing, and I guess a number of people took exception to it.

However, there was one thing that went on during that year that I was really very proud of. My predecessor had been Benny Wyatt, later a commodore; and very shortly before he was detached he had gotten up a sort of a roman holiday in which everybody in the battleships and cruisers was invited to bring in ideas as to how they could improve the recovery of the battleship and cruiser planes. In general, they hadn't come up with very much, but there was one fellow from a cruiser by the name of Ott - I don't know what ever became of him in later years - who brought up an airplane that had a hook put on its keel, and he spread a rope net along the side of the ship towed from a boat boom and he landed his airplane short of this net and taxied up to the net. As you taxied one of those float airplanes, the nose would be pretty high, and as soon as you cut the gun the nose dropped. So he taxied onto this net, cut the gun, the nose dropped, and the hook engaged the net, and there he was. It seemed to be pretty good, except that, shortly, the net drifted over toward the ship's side, his airplane bumped its wing tip against the ship's side and busted up the wing tip, and everybody said, well, that's that.

I must mention that at this affair, there was also exhibited a device that had been I believe designed in the Bureau of Aeronautics and built by the Bureau of Ships called a plane trap. This was a large metal affair that was lowered over the ship's stern, sort of a clam-shell bucket arrangement. They had one airplane that had been equipped with a rod going forward from the plane's float with a big knob on the end of it, and the object of the game was to taxi up in the ship's wake and put this knob and rod into this clam-shell, which would then grab this rod and there the airplane would be under tow, and they would hoist the airplane in with the after airplane crane.

This worked very well and everybody left saying, okay, the plane trap is fine.

Q: It would require calm seas, though, wouldn't it?

Adm. S.: I really don't know. Somehow or other, I guess by correspondence, I found out that the plane trap would be installed in the battleships and cruisers, as they had their overhauls every year and a half, so it was obvious that it would be about three years before - three or four years - all the ships were equipped, and the plane trap cost about $50,000, which was a lot of money in those days.

So, I thought, gee, this net business almost works and I should think if we put some vanes on the spreader bar on the front of this net, we could hold it away from the ship's side, and we'd have something that we could use before the plane traps got installed. I got to the admiral with this idea and he said, yes, let's give it a try. So he designated Commander, Battleships, to give it a try.

He did, and it worked beautifully, and in three or four months we had more damned varieties of nets being towed in various places from ships, and instead of just being able to recover airplanes at 3 or 4 knots, which was the best I had hoped for, I'd been picked up by the California at 14, and some of the cruisers even picked up airplanes at 18. In calm weather, some of the ships picked up three at once. They had a net out on each side and another one aft. All three airplanes would land, taxi up there, put them on and, in a matter of three or four minutes, they'd have all the airplanes on board and they'd go on about their business. It was so successful the Navy Department cancelled the plane trap.

Q: Very smooth!

Adm. S.: I was not the inventor of this thing, but I saw its possibility and I was in a position to put Admiral Reeves's authority behind trying to work it out, and it worked very, very well indeed. I don't know whether the battleships and cruisers were still using it in World War II or not. I just don't know, but for several years it was very, very useful to us in getting our airplanes back.

Q: Did you get a commendation for that?

Adm. S.: I don't believe so. There was no reason why I should. Ott was the one who thought of it.

Q: What was the overall mission of the Battle Fleet at that time?

Adm. S.: It was to maintain itself in readiness for whatever might eventuate. Admiral Reeves really believed that the Japanese might jump us. We spent a great deal of time also on the early stages of amphibious warfare, but that was run primarily by the Commander in Chief, U.S. Fleet, Admiral Sellers, over in the Pennsylvania, and his very brilliant operations officer, Commander Frost.

Now, I say I got on people's nerves. Frost also got on people's nerves. He was forever writing instructions about this, that, and the other thing. He had us all rushing around on exercises where each ship was supposed to represent three or four ships. The idea was to teach the captains of ships something about the handling of larger units. Well, that was all very fine, but if you had a destroyer screen - here was one real destroyer and then there were three or four purely hypothetical ones, before you got to another real one, if somebody tried to come through that on a dark night, it was very easy to get through the screen!

Q: Indeed yes.

Adm. S.: Well, as I say, I had a delightful year there. Our cruise that year wound up on the East Coast. We went up to New York, and Admiral Reeves succeeded Admiral Sellers as Commander in Chief, U.S. Fleet, and issued rather a famous directive. His General Order No. 1 was a list of all the things that Frost had put out on tactical exercises, marked references a to n, and all General Order No. 1 said was "References a to n are canceled," signed J. M. Reeves.

Q: He must have felt them a thorn in the side, too, then?

Adm. S.: Yes, I know he did.

Q: Did you continue in the same job when he - ?

Adm. S.: No. The aviation aide to the Commander in Chief, U.S. Fleet, didn't have really very much to do with actual aviation in the fleet. His chief business was being fleet athletic officer. Andy McFall had been Sellers's aviation officer and he had been the fleet athletic officer. Well, I went to Admiral Reeves and pled that I had a chance to get a squadron if I could get out of the staff and would he kindly let me go. He conceded to that -

Q: Do you infer that you didn't really enjoy staff work?

Adm. S.: I enjoyed working for him very much, but staff work in general, no. He got Frank Wagner, later a vice admiral, and now dead, too, as his aviation aide, as Commander in Chief, U.S. Fleet, and I was given the job of squadron commander of Scouting Squadron 1. We were down at Norfolk, as were all the other aircraft squadrons at the time, the Sara and the Lex being on the East Coast, and the Ranger just going into commission. We in VS-1 were supposed to be the Ranger's squadron -

Q: The Ranger was a carrier from the beginning?

Adm. S.: Yes.

Q: She was not converted from something?

Adm. S.: No, a comparatively small vessel, about 14,000 tons. She was rigged so that she could land airplanes over the bow as well as over the stern because she was given unusual backing power. She could make about 25 knots astern.

Well, she wasn't ready when the fleet prepared to return to the West Coast, so we were embarked in the Saratoga and went back in her. Admiral Butler, for the third time, was Commander, Aircraft, but this time he had a very different chief of staff. He had Kelly Turner as chief of staff and Turner really ran everything, and he ran it plenty, too! He ran it hard.

Q: Kelly Turner?

Adm. S.: Kelly Turner, yes.

We got down to Panama and Admiral Reeves, as I say, was a little hipped on the subject of the Japanese being about to jump on us, so he arranged for a sudden and rapid transit of the whole fleet through the canal. It made quite a stir at the time. We got the whole fleet through in something under forty-eight hours, and we went back north.

We got put ashore at the air station in San Diego and operated from there. In the course of that year my squadron operated from all the carriers the navy had. At one time or another, we operated from the Langley, from the Saratoga, from the Lexington, and, later, from the Ranger. I was very proud of this.

Q: Do you want to tell me about Kelly Turner and his tour of duty on the staff of Admiral Reeves?

Adm. S.: No, Admiral Butler.

Q: Admiral Butler, I'm sorry.

Adm. S.: Turner was very anxious to qualify us all in night operations and we were turned to in an extremely ambitious campaign. First off, we did a lot of carrier type landings at night on the beach. Then we went out in the ships. We were trying to operate full carrier air groups at night. Now, as you will recall, we never were able to do anything of that sort during World War II.

Q: No.

Adm. S.: At the most, during the War, just a few airplanes. Well, back in 1935 we were trying to put all seventy or eighty in the air at once, and this resulted in some events you might call contretemps!

Q: Yes!

Adm. S.: One operation we were supposed to fly up to Long Beach and make an attack on the battleships at anchor up there. We were actually at the air station at the time. I had a bad idea, which was that if we were trying to operate at night on board ship the ship would not be able to line our airplanes up in such a fashion that we could go off in a known position with respect to the other members of our squadron. We would be just helter-skelter. So for this night operation, we just lined our airplanes, VS-1, up in helter-skelter fashion, took off that way, and tried to get together, and we proved conclusively that it was not a good idea, that if you were going to get together at night you had to go off in a planned sequence. This resulted in a great deal of chatter on the voice, all of it being down around Point Loma.

Eventually, we did get together, got up to Long Beach, did our stuff up there, returned without anything untoward, and the next morning Turner sent for me and he gave me pluperfect hell for all this chatter that we had on the radio. Eventually, I was able to break in and convince him that we were trying to do something and that we had proved that it was impractical, we would not do it again, and I was able to point out, which he also admitted, that once we got together we hadn't said a word until we got home again. So I got an apology from Kelly Turner, which not many people have had!

Q: That was quite an achievement!

Adm. S.: I've also had an apology from Rickover!

The big do, however, of all this is that we were all embarked in the carriers, the battleships were at sea, and we were to make attacks upon them. My squadron was in the Lexington at that time and we took off right after VF-3, whose squadron commander was Miles Browning, who was chief of staff to Admiral Spruance at the Battle of Midway.

Well, we took off right after Miles Browning's squadron, so I followed Browning and I followed Browning and I followed Browning, and after a while I began to realize I wasn't catching up with Browning a damned bit. And after a while I discovered I was following Canopus or Polaris or some star! It wasn't Browning.

The job my squadron had was to drop flares on the battleships to illuminate them for attack by the dive-bombing squadrons and so forth. I don't recall just why we were in two separate divisions, but we were. We went in and we dropped our flares and we illuminated them. Then the question was trying to get together again and we were having a very bad time with that. Meanwhile, a famous remark was made. One of the dive-bombing squadrons was coming down and ran into fog which was beginning to creep in, and Country Moore shouted, "Second Division of bombing 3. This is So and So. I'm in this cloud and the rest of you get out of it"! That caused a great deal of amusement round about.

Eventually, I gathered up nine planes of my squadron and I knew that my exec, Freddy Harper, had the others, the rest of the men with him, so it was just a question of getting back to the ship.

I went back to where my plot said the ship should be and there was a nice big carrier down there, but I noticed that she was launching planes. I couldn't see any reason why the Lexington should still be launching planes now that the battle was all over. I called Freddy and Freddy said that he was over the Lexington, and this just didn't add up because he wasn't anywhere near where I was. Eventually, I found the Lexington about twenty miles away.

Meanwhile, I got over there and found they had a red light on the stern and they told me to come in and land. I said, "I will as soon as you turn on the green light."

They said, "We've got the green light on." I said, "No, you haven't. You've got the red light on." Well, it finally turned out I was talking to the wrong ship! Eventually, I got on board the Lexington, taxied up forward, climbed out, started up to the bridge to report in, and I saw a couple of fellows - no, I looked aft and I saw a Fighting-6 plane come in. Well, Fighting-6 was a Saratoga squadron. My God, was I in the wrong ship after all this! I looked wildly around and I found that I knew the people who were there and knew I was in the Lexington.

Well, it turned out that someone in Fighting-6 had got mislaid. Dixie Ketchum came in with about six of them from the wrong ship. There they were without a nickel or a toothbrush, a heavy fog set in, and we had to stay at sea for damned near a week, and there they were stuck on board.

We had a great deal of fun, sport, and amusement with Turner's efforts to fly full carrier air groups. So far as I know, this effort was given up completely the next year, and it was very unfortunate because by the time World War II came we had to build up a night capability from practically nothing.

Q: Yes, we were far behind the Japanese in that technique.

Interview #4 with Rear Admiral Malcolm F. Schoeffel,
U.S. Navy (Retired)

Place: The residence of his son, Captain Peter Schoeffel, in Alexandria, Virginia

Date: Thursday morning, 31 May 1979

Subject: Biography

By: John T. Mason, Jr.

Q: Sir, after somewhat of a hiatus we're going to resume this very interesting story.

It was in June 1935 that you left the Ranger and came back to Washington to the Division of Fleet Training.

Adm. S.: Yes, that's right, and I spent a year there. I have been trying to think who else was there at the time and I have great difficulty in remembering with two exceptions. The officer in charge was Captain Fairfax Leary and the man who had the battleship desk there was Ching Lee, afterwards Admiral Lee who commanded the battleships in the Pacific during World War II.

Lee was a lot of fun. In his early days he had been a great pistol shot; and one time, not having much to do around the office, he had bought himself a small rubber-band pistol that shot bee-bee shot and he had some celluloid birds on spindles. He would set them up and sit at his desk and shoot at them.

Well, our desks were arranged in a rather peculiar fashion. Inside the wall that ran along the public corridor there was another corridor that went the whole length of our office space -

Q: This was in Old Navy?

Adm. S.: Yes, the old Navy Department building - and each desk had a little cubbyhole off the inner corridor.

I was sitting at my desk working away at something or other when suddenly I heard a wasp go by my ear. I looked around. I could see no wasp. Shortly, another one. Then I heard a chuckle, and I looked around the hall into the next cubbyhole and there was Lee with his feet up on his desk shooting these damned little birds with bee-bee shot that was ricocheting off the wall and catching me.

Q: Tell me a little more about him. He was a mathematical genius, wasn't he?

Adm. S.: I really don't know about that, but I know that he was a very pleasant shipmate in our shore job there and he had a reputation of having been one of the best rifle and pistol shots the United States ever had.

I was responsible for keeping track of the aircraft

gunnery exercises and getting up the rules for the next year and preparing an annual Report of Gunnery Exercises, the aviation part of it. I also had as an extraneous duty being in charge of the photographers who worked with the Fleet Camera Party. I do not recall whether there was an Atlantic Fleet Camera Party or not, but there certainly was a Pacific Fleet one, and they took motion pictures of all, or practically all, of the gunnery exercises of the battleships and, I suppose, the cruisers and destroyers.

Q: The purpose was what?

Adm. S.: To plot the fall of shot very accurately. They maintained that they could do this with a great degree of accuracy, and they may have been right, I cannot be sure. But their motion-picture cameras were getting old and run-down and we had to buy some new ones. I was given the job of preparing the specifications for them. They had a man in charge of the photographic lab there in our office who said:

"Oh, nothing to it. I've got the specifications all ready."

Well, it turned out that what he meant was that he wanted to buy this camera or that camera as a purely proprietary article, and I knew from my experience in the Bureau of Aeronautics that that sort of thing did not go, and I had to prepare some performance specifications so that the various camera manufacturers could compete. Also, nobody seemed to know where the money was going to come from. The Office of Fleet Training didn't have any money. However, I applied to the chief clerk and he said:

"Oh, we'll get them to charge it to the shipbuilding fund that's just been set up."

I thought "Well, how much of that do we get?" He didn't know, but he said:

"Oh, it's a huge fund."

This happened to be the year in which Congress had appropriated something like 250 or 300 million for building a considerable number of auxiliary craft that the Navy badly needed in those days. In those days it was a huge fund!

Anyhow, after a great deal of sweating, I was able to get these specifications prepared and we got bids from several camera manufacturers. We recommended awards and somehow or other the Fleet Camera Party got new cameras! It was a very loose operation because I didn't actually know anything about photography.

Q: That was a curious title, "Camera Party."

Adm. S.: The Fleet Camera Party was a group of photographic people who were Navy men. They were quartered in one of the vessels of the Train, I don't recall which one. They went out with their cameras whenever there were firings, got their pictures and plotted the fall of shot.

After a year of this, I felt that another year would be very boring, just cutting out paper dolls; and I sort of aired my views among some of my contemporaries and one day in the back corridors, I ran into Fuzz Sherman, otherwise Forrest Percival Sherman, later Chief of Naval Operation. At that time he had the Aviation Desk in the Bureau of Ordnance and his tour of duty, in his mind, was up and he wanted to get to sea. He thought he had it all arranged for Art Davis, later a vice admiral, to relieve him, but Art had other ideas and slid off sidewise, leaving Fuzz stranded.

Well, the powers over there in the Bureau of Ordnance weren't very helpful because they said, "Go find yourself your own relief!"

As I say, we met in the back corridor and he said:

"Red, I understand you're not at all desirous of spending another year in Fleet Training. Would you care to come over to Ordnance and relieve me?"

I fell on his neck and practically kissed him on both cheeks!

So, I went over to the Bureau of Ordnance and was there for the next two years. Whereas Sherman had been entirely on his own at the Aviation Desk, had no assistant whatever, I got an assistant, Sherman Everett Burroughs, now a retired captain living out in Coronado and a most capable man.

Q: What was your title there?

Adm. S.: My title was just Officer in Charge of the Aviation Desk.

The Bureau of Ordnance in those days was a pretty small place. I think the total personnel, officer and civilian, was about forty and we occupied rooms in one corridor on, I think, the second deck of the Old Navy building. Admiral Stark was Chief of the bureau and the Assistant Chief was Commander Hank Markland, a very dour character who I know never made admiral. I think he even missed making captain but, to my way of thinking, he made a very fine Assistant Chief there.

About the only other person I remember - well, Fred Entwistle was there and also Jerauld Wright, later four star, Jerry Wright. I remember one day I was in trying to sell some idea to Commander Markland when Wright suddenly rapped on the door and asked if he might come in on a rather urgent matter. Yes. He said he would like to get immediately ten days' leave for the Feast of the Passover. Markland said never a word, just reached for the papers, signed them, and Jerry went out. Markland turned to me with wonder in his face and said:

"That's the first time I ever knew that Jerry was one of the Chosen People."

I laughed and said:

"That's not what he means, Commander. He means that he just wants to be out of Washington when the selection board meets."

My chief business in those days was trying to buy and maintain machine guns for our planes. Burroughs and I spent a good deal of time poring over proposals from various European outfits that had 20-mm aircraft guns. Up to the time I left, we'd never gotten around to actually buying any of them -

Q: These were like Bofors?

Adm. S.: Yes, there were Bofors and there were Oerlikons and there were three or four others. As I say, we never actually bought any of them.

Q: Did you have a relationship with Dahlgren also?

Adm. S.: Oh, yes, close relations with Dahlgren.

Shortly before I left the Bureau, a very considerable amount of interest in improved bombs was stirred up and Admiral Stark - no, by that time it was Admiral, oh, a fellow with a German name, but I'll come back to that (Furlong) - set up a bomb board, of which I was a member. The senior member was the Commander of the Naval Gun Factory. I can't remember his name but he was a lot of fun to work with, and the junior member, the recorder, was Jack Snackenberg, later a rear admiral. He was a very sharp cookie.

We hadn't actually arrived at any conclusions by the time I was detached. At the end of my first year there,

Admiral Stark was detached and I don't recall just where he went at that time. Now I must remember the name of the man who relieved him. This fellow was later summarily relieved by Mr. Frank Knox when Knox became secretary of the navy, Admiral Furlong. Practically the first act Knox did after sitting down at his desk was to say, "Get him out of there."

Q: What had he done to offend Knox?

Adm. S.: As a matter of fact, it was for not getting things done. Furlong was trying, back in '41, to carry on vastly expanded business in the Bureau with almost exactly the same organization that had been set up in World War I, only it had been proliferated here and there. Whereas in World War I the Bureau had eight or nine sections, by that time the number of sections had grown to over thirty. He worked like hell but he just could not keep up with the job.

Q: This was after you had gone by some time?

Adm. S.: Yes. I'm talking about 1941 now.

Anyway, in those days (1937) the Bureau of Ordnance got an annual appropriation of around 30 million dollars. It also got money from shipbuilding appropriations, but that 30 million was the appropriation for Ordnance and Ordnance Stores and was its life blood. I had been filled with admiration listening to Admiral Stark defend his estimates before congressional committees. He was very smooth, very convincing, and Furlong, unfortunately, was not. He had a terrible time before the congressional committees. I remember very well that one day they were attacking the retention of the Navy's armor factory in West Virginia. This armor plant was constructed immediately after World War I. I suppose it was intended to build the armor for our ships that were scrapped by the Disarmament Treaty in 1921. Well, the plant was shut down and had remained shut down all the intervening years and, in an attempt to save a little money, the congressional members were attacking the retention of it. The Chief was trying to support it and he did a very, very poor job. Finally, they asked him some extremely embarrassing question, and I can remember, he sat there with his head bowed for, it must have been, a minute and sweat broke out all over his forehead in great drops and finally he said, practically in a whisper, "I'd keep it."

He couldn't support this statement of his in any way. However, it was kept. I do not know whether it was used in World War II for armor, but I imagine it was. It was a fine big plant, I understand. I never saw it.

Q: Tell me a little more about that bomb study. What was the nature of it? What kind of bombs were they interested in?

Adm. S.: Aircraft bombs, and just improving the design, the

fusing, and so forth, trying to build bombs of better design than the ones we had. I don't recall what were the arguments against the ones we had, but it was an attempt to improve.

Q: Why were not your efforts with the Bofors and other guns resolved? Why wasn't there some decision made in this area, because there had to be later on?

Adm. S.: Yes, but at that time it was an open question, it really was, as to whether airplanes should be armed with a few large guns, such as 20-mm, or a greater number of small guns such as 30-caliber. I had always been a strong proponent of the "many small guns" idea. I think the war proved me completely wrong, but that was the possition I had always taken. But we still did not want to neglect the possibility, and we got proposals from quite a number of European companies. They would send their representatives in and they would talk a wonderful story, and it was very difficult to sort these stories out and try to figure out which ones really made sense, if any of them. So, but the time I left, there was no decision. In fact, the United States fought the war with its airplanes armed with 50-caliber guns, and most adequately. That proved to be a most successful gun, the 50-caliber Browning.

In June 1938 I left BuOrd and went to sea as navigator of the Saratoga.

Q: Who was the skipper:

Adm. S.: The first one was Albert Cushing Read, the man who had flown the NC-4 across the Atlantic back in 1919. After a year he was relieved by Captain Bobby Moulton.

There was nothing very striking about those two years in the <u>Saratoga</u>.

Q: Were you operating in the Pacific?

Adm. S.: Yes. I learned a great deal about shiphandling from Captain Read.

As an example of easy ways of doing things, our anchorage was up at Long Beach Harbor and we very frequently had to go from Long Beach down to San Diego to embark aircraft and so forth, and on our way back and forth, we were almost certain to encounter other vessels out there. We would be in his sea cabin and it would be reported to him that there was a steamer just sighted on the horizon, slightly on our starboard bow, the bearing not changing. At this point we would just change course one degree to the right and that was all that was necessary to handle the situation. That would just pass us astern of the other craft. It wouldn't take us off our course to any extent whatever.

He was an extremely taciturn individual. He had very little to say, but when he said it you jumped. As it was said, of Mitscher, "You could hardly hear a word he said but you had to hear every god-damned word he said!"

He left at the end of the year. He went to Pensacola, to take command down there.

Q: Training?

Adm. S.: Yes, and he was relieved by Bobby Moulton, who was in the same flight class I was in in 1921 at Pensacola.

Moulton was a very different person. To look at him, you'd say, "Well, here's a farmer." He always had his glasses way down on the tip of his nose. He'd look at you over the top of his glasses and he did a great deal of talking, but he was a very pleasant man to work for. He was a real gentleman. I'll tell you a yarn to show what a gentleman he was.

We went out to Hawaii with the fleet in the winter of 1940. We were to proceed along with the rest of the fleet to anchorages in Lahaina Roads. I had never been there, and in the quartermaster's gang we had a little fellow by the name of White, a first class quartermaster, who was the only one of us who had ever been at Lahaina Roads. He was a very excellent man in every respect. We had a meeting and he made something of a speech on the subject of finding your anchorage in Lahaina because, he assured us, it was very easy to take your bearings on the wrong place and get yourself anchored in the wrong spot. He had seen that happen several times.

So we proceeded into Lahaina, thinking we were all fixed, and we got the wrong spot for our bearings so we anchored in the wrong place. Shortly, I had to go to Captain Moulton and say:

"Captain, we're going to have to shift anchorage."

Naturally, that upset him, but he kept his temper and we shifted, and darned if we didn't get the wrong spot the second time.

Q: What makes it so difficult?

Adm. S.: The places upon which you took bearings were very difficult to see and other places looked just like them, so you would put your alidade on the wrong chimney or the wrong what have you and you would get anchored in the wrong place.

Q: You needed Loran, didn't you?

Adm. S.: Yes! So I had to very shame-facedly tell Captain Moulton this, and poor Captain Moulton said:

"Well, I'll have to put my tail between my legs and go and tell Admiral Halsey," who was on board as ComAirBatFor, "about this."

So we shifted the second time and this time we got it right, thank God.

Then we went out on a big exercise and we in the _Saratoga_ were attached to an outfit the core of which was about half a dozen battleships. They cruised in a V formation and our station was right in the middle of the V, across the base. One day we had operations out there and went tearing off as the wind demanded, practically out of sight of the battleships most of the time. Eventually, in the late afternoon, we were getting in the final flight and headed back for them hell bent for election. Poor old Moulton was a little nervous because we seemed to be headed for a fine collision with the stern of the rear battleship on the port wing of the V, but I was able to assure him that we would just miss it.

Well, we went sweeping by the stern, flashing by the stern, just as the last airplane came on board, and I said:

"Left full rudder, all engines ahead standard," and we swung right square into station, the most perfect thing that ever happened. It was one chance in a hundred million that a thing like that should ever happen because it was purely happenstance. At this point, Halsey leaned over from the flag bridge and called out:

"Captain Moulton, that was a very smart maneuver."

At this point, I say Moulton was a real gentleman because he just motioned toward me, who had anchored them twice in the wrong place and said:

"There's the man who did it."

That series of exercises had another remarkable affair in it. It didn't have anything to do with me or with the Saratoga. I forget who commanded our side in that exercise, but he was a battleship officer who was very highly thought of. He was a very excellent man.

We were proceeding along at night - by that time the battleships had been placed in column, and he was suddenly called onto his bridge and looked out the port hand. There, in the moonlight, was the whole enemy fleet, also in column, all lined up practically broad on his port beam. He had by happenstance crossed the T perfectly and all that he had to do was "Ship's right ninety", go to general quarters, and open fire with all the after turrets, and he had that battle won.

We were just beginning to use voice radio communications from ship to ship at that time. I don't think they called it the TBS yet. Anyway, he didn't wait for any of his staff to do the job for him. He grabbed the transmitter himself, pushed the button, and said:

"Turn 9, emergency turn 9. Execute."

His flagship started to make the turn and, to his utter horror, all the other ships except one followed him around in the column, just what he didn't want them to do. Well, at the critique afterwards he explained this:

"It wasn't until after this episode was over that I discovered that I should have pushed the button and waited ten or fifteen seconds for the set to warm up. The result was - I just pushed the button and shouted into it - the results was that nobody else got any of the message, except one ship got just the word 'execute.' That was all. There I was at one minute in a position of maximum advantage and then, before everything was all over, I was in a position of very considerable disadvantage!"

After this exercise, we were anchored off Honolulu, when Captain Moulton died very suddenly of a heart attack, as people often do. So the executive officer, Commander Jimmy Shoemaker, took over in his place, naturally.

I want to go back for a moment to say that during the time when Read was captain, the executive officer was DeWitt

Clinton Ramsey, later four-star, "Duke" Ramsey, and it was a strange coincidence that he and my father had been messmates in the Army in the old days out in the Philippines and were great friends. The old Duke made a great executive officer but he would listen to any sailor's tale of woe and weep with him. He was full of the milk of human kindness. Shoemaker was not!

I had orders back to Washington again, this time to the Division of Ships' Movements in Operations.

Q: Did you want to leave the Saratoga at this point?

Adm. S.: I was about to say we were out there in Hawaii, this was the summer of 1940 and I felt sure that a war with Japan was coming on. The upshot of it was that I requested to be allowed to continue on sea duty. However, the people up the line said, "Don't be a fool, young man," and my request was turned down, so I returned to the United States, picked up my family, who were living in Los Angeles at the time, and we proceeded east as far as Chicago by the very first night airplane semitranscontinental service that was put into effect. We were the first family that bought tickets for this. I forget which airline it was but they were proceeding on the assumption that air transportation at night would be like a pullman car, so the airplane was fitted up with lower and upper bunks and in place of a porter we had a couple of registered nurses as stewardesses, who were very competent and thorough.

Q: What was the make of the place, do you remember?

Adm. S.: No, I don't recall. It was probably a DC-3, but I'm not sure. That was about as big as we had in those days.

The airline was very much impressed with this family traveling with them -

Q: How large was your family then?

Adm. S.: There were five of us, my wife and three children.

They sent a limousine over to take us to the airport free of charge and they doused my wife with gardenias all over the place and they had this, that, and the other things for the kids.

Q: And pictures?

Adm. S.: I don't recall any pictures. I don't know about that.

In order to get to Chicago at that time the airplane had to stop three or four times to refuel, and my elder daughter, poor kid, had a terrible time with her ears. Every time we came down she was in agony and would stay that way until we got up again. Luckily, we made Chicago all right on Saturday morning.

Shortly before we left California, my wife had turned in our old automobile and put up the price for a new one to be delivered in Chicago, and it was to have licence plates, insurance, and all the necessary papers, with it. So we went around in the middle of Saturday morning to the automobile place and they'd never heard of this proposition. We finally convinced them that they really had our money and that they really owed us such and such a type of car, and they finally admitted that, yes, they had that type of car out on the lot so they brought it out. But as far as any licence plates or papers were concerned, they just gave me hollow laughter.

This was the Saturday before a Monday holiday, so if it was a question of going to the proper place in Chicago to get all these plates and papers legally, it would be necessary to stay over until Tuesday, which we didn't like the sound of at all.

I was in despair, but my wife was wiser than I. She said:

"Look, just sit down here. We'll all just sit here and we'll all just stare at him and after a while he'll do something."

And that's just what happened!

After a while he came around and out of the corner of his mouth said:

"If you go round to the shop and look So and So up, I

think you might find a pair of licence plates, and if you give one of the boys a couple of dollars I think he might put them on for you."

We got that done and, without any papers, we set off. These were Minnesota licence plates. Neither I nor any of my family had ever been in Minnesota. We drove east being very careful to obey every traffic sign, stay within the law completely, and all across the middle west we would run into other cars with Minnesota plates on and they'd yell at us: "Minnesota, where are you from?" We had an easy answer for that. We said "Rochester." Well, it was Rochester, New York, we were from, but they all took it for granted it was Rochester, Minnesota.

We got to Washington without getting pinched and there I had a relative who had an "in" with automobile dealers and she got a dealer somehow or another to fix everything all up for us. So we got legal, eventually!

Well, I went to the Ships' Movements Division in the summer of '40 and I found this a much more interesting job than the one in Fleet Training had been.

The only other person I can remember there was my classmate Bill Callahan, who had the Auxiliary Ships' Desk. He was later a vice admiral and commander of the Naval Transport Service.

Oh, yes, Finley France was there, too. I don't recall what job Finley had.

In the early months of 1941 we were much interested in

Schoeffel #4 - 183

getting PBY patrol planes flown east from San Diego, over to the Atlantic side. This was a very trying hop for those airplanes at that time. We had one considerable group flown down to Mexico, the Pacific side of the country, and then across the Isthmus of Tehuantepec and come on up. Somehow or another, we got word that German saboteurs were waiting for these airplanes down there in central Mexico and intended to try to destroy them. This caused considerable jitters but nothing happened. The airplanes got through all right and no vandals showed up.

Q: They were to be used where in the Atlantic?

Adm. S.: I don't recall whether they were being delivered to England at that time or whether they were just to be part of the Atlantic air squadrons. I don't remember.

Q: Admiral Richardson wanted some out in Hawaii, too, didn't he?

Adm. S.: Oh, yes.

An attempt was made to fly some of them across overland, across Arizona, New Mexico, and Texas, by making use of some of the artificial lakes behind the dams on that route. One group of about half a dozen of these planes was coming by that route and got over central Texas when they were flying at an altitude of 16,000 or 17,000, which was fairly high for those days. They ran into some terrible upper-air weather and I believe that one of the planes disintegrated in the air as a result of the terrible buffeting it took. I know that some of the men bailed out and they were flung all around Texas. Most of the airplanes did get through after a really harrowing experience. Some of them got down in small lagoons on the east coast of Texas and then these lagoons were too small for them to fly out without great difficulty. But they were eventually all flown out and got across.

Q: With the imminence of war, ships' movements became much more important, didn't they?

Adm. S.: Yes. It was still a small division. Each one of us had our desk there, by types, and each one of us ran his own. We had no large plotting room. There was a Captain Brainerd there, who was the number two man, and I remember his saying that they were getting ready to establish what he called a War Room somewhere in the building. It was established later but not in my time there.

During that time, of course, Admiral Richardson was relieved by the President and was replaced by Admiral Kimmel. I didn't know Admiral Richardson at all then, but I had had some dealings with Admiral Kimmel when he was a captain and was the Navy Department's Budget Officer while I was over in the Bureau of Ordnance! and I formed an extremely high opinion of Admiral Kimmel. I remember thinking to myself that with Kimmel out there the Japanese will not be able to "Port Arthur" our Pacific fleet. Unfortunately, this was a very wrong judgment, but it was the way I felt about it.

In the spring of 1941 the President brought in Mr. Frank Knox as the new Secretary of the Navy. As I said earlier, his first action, practically, was to fire the then-chief of the Bureau of Ordnance, Rear Admiral Furlong, and replace him by Captain W. H. P. Blandy. I have been told that Knox made a habit, whenever he went to a new job, of immediately firing someone from a highly responsible position. The idea, apparently, was just to "encourager les alltres" as the French say. Furlong was sent as Commandant XIV Naval District at Hawaii where I believe he served faithfully but without distinction throughout the war.

Blandy was then the navy's hotshot antiaircraft man and he was moving heaven and earth to get the navy's antiaircraft defenses improved, which he did, in the long run. Blandy, when he was sent to BuOrd by Mr. Knox, said that he wanted absolute carte blanche for quite a number of additional officers for quite a number of additional officers for the Bureau. I think it was sixty he wanted. He didn't know me and I didn't know him and I don't think that he asked for me, but he did ask for my friend and mentor Mike Schuyler and I imagine it was Schuyler who told Blandy to ask for me. So I found myself picked up out of Ships' Movements and sent back to the Bureau of Ordnance. This time I was Aviation Assistant to the Director of the Research Division.

Blandy reorganized the Bureau completely. It had been previously organized in what was called "Type Fashion." There was the Main Battery Desk, there was the Secondary Battery Desk, there was the Antiaircraft Battery Desk, and this, that, and the other thing. Each one of these desks took care of its own type of material from its inception to its eventual death and burial.

Q: This was a Blandy idea, was it?

Adm. S.: No, this was the old idea, a hangover from World War I, and it had worked very well back in the twenties because responsibility for material was very definite and in one spot. But by 1940 - '41, this was - by 1941, the idea had changed and the thing to do was to have a - well, anyway, the upshot of it was that the Bureau was reorganized on so called "functional lines" into a Research Division, a Production Division, a Planning Division, an Administrative Division, and a, it wasn't utilities but a division that handled all the real estate.

So I found myself in the Research Division and I was the bull aviator of the Bureau of Ordnance. At first, really the chief part of my job was to try to find some people to handle aviation ordnance matters in the various divisions and sections of this reorganized bureau. It was extremely difficult to get anybody with any experience in aviation ordnance at all. They just weren't to be had, but I did manage to pick up a considerable number of young naval reserve officers, most of whom didn't know a machine gun from a lead pencil, but they were told to learn while doing and most of them did a very fine job.

Q: Well, they came from very good backgrounds, didn't they?

Adm. S.: Not necessarily.

Q: I thought they were professional types, lawyers and -

Adm. S.: Not necessarily, no. Some of mine were right off the farm.

Speaking of people with professional background, it was during that time Blandy brought in a lot of Naval Reserve people who were primarily businessmen. He said he thought he could get technicians elsewhere and he wanted some businessmen. Word soon went around that he had brought in a g great prima donna, one Lewis Strauss. We all "ohed" and "ahed" about this fellow from the banking world who had been Herbert Hoover's righthand man over in Belgium and all the rest of this. My first meeting him was amusing.

Blandy had Captain Glen Davis, later a rear admiral, as his Assistant Chief, and Davis sent for me one day. I went down to his office, walked through the outer office, peeped through the door, saw that Davis was busy with somebody else, and sat down. A large, handsome commander was pa pacing back and forth in the outer office and I thought he looked like Strauss. I went up to introduce myself and it was Strauss, and he said to me:

"Has the Assistant Chief sent for you, too?"

"Yes."

"Do you know what it's about?"

"No."

"Aren't you nervous?"

"No, what have I got to be nervous about?"

"Well, I'm very nervous. All my life I've been sending for people, and just now I'm beginning to find out how it feels!"

Strauss went in there and shortly he came out with a big grin on his face and whispered:

"He just wanted some information."

In later years we became very good friends with both Strauss and his wife Alice.

I finally managed to get people to handle the ordnance aviation aspects, but, outside of that, I didn't accomplish very much myself, except for one thing and that was the Joint Chiefs of Staff had set up an international bomb board with representatives from from the British Air Ministry, the British Ministry of Munitions, representatives from Army Ordnance, representatives from Navy Ordnance, and from the Navy's Bureau of Aeronautics and from the old Army Air

Corps. I was the Navy Bureau of Ordnance representative. We worked along there and eventually came up with designs for bombs that were easily manufacturable and that could be used by the airplanes of both the British and the United States, standardized bombs.

I eventually became the chairman of this committee, and we standardized on armor-piercing bombs, semi armor-piercing bombs, general-purpose bombs very successfully. Those designs were turned out by the hundred thousand and million maybe, and were used worldwide later on in the war.

Q: What was the range in weight of these bombs?

Adm. S.: We ran up, as I recall, to a thousand pounds or somewhat more for the armor piercing type.

We also standardized a form of incendiary bomb, but this was by no means so successful. This was designed primarily on the basis of British criteria, because we in the United States had no background or experience at that time in incendiary bombs. At least no background worth anything.

I know we in this committee felt that the design that the British wanted and was suited to European conditions would be very unsuitable for use against the Japanese because it was a magnesium bomb and had a rather strong case, the idea being to carry it through a tiled roof. Because we were assured that the British experience had been conclusive that for the type of building construction used in Europe the incendiary bomb that caused the greatest degree of difficulty was one that went through the roof, lodged among the rafters, and caught fire there. We knew that our magnesium bomb, if dropped on the ground, for instance, would go into the ground and you wouldn't know whether they ever went off or not until you dug them up because no fire could come up. So it was fully expected that they would pass through the light Japanese roofs, go into the ground, and be of no value, which I think is just what happened.

But just about the time I was detached some people came in with proposals for petroleum not magnesium, incendiary bombs, and these were eventually manufactured in very large numbers and used against Japan. I had nothing to do with them except to read the very first proposals that were made along that line.

Q: Where were most of these bombs manufactured?

Adm. S.: Oh, the larger bombs all around. I visited one place out in Wisconsin, near Milwaukee, where they were manufacturing the general-purpose bombs. They just had miles and miles of steel tubing and they just put it through something that would close the nose and then the machine would form the afterbody and they would just cut it up, by the mile.

After the war was over, I was awarded an OBE by the British from my part in that bomb committee. I was always amused because the paper said that this entitled me to a grant of dignity from the King of England. I never got the grant of dignity but I often wondered what the hell it was!

Q: They were awarded to Britishers after the war, but I guess nonBritishers didn't qualify.

What were some of the other things that were turned out in aviation ordnance?

Adm. S.: There wasn't a very great deal that was turned out successfully. We fought the war with our 50-caliber machine guns very successfully. We got them from Army Ordnance. We got great quantities of 50-caliber ammunition, of course. We supplied the Army Air Corps with all their Norden bomb sights.

Q: By that time, the Norden bomb sight had been fully tested?

Adm. S.: Yes.

We supplied numerous gadgets, none of them of any great importance. We worked hard on trying to get some form of usable aircraft fire control. We never achieved anything of real value. In fact, nothing of real value was ever achieved in that particular field until the whole problem was completely handled by electronics, and at that time we didn't have very much in the way of electronics.

Q: What about that special fuse, that contact fuse?

Adm. S.: You mean the antiaircraft VT fuse?

Q: The VT fuse.

Adm. S.: I had nothing to do with that. That was an antiaircraft affair and it was handled within the Bureau largely between the Chief Assistant for Research, Captain Sam Shoemaker, and that very brilliant pair of scientists - one was Tuve - and what was the name of the other one?

Q: They were from Baltimore, weren't they?

Adm. S.: The Carnegie Laboratory. I used to see them in Shoemaker's office quite frequently. One of them, I forget which, was a rather rough egg, and so was Shoemaker. They would get together and they would put their feet up on the desk and smoke more damned horrible cigars and really pollute the atmosphere, and just talk things over.

Q: Did you have anything to do with our allies, the Russians? In supplying them with anything?

Adm. S.: Not to my knowledge. They were supplied but I had nothing to do with that aspect of things.

There was the torpedo business, which was not definitely in my hands but I was very interested in it. Just before World War II broke out, the Navy was endeavoring to develop three types of torpedoes. There was the Mark 11 which, I think, was a submarine torpedo. I think that was the title of it. Then there was the Mark 13, an aircraft torpedo, and the Mark 15, which was a destroyer torpedo. These were well along in their development by 1941, but by no means completed.

We were having great difficulty in getting aircraft torpedoes into the water from reasonable altitudes and at reasonable speeds, and we were having great difficulty in getting suitable airplanes to test them at the higher speeds because the Bureau of Aeronautics had plenty of other uses for practically all its airplanes.

Q: Where was the testing taking place?

Adm. S.: Up at Newport. These developments were all run by Newport, which had become a very closed monopoly on the subject of torpedoes. There weren't any competitors in the United States. I don't remember the name of the man who had the Torpedo Desk in the Research Division then, but he believed that Newport was the place to do all this stuff, that they had the knowledge, they had the experience, they had the background, they had the facilities. So he was more or less a go-between between the Bureau and Newport. He had ideas of his own but when the reports began to come in of submarines having plenty of duds, he was really under fire and I think Blandy finally got rid of him.

There has been a vast amount of criticism of BuOrd, primarily by submariners, for torpedo troubles early in the war; and I think a few words for the defense are in order. First, let me mention the magnetic exploder that never worked. Both the German's and the British also had magnetic exploders that didn't work and had to be thrown away. I don't know whether the Japanese or the Italians had the same experience. Possibly the failure of ours was due to the then-unrecognized deep running of the torpedoes. I presume that when that trouble came to light the exploder was re-examined; but I do not know.

As for the contact exploders, the Bureau had every right to expect them to function properly. Shortly before the war two old destroyers had been used as targets off San Diego and everything worked to the Queen's taste. It was later found (by Subpac, not by the Bureau) that the duds in action occurred when the torpedo hit its target at, or very near to, right angles; while detonation ensued from a more glancing blow. I can only assume the shots against the test destroyers came in at an angle.

As for the excessively deep running of the torpedoes (also first confirmed by Subpac) I cannot say anything in defense of either the Bureau or of Newport. I can think of a possible reason for the situation, but a "reason" and an "excuse" are miles apart. As I have said Newport had an absolute monopoly on torpedo development and (almost) on manufacture. Newport was dominated by the Shop Superintendants, worthy men who had worked up from the bench and the lathe but generally of very modest education. In their minds they "knew all the answers" and they had the few Naval officers there similarly hypnotized.

The depth of a torpedo was controlled by a hydrostatic mechanism and, when one was tested for depth, the test mechanism was also hydrostatic. Therefore any phenomenon that affected one also affected the other; and therefore all torpedoes tested at Newport seemed to run at the correct depth - unless they positively broached or stuck in the mud. Newport and the Bureau were very, very remiss not to recognize this situation earlier.

We tried all kinds of ideas about getting a torpedo into the water better and eventually, after I left the bureau, somebody came up with a collapsible tail vane arrangement that worked. So by the end of the war, our torpedo planes were able to release torpedoes at altitudes of some hundreds of feet and at speeds up to 250 or so knots, and the torpedo would go into the water and function. Before the war, we had considered that the maximum altitude was about 15 feet and we considered a speed of 100 knots as very, very high indeed. The same torpedo but just with this gadget attached to it, this tail vane.

We were also much interested, and so was Newport, in flying torpedoes, that is, putting wings on them. The British had worked on this -

Q: The Germans had it, too, didn't they? Oh, I guess they had a bomb.

Adm. S.: Yes, they had a flying bomb.

Newport worked hard on putting wings on torpedoes but nothing ever came of that. I was much interested in the efforts of another program that eventually came almost to nought. It was called the Elk or something like that.

This was a flying bomb, and the idea was that it would be controlled by radio from the airplane that released it. The bomb carried a television transmitter and there was a receiver in the parent airplane where an operator was then supposed to guide the flying bomb into its target by radio. It turned out to be a good deal harder job than anyone had thought at first. Targets were set up on an uninhabited island out in the Cheaspeake and they'd take these things out there, fly them at the target. Everything would go beautifully and they'd get down close to it and then the damned thing would fly just over the target. The people in the airplane had the television picture and they thought they were flying their bomb right into the target when actually, due to the angle of attack of the wings of the bomb, it was proceeding on a course slightly above the target.

I think I've heard that these were used in one case down somewhere in Indonesia. They were used against a couple of Japanese tankers that were alongside a dock down there. No, I'm talking about another flying bomb. The one I'm thinking of now was not the television-controlled bomb, it was some form of radar-control, because the radar was unable to distinguished one tanker from the other, so it did the best it could and flew the bomb between the two tankers!

Q: It compromised.

Adm. S.: The story was that it hit a lighthouse and demolished it. I don't know the truth of that, but I do know that years later when we got into so much trouble with the Koreans hiding their railroad trains in tunnels where it was very difficult to get at them, these things were broken out again and an effort was made to use them against the tunnels. I don't know with what success.

Shortly before I left BuOrd, that tour of duty, a little fellow with a Scottish name who had been a professor of physics up at Yale University came down - I think his name was McEwan. He was in the naval reserve, and he came down and was put in charge of the Mine Section, in Research. He was working hard on the very first of the target-seeking torpedo devices. He called it a mine to keep this hush-hush, if possible. It was not a very high-powered affair because I think its maximum speed was something like 8 or 10 knots, but it was target-seeking under water and, I believe, did achieve a few successes toward the end of the war.

Then, along in the spring of '43, I managed to get to sea.

Q: Had you been itching to get to sea?

Adm. S.: Yes. I managed to get to sea and was sent to Camden, New Jersey, as Prospective Commanding Officer of the then-building light carrier USS Cabot. The New York Shipbuilding Company built ten of these vessels. They had originally been contracted for as cruisers.

Q: What kind of tonnage?

Adm. S.: 17,000 - then it became apparent that we were going to have cruisers running out of our ears and that we needed more carriers, so it was decided to convert these to light carriers, and a very successful job it turned out to be.

My ship was already launched and about the first of June we were turned over to the Philadelphia Navy Yard, where we went into commission.

Q: This was in the year 1943?

Adm. S.: 1943, yes, early '43. Then we proceeded out and went down to the Chesapeake for a little while for some operations, picked up our air group, went on down to Trinidad, operated for a month down there on a shakedown cruise, getting the air group in applepie order.

Q: How big an air group did you have?

Adm. S.: We had thirty airplanes. We had eighteen planes in the fighter squadron and twelve planes in a torpedo bomber squadron.

Q: And the complement, the crew?

Adm. S.: It ran around, if I recall correctly, about 1,500.

Q: How many of them had had any sea experience?

Adm. S.: Very few, at first. They got plenty before they got through!

Q: Of your officer personnel, what percentage were academy men?

Adm. S.: There were very few. My Exec was a Commander

G. A. T. Washburn, and golly he was a tower of strength. The Air Officer was named Chapin, and the Navigator was Miller, the First Lieutenant was Hodges, and we had one Naval Academy ensign. All the rest were reservists or mustangs. Of course, some of them didn't turn out well, but most of them turned out splendidly.

Q: How did you whip them into shape?

Adm. S.: Learning while doing!

Q: This was in Chesapeake Bay and down around Trinidad?

Adm. S.: What?

Q: During the shakedown cruise in the Caribbean and - ?

Adm. S.: Not only in the Caribbean, we went into the Gulf of Paria down there.

While we were down there we had one amusing incident, as it turned out in the long run. Before the United States got into the war, a German submarine had gone in there and had created quite a panic over at the main port of -

Q: San Lucia?

Adm. S.: No, wonderful old Spanish name, the main port on

the island of Trinidad. Well, never mind. Port of Spain.

We went forth into the gulf and, although we had a destroyer escort down there, he had some maintenance to do so he stayed behind, and they gave us a couple of small motorboats to act as plane guards. One day we were down in the southern part of the gulf and we were just about to land our air group when a most perplexing message came in. Port of Spain, that was the name of the town. The message came from the Naval Base up there and it said:

German submarine reported such and such a latitude and longitude," which plotted just about ten miles dead to windward of where we were at the moment, with the air group all in the air ready to come on board. If we took them on board we would practically go right through that spot where the submarine was reported to be. And the dispatch went on:

"If you plan on staying out tonight, suggest you keep your escorts with you." I thought this indicated a very non-chalant view by the Naval Base. With my hair standing on end, we told the air group to go to the air station on the island, while we turned hard around and went steaming north as fast as we could for Port of Spain, sending dispatches to the effect "For God's sake, get our destroyer out here and have the gate wide open for us so we can slide right in." We got up there and nothing had happened. The destroyer was peacefully at anchor, the gate was closed, but they got the gate open and in we went. I went ashore and I met the Chief of Staff on the dock and I never saw a madder man in all my life because he said they'd had five people check the latitude and longitude of this dispatch to make sure it was right and they'd all got the latitude in error by two or three degrees. The submarine was actually way out to the north.

Q: Out of the gulf entirely?

Adm. S.: Out of the gulf entirely. Those things happen.

Q: Did you have any problems with the training, the shakedown?

Adm. S.: Nothing in particular. We did lose one airplane and its crew. We catapulted one of the torpedo bombers and it got in the air, reared up, stalled, went in, and we were not able to save any of them. But, aside from that, we had no particular problems.

Then we returned to Philadelphia for a post-shakedown touch-up and had an amusing experience on the way up.

As we were going up the Delaware there was a very thick fog lying over the east side of the river and it had an extremely sharp cutoff. It got to the point where you could stand on the port side of the bridge and hold your arm out and have it in the fog and the rest of the bridge and the ship were in the clear. After a while we came to a place where the damned fog came across the river and we had to anchor, whammo, right square in the middle of the river. Well, the tide was ebbing and that was fine because I wasn't at all sure that if the tide started to flood we could turn around our anchor without our stern running aground somewhere. But this didn't come off. Eventually we were able to get under way.

Q: Did you have any kind of radar?

Adm. S.: Oh, yes, but we didn't have it up on the bridge. It was down in the CIC. We had heard stories about the wonders of radar but we knew very little about it. The pilot and I went down to look it over and try to figure out whether we could see well enough to get the ship under way in this narrow river, and we decided we'd better not try it. So we just stayed there.

Finally we got going and we got up opposite Wilmington and the exec, the doctor, and the first lieutenant all waited upon me to say that they had a problem. The river was so polluted that our evaporaters didn't have a high enough temperature to kill the bugs in the water while making fresh water. In other words, the only fresh water we had was what we had previously made and was in our tanks, and there was just enough to wash the dishes after dinner. We had to close all the washrooms and tell everybody they couldn't wash their hands and faces or any of that foolishness until we got some more fresh water.

Q: And your only source was the Delaware?

Adm. S.: Yes.

We sent frantic messages up to the Navy Yard, "For God's sake send us a water barge." Well, they only had one water barge and it was up at Trenton and it would take twenty-four hours to get to us. All this was going on while we were lying at anchor in the river.

However, as I say, eventually the fog cleared enough and we got up alongside the dock and we got connected up to fresh water and the situation was saved. But we were almost in the position of the Ancient Mariner, right in the middle of the Delaware River!

Q: What special knowledge did your crew acquire on damage control?

Adm. S.: They had a fire school in the Philadelphia yard that was extremely interesting. I learned many things about the control of fires that I had never heard of before.

Q: Knowledge from the fleet was coming in at that point?

Adm. S.: Yes, and they had gotten hold of a lot of professional firefighters down there and they set up this fire-fighting school. These people knew how to do it. All of us had always taken it for granted that if you had a gasoline fire you wanted no water around there whatever. But they showed that if you had a spray you could put out the damnedest oil or gasoline fire with a good spray.

Q: A water spray?

Adm. S.: A water spray, yes, and they had a mock-up of a ship's bridge and the structure below it. They would sprinkle that with oil, set fire to it, and there would be the daggonedest collection of fire and smoke you ever saw. They'd put on their asbestos suits and take their various sprays and things, walk in there, and heave it all out in five minutes flat. It was a most heartening thing to see what real first-class knowledge could do in a case like that. We never had occasion to use it on board the ship when I was there but they did later when she was kamikazied and they used their knowledge very successfully.

Well, as I say, we went back to the Philadelphia and had a post-shakedown overhaul. Golly, things were polluted around there. The air was. The white paint all over the ship would turn the color of brown clay in a very few days. There just wasn't anything you could do about it. The gold stripes on a blue uniform would be all corroded, completely horrible-looking.

Q: There was very sparse use of paint on the ship, wasn't there, as you were preparing to go into battle?

Adm. S.: Yes. We didn't build up these thick layers of paint that we used to. We didn't do that any more because burning paint had proved to be one of the worst things in a fight.

Q: What about the question of spare parts? Did you lay up any on board ship?

Adm. S.: We had an allowance of spare parts but I don't recall that we had more than our regular allowance.

Q: It seemed to me that some of the skippers took extra precautions in taking on spare parts, anything they could get their hands on.

Adm. S.: Well, any boatswain's mate worth his salt would go on board his sister destroyer moored alongside and when his opposite number wasn't looking would steal his boatswain's chest from right under his eyes.

I don't recall any particular episodes there.

While I was there I got invited over to the commissioning of a small, experimental ship that had some very experimental engines in it. I do not recall the nature of these engines, but the ship had three or four young reserve officers on board. I went over for their ceremony. I happened to be the senior officer afloat at the time in the yard. They were all full of protocol and coffee and cake and we had a very fine time. They later on achieved a measure of fame under the name of the "Flying Teakettle" or something like that, because this experimental engineering setup proved to be a complete failure. They could get their little ship as far as the mouth of the Delaware River and then they would find they were out of water and they would have to get some water from the beach. They would go back to the Navy Yard and the Yard would try to find out what became of all that water but never was able to really determine what happened.

This poor little teakettle never did get to sea. I think they got out and maybe got around to the Chesapeake but that was as far as they ever got. They had a terrible time. I didn't hear about this until years afterwards when it was written up very amusingly in the New Yorker and I think it was made into a movie. But my heart bled for those poor young fellows when I found out what a disappointment this craft had been to them because they were so proud of their experimental affair.

When we left there we were sent up to Rockland, Maine, to run the standardization trials for our class of ship. We got up there and the standardization party came on board and they started explaining to me that they wanted to get the ship going at 110 per cent of her full power. They were talking about 10 per cent over full power, and then apply full rudder. I was aghast because, in the course of our shakedown cruise, we found out that if we were running along at 20 knots and we put on a good deal less than full rudder, the ship would heel so that everything that wasn't nailed down would fall over. We had busted crockery and so forth all over the place. So I had issued orders that we would never use more than just standard rudder if we were making over 25 knots. I said:

"My God, she'll capsize!" and I described how she heeled.

Q: What was the need for this, anyway?

Adm. S.: It was a standard test, I guess. It was finally agreed that we would approach this subject with caution. We would work into it and see what happened. As it turned out, everything was perfectly okay because no matter how fast we went she heeled just so much and then she stuck there. In fact, the faster we were going the sooner we got out of trouble because as the ship turns it goes thisaway and here we've got the ship trying to go sidewise through the water before it gets going over where its headed, and as a result it slows down very rapidly. We could go into one of these turns making about 36 knots and put that rudder over, and by the time we'd turned 90 or 120 degrees we wouldn't be making over 12 knots through the water and the ship would be coming back to an even keel. But if you really wanted to have some fun, the thing to do was to let her turn about 60 degrees, then put the rudder amidships. Then she really would stand on her ear!

We went through all these standardization trials up there, then went back, picked up a couple of destroyers, and headed for the Pacific.

Interview #5 with Rear Admiral Malcolm F. Schoeffel,
U.S. Navy (Retired)

Place: His son's residence in Alexandria, Virginia

Date: Friday morning, 1 June 1979

Subject: Biography

By: John T. Mason, Jr.

Q: Well, Sir, I think we're raring to go this morning. Yesterday, when we broke off, you were skipper of the Cabot and you had completed all the preliminaries and were, I think, in Hawaii.

Adm. S.: No, we were just leaving Philadelphia.

Q: Oh, yes, all right, Sir.

Adm. S.: To go to the Pacific. We stopped off in Norfolk and at that time Commander, Aircraft, Atlantic Fleet, made it a policy to man ships to 104 per cent of a complement to take care of expected attrition very largely from men missing a ship.

In this connection, I want to speak on the subject of the morale of our crews.

In World War II the morale of a crew, at least of the

crew I had in the Cabot, was very much better than the morale of the crew of the Oklahoma that I had seen in World War I. I think this was widespread, Navy-wide, in both wars. I think we had a much better spirit in World War II than we did in World War I.

Q: Why was this? Because of Pearl Harbor?

Adm. S.: Because the whole country was really behind World War II. The whole country was not behind World War I, and a great many of the men in World War I were truly draft-dodgers. That's why they were in the Navy. A very small indication of this - I remember that on board the Oklahoma we frequently had great difficulty in getting the enlisted men to stand and salute the colors at colors. Nothing of that sort did I ever hear of in World War II, quite the opposite.

We were built up to 104 per cent like the other carriers that were sent out.

Q: Why the magic number of 104? Why not 105?

Adm. S.: Because statistics showed that 104 per cent was the right figure! They had the statistics and George Murray, who was Commander, Aircraft, at that time told me that that was the reason.

Q: I see, all right.

Adm. S.: This proved to be about right in our case because there were a number of men who missed the ship, and, later on, when we were out in Hawaii a good many of them were returned to the ship. I got them all together at a special mast and I said to them:

"You men have all had some form of punishment for missing the ship. Therefore, I can do nothing further in that line, but I want to tell you my eyes and the eyes of the other officers of this ship are on you. I am having a detachable piece of paper put in your records saying that you were returned and the supposition is that you missed the ship because of cowardice. I cannot expect you to perform heroic deeds but, when we get into action, if you perform your duties meticulously well, I will have these slips of paper removed from your records."

I think this was very salutary. I think it had a big effect on those men because the reports came in after we'd been in action and practically all of these slips, if not all of them, were pulled out and thrown away.

Q: What inspired you to tell them that?

Adm. S.: It just seemed a good idea, that was all. I felt very strongly that most of them had missed the ship because they had a yellow streak, either that or, in the case of many of the Italian ones - and most of those who had missed were of Italian background, Mama fell upon their necks and wept all over them.

Well, we set out with two destroyers and got down to the Panama Canal. Although my ship was a light carrier, we had to have some gun sponsons takens off on the Atlantic side in order to get through the locks, and, even with them off, the canal authorities laid us right up against one side of the lock and we went through with a terrific screech of steel on concrete. Then we got our gun sponsons put back in Balboa, and off we set for San Diego.

On the way up we had a small incident. Our radar - and I'd like to refute the people who try to talk about radar showing UFOs coming in from outer space. By this time we had been in commission long enough to have experience with our radar and to know that the ghosts that tended to follow us around at night were probably nothing material at all. Off the mouth of the Gulf of California in broad daylight and perfect weather we were refueling our two destroyers; one alongside was refueling and the other one patrolling ahead, when our radar picked up a very strong blip from three or four miles away on the starboard bow. We immediately sent the patrolling destroyer over there to investigate and got ready to cast off the one that was fueling.

This destroyer went over there and shortly reported that they could find nothing. The blip was still there.

We had vectored them right through the blip, but they said there was no bird, there was no wreckage, there was no sea-turtle there, just nothing. Well, that blip continued out there and the destroyer went all round it and they listened and everything else. Whatever it was it was something that was quite immaterial.

Q: The destroyer had radar also?

Adm. S.: I don't remember. Probably not at that time.

Well, we went up to San Diego, stopped off there, shoved off, went out to Hawaii, and upon arrival there - no, it wasn't upon arrival, I guess it was after a week or so, because we were sent out with the Yorktown for air exercises in the vicinity of the Hawaiian Islands. We spent Christmas Eve alongside a dock at Pearl and that evening I was told a lot of mail sacks had arrived so I went to the quarter deck to gloat over them. But I didn't gloat long, for seven million cock roaches were streaming out of those sacks and making for parts unknown. So I sent for the Exec, the Supply Officer, the boss Doctor and the First Lieutenant and reminded them of the mandate I had laid down at commissioning, "We cannot keep vermin from entering the ship but we can run it so they all starve to death." I really don't know what my boys did but I never saw another roach.

Jock Clark, later four-star, had the Yorktown at the

time. We had half a dozen destroyers with us, and the way Jock yapped at those destroyers all the time on TBS was a caution. He was continually shouting at them, "Small boys, get going! Small boys, get going!" or words to that effect.

Q: That's typical Jocko.

Adm. S.: Well, he didn't yap at me so I had no reason to complain, but I wondered what he thought he was getting out of it.

We had some rather heavy weather out there but we got through our exercises without smashing any airplanes, went into Pearl, and the Fifth Fleet at that time was just about to shove off for the attack on the Marshall Islands.

Q: This was under the command of Spruance?

Adm. S.: Yes, under Spruance's command. We in the Cabot were assigned to Task Group 58.42 under Alfred Montgomery's command. I had been Montgomery's exec when he was squadron commander of VT-2 back on North Island, so I knew Montgomery pretty well.

Came the day to get under way and there was a wind that absolutely pinned the Cabot to the dock. We could not get her to push her nose out enough to go ahead or astern to get clear of that dock.

Q: It must have been an unusual wind.

Adm. S.: It was a damned unusual situation! All the rest of the boys went past and out to sea and there was the <u>Cabot</u> still alongside the dock.

Q: You must have had Jocko hollering at you on that occasion?

Adm. S.: Jocko had nothing to do with it. I was under Montgomery's control by this time.

Finally, we got a tug, and the tug pulled us out and we went out with my tail between my legs. We got out there and fell in and, as far as I recall, Montgomery never said a word about it. I know I did not get severely bawled out, as I had expected to be.

Q: This was an act of God, anyway, wasn't it?

Adm. S.: Maybe so, but captains are supposed to be able to handle such things!

We went way down south and we passed through that point at 180 degrees longitude, zero latitude, where a polliwog becomes not just a shellback but a golden something or other. We were allowed to take enough time off to initiate our polliwogs, and then we turned and headed north for the Marshalls, going up the west side of the Gilberts. Weather absolutely cavu, absolutely perfect. We were expecting

Japanese airplanes to come out and spot us at any moment, particularly since another one of the task groups was not maintaining any sort of radio silence on their TBS. They were jabbering all the time.

Montgomery had told us, "You keep quiet. If you have anything to say, say it by light or wigwag and keep the TBS for essentials." But this other outfit was just jabbering. We were all scared to death that this was going to bring the Japs in.

About that time, the <u>Indianapolis,</u> which was Spruance's flagship, showed up on the horizon and came over and fell in with us. Very soon a rather dramatic little incident occurred. A very deep voice came over the air:

"All Hands," which was the call for everybody, "this is Bad News."

That was a very well-chosen pair of words because it absolutely described the situation and also it was Spruance's administrative call, "All Hands, this is Bad News. Pipe down! Out." After that there was complete silence.

After the war was over and I was on Spruance's staff, I asked him if he had done that himself, and he maintained that he didn't know anything whatever about the incident!

We went on and we arrived off the Marshalls. Came the first day of action and we went into battle, all keyed up, of course. Our airplanes flew off and shortly came back and reported that their squadron commander had shot down a couple of Japs, other people had done so and so, and the whole operation was probably best summed up by one of the enlisted men in the flight-deck crew. He said:

"Hell, this ain't my idea of no battle. This is just a hell of a lot of hard work!"

Q: The Japs obviously hadn't come near?

Adm. S.: No. We just overwhelmed them and then we took part in the covering of bombardments and the landing and so forth.

We had only one casualty. I don't know whether that was due to Japanese action or whether his engine just decided to go dead, but the pilot put his plane down in the water and a destroyer had him out in nothing flat. This young man, in the course of time, became rather adept at ditching. He seemed to get into trouble from time to time, but he always ditched and he seldom got anything worse than his feet wet. I can't remember his name, but he was quite a dashing young pilot.

Q: How accurate did these reports from the pilots turn out to be? Were you ever able to verify them?

Adm. S.: When I was on Admiral King's staff in Washington, I came to the conclusion that we should take our claims of enemy losses and divide them by three, and as a general average, if we took a third of our claims - our claims had been made in good faith by the people making them - then we were pretty close to correct. I was able to arrive at this result by reading in the Magic intercepts that were passed around Admiral King's staff what the Japanese said about their own losses. Then, of course, we took the American losses that the Japanese claimed via Tokyo Rose and we divided them by 10,000, and we came somewhere near the correct answer.

Following the capture of the Marshalls, we went in to Majuro. For a while that was our anchorage. A couple of amusing things happened on the way in there. The entrance is a very narrow one through the reef, then there's a very large lagoon in there. We were informed that we would be met at the entrance by pilots who would take us in. My only experience with pilots up to that time had been old sea dogs whose fathers and grandfathers had been pilots before them and they knew all about local conditions and all about how to handle a ship. I'll come back to the pilot in a moment.

For some reason or other we were told off to fall in with a cruiser division before we went in to Majuro. This cruiser division was commanded by some old sea dog whose name I can't remember but who had spent a year or two with the British earlier in the war. He was so imbued with British methods of doing things that he insisted upon using the British signal book for his tactical signals within the division.

Q: How confusing!

Adm. S.: Well, he ran up a signal and I was very promptly

apprised that this was the British method of signaling. I had a little bit of a bridge that was not much bigger than that rug and I was up there all by my lone and I didn't have any British signal book around. I had to scream for the ship's secretary and he had to go down and break open the ship's safe and get the British signal book. He brought it up and I think the signal was "left 25 degrees" or something like that.

Q: By the time you got this information, it could be quite outdated!

Adm. S.: Yes! Meanwhile, the division commander was making noises in my direction, "Why don't you two-block my signal" and so forth. I wanted to reply to him:

"You silly ass. If you'd used American signals, I would have done so a long time ago."

But I didn't say anything and I finally got my signal two-blocked just about the time he wanted to haul down, anyhow had to haul down.

We went off and stood in to Majuro. The pilot boat came alongside and the pilot came up on the bridge. He was a very natty-looking young junior lieutenant and he handed me a big blueprint which, he said, showed the swept channel into Majuro, to the anchorage. Thinking of him as being the grandson of some old sea dog, I asked him if he wanted to take the conn. Oh, no, indeed, he didn't want to take the conn. It turned out that he was essentially a dentist from somewhere in Iowa and he was attached to an LST that had been in Majuro for a few days with the first outfit that went in there. The morning of our entry his ship had been directed to tell off a number of officers to go out to the entrance and be pilots, so that was the extent of his pilotage.

Q: His knowledge of the lagoon was pretty limited, wasn't it?

Adm. S.: It was very limited, very limited.

We didn't know whether there were any mines in the lagoon. We thoroughly expected that the Japanese had mined the lagoon very well. As a matter of fact, they hadn't mined the Majuro lagoon. We didn't know it.

Q: Were there any minesweepers with your unit?

Adm. S.: With the first outfit that went in, yes, and they had swept the place up to where the anchorage was to be, and there were anchorage buoys laid out up there and things of that sort. However, there were a lot of coral heads in this lagoon. We in the Cabot had read up all that we could on the subject of going in to these atolls. The pilot books strongly recommended putting a very good lookout aloft, as far up as you could get him, because he could see the coral heads better than you could from a lower altitude.

Q: The water was very clear?

Adm. S.: Yes. So I had the exec Gat Washburn way up at the foremast head, and he could see the coral heads all right, but there weren't any along this swept channel that we followed. We could see them off to one side or the other -

Q: They're almost as dangerous as mines, aren't they?

Adm. S.: If you hit one, but you can see so far down into the water that you see a coral head and there may be 100 feet of water over it, but I don't know offhand the immediate answer as to how you tell how much water there is over the coral head.

Well, we got in to our anchorage and, golly, that was an impressive sight there, those great task groups both at sea and in their anchorages. Such masses of ships! Everybody liked ot get up on deck and just look around and say, "My God, look at these ships! Ships everywhere!"

We hadn't been there very long, a few days, when a tanker came in and the poor tanker captain missed a very important buoy where you were supposed to turn hard right, so the first thing he knew he was on a coral head. I don't think it damaged him very much, probably nothing much but his self-esteem.

Q: It didn't cause a leakage of his precious oil?

Adm. S.: I don't recall any leakage visible.

Well, as I say, we stayed around there a few days and then we set out for the first attack on Truk. This really had a lot of people looking a little cross-eyed because Truk had a horrendous reputation.

Q: Yes, it did. A bastion.

Adm. S.: It was fourteen Gibraltars rolled into one, as we understood it.

We got going and set off up to the north and along about three o'clock one morning very soon after we got under way, I was called out of my little sea cabin, which was way down on the flight-deck level - I had to climb quite a distance to get up to the bridge - and we could see shooting going on over the horizon ahead of us. One outfit was putting out a lot of gunfire, using white tracers, and another outfit was shooting back, using red tracers. We didn't know what was going on and our Task Group Commander had nothing to say on the subject, so I just went to general quarters and stood by. After a while this firing died down. I think it was the "reds" that quit and the "whites" kept on going. The whites were going from west to east and the reds were shooting back from east to west. All of this dead ahead, all of it over the horizon, no gun flashes visible.

Montgomery never said anything. I heard later that one of our destroyers operating independently had come upon a barge laden with Japanese troops and artillery escaping from the Marshalls. Our DD opened fire and the Japs used their improvised armament to shoot back. The Japs were brave men.

Everything having calmed down, I secured again, sent everybody back to his bunk. I don't recall whether it was that morning or the next morning that we made the actual attack on Truk. I know that the afternoon of the day before the attack we in the Cabot, who had by this time established a reputation for having one of the best radars in the group - we could pick up airplanes farther away than almost anybody else.

Q: Was yours a different model from the others?

Adm. S.: I don't recall whether it was a different model or whether it was just a little better tuned or what. But we picked up a Japanese airplane headed for the group about ninety miles away. We watched him coming and we expected he was going to spot us, and then, when he got about seventy miles away, he turned off to the right and disappeared. He never saw any of us.

Finally came the morning of the attack. I might say at this time that in our group we had, as I recall it, three big carriers and there were two of us CVLs, and we in the

CVLs did the combat air patrol and the antisubmarine patrol. At this time we did not participate in the strikes. I guess we only had one CVL because if we'd had two they certainly would have used the planes of one to go along with the strike force.

Q: Yes, because that was a massive attack, wasn't it?

Adm. S.: We in the Cabot were flying the defensive patrols and our strikes were launched at just about dawn and our strike force absolutely got over the outer reef of Truk before the Japanese knew anything was coming.

We feel that we did a rotten job at Pearl Harbor, the Japanese attack coming in undetected. But imagine the terrible job that the Japanese did at Truk. The war had been under way for two years. We had just struck the Marshalls, conquered the Marshalls, we'd conquered the Gilberts. There was absolutely beautiful weather. And they let us surprise them completely!

Q: Did they have radar, or what was their provision - ?

Adm. S.: They had some radar. I don't think it was as good as ours.

They had sent most of their combat ships out of Truk before we got there. There were only a few of them left in the lagoon, but there were a lot of airplanes there and a large number of merchant vessels. Our airplanes shot up the Japanese airplanes and they sank the merchant vessels and some of the combatant ships. One or two of the combatant ships got out and went hightailing it to the westward. Some of our cruisers and one of our battleships, I think, took out after them and shot at them. I don't recall whether they hit them or not.

Q: Was this a dawn attack?

Adm. S.: Yes, and we kept up the attacks most of the day.

I don't recall whether we went back to Majuro after that or not, but shortly thereafter we participated in two other big strikes. I don't recall which came first. One was covering MacArthur's invasion of Hollandia. We went down and took part in that, then we went out to those islands far to the westward which were not too far out from the Philippines.

Q: The Ellice Islands?

Adm. S.: No.

Q: The Carolines?

Adm. S.: It was beyond the Carolines, the ones that ran down to the south from the Carolines. South from Yap.

There, the objective of our torpedo planes in that attack was to lay mines, which was something that none of our airplanes had ever done before.

Q: They weren't very fond of that kind of a task, were they?

Adm. S.: Well, they had no qualms about it. The only trick to it was that you had to be very careful of the location where you laid your mine and you had to be able to come back and tell just where you actually put it.

Q: It was an anchored mine, was it?

Adm. S.: Yes. They were influence mines of some sort. I don't recall what the influence was.

We had much success in all these operations, and I guess Hollandia was the first of those two, because I remember that as we laid back through the Marshalls from the island operation - the Ryukus, the island operation - we made a second attack on Truk. In preparation for this attack we were met while at sea by one of these replenishment carriers, a CVE, that had relief pilots on board.

I made it a practice in the Cabot whenever we went into action to follow the old regulation that you hoisted your largest American ensign as the battle flag. Nobody else did it. The upshot of it was, I was told later, that the pilots found they could identify 58.2 from the other task groups very easily because if they could see the great big American ensign up there they knew it was the Cabot in good old 58.2!

Anyhow, as we departed from Truk, we had all our airplanes on board but we had a clear deck and the other people generally didn't have clear decks, when a lone fighter showed up, an American fighter. We took him on board and here was a poor little replacement pilot who had reported the day before to one of the big carriers in another task group, and he had been shoved off to go and participate in the attack on Truk, and all they had told him was, "You just stay with your section leader." So he stayed with his section leader and his section leader got shot down. What was the poor fellow to do? All he knew was to take off to the southward. He went down somewhat to the southward and he soon sighted a bunch of American carriers, and we were hospitable and took him on board. We informed his ship that we had him and we would send him back tomorrow.

The next morning we got him up on deck and this young fellow had never had a catapult shot. This was all news to him, so we had to instruct him in that. Then our flight-deck people said to him, "You take off and your task group is right over the horizon, just over there to the right."

He took off. Everything was hunkydory. Then he disappeared to the left, and I don't know what ever became of him. Oh, the complete inexperience of some of the pilots who were sent out as replacements was unbelievable.

Q: How could that happen? Because they were trying to turn them out too rapidly?

Adm. S.: Yes. You see, a great many of them had gone through flight training and then had gotten their carrier training with three landings on one of these Wolverine, side-wheel carriers up in the Great Lakes, and that was all the carrier experience they had.

Q: There must have been a lot of casualties with such pilots?

Adm. S.: Yes, I'm sure there were.

Q: Was any study ever made of it?

Adm. S.: Oh, there was a great deal of effort and thought being put into this, and we had an outfit back in Hawaii called I think it was Task Force 100, whose job was to get these replacement pilots adequately trained before sending them out.

Q: They arrived out in Hawaii and then discovered they needed more training?

Adm. S.: Well, it was these experiences out in the forward area with these extremely inexperienced replacement pilots that led - I think it was John Towers who was Commander, Aircraft, Pacific, at that time, to form this Task Group 100, which was just getting under way. I think Raoul Waller was in charge of it but I'm not sure.

As an example of lack of experience, when we were running south, just before the Marshalls attack, one of the big carriers had a night fighter on board. I don't know how this came about, but his airplane was an F4-U. The F4-U later on became a very favorite carrier airplane, fighter airplane, in the Navy, but at that time it was pretty brand new and it was thought to be very tricky. I thought it was very strange that they would assign such an airplane as a night fighter.

It was decided to launch this fellow one night and give him some practice and give the ship some practice, I suppose. Well, he got off and I don't know what went wrong, but eventually he ditched. It's damned difficult to ditch at night successfully and in an airplane like an F4-U, I thought it was an excessively hairy operation. But the pilot got away with it. He found himself in the water. He had a little flashlight and he flashed his flashlight, and somebody saw it and he got picked up. I want to tell you that young fellow really was living on borrowed time, but he was picked up!

I heard afterwards that his total carrier landing experience was three on the Wolverine. I may have been misinformed, but that's what I was told.

Q: Was it not true that Task Force 58 learned fairly soon that it wasn't really feasible to have night fighters and day fighters in the same carrier?

Adm. S.: Yes, and later on, particularly during the Iwo Jima operation, they had a whole small division of carriers, night carriers, out there.

But, you see, we had flown full carrier air groups at night back in '34 and '35 when Kelly Turner was running AirBatFor, but following that we had given it up completely, and apparently there was no need felt for anything of the sort until the Gilberts operation when the Japanese started coming out at night, trying to attack our ships, and they did sink one of the CVEs at that time. Butch O'Hare volunteered to make himself into a night fighter then and there. He went out and I don't know how successful he was, but he was lost at that time in one of those night operations.

Well, returning to our second attack on Truk. The second night there, there were still some Japanese airplanes around the island and they were coming in at night, and our destroyers and cruisers and battleships and big carriers were firing at them, using these new VT fuses. You could see these little extremely instantaneous spots of light as these things exploded. We in the Cabot had only some Bofors 40-mm and a good many Oerlikon 20-mm, so we weren't doing any shooting but we were certainly standing by and watching.

Q: Both types of guns that you hadn't really taken over earlier?

Adm. S.: Yes.

We were naturally watching with much interest. I'm getting a little ahead of myself, but I'll come back later.

Soon the Intrepid, which wasn't far from us, got in the way of a Japanese torpedo and had a large hold opened in her port quarter. Montgomery very promptly directed her to return to Majuro and elected a cruiser, a couple of destroyers, and the Cabot to escort her back there. Tommy Sprague, later a vice admiral, was skipper of the Intrepid at that time. The fleet was getting ready to proceed directly from Second Truk to the attack on the Marianas, the first raid up there. So they went off to raid the Marianas. We in the Cabot did not go on that expedition. Therefore, I have ever since been in the position of blaming Tommy Sprague that I never became a vice admiral, because every carrier captain who went on that first Marianas raid got some decoration, I forget which, that permits oneupmanship on retirement and I never got one! So it's all Tommy Sprague's fault!

Q: It was a costly diversion.

Adm. S.: No, it didn't cost me a nickel, nor anybody else, except you do like to call yourself by that title!

As I say, I'm getting a little ahead of myself. In the course of the second attack on Truk, some Jap airplanes came out by day also. It was a day of low clouds, poor visibility. We knew that there were a couple of Japanese torpedo planes headed in on us, and the Yorktown opened fire. We could see all these bursts over there. She was just off on our starboard bow. She did not shoot down these two Japanese airplanes that passed a very low distance over her flight deck, but evidently they had been well shot up because immediately after passing over the Yorktown they both reared up in the air and then dove into the water right ahead of us, perhaps half a mile ahead of us. Finis.

Then another one came in. One of our fighters was on the catapult at the time, the catapult was fired, the pilot found this Japanese airplane right in his sights, right ahead of him, and before he even pulled up he shot down the Jap!

Well, we got back to Majuro and laid around there. Then all the boys came back from going up to the Marianas and we were to get ready for something else when I got a dispatch announcing that I had been promoted to rear admiral and that I was detached from the Cabot.

Q: You must have had mixed emotions at that point?

Adm. S.: I certainly did. I didn't want to be detached.

Schoeffel #5 - 234

Q: But you wanted to be a rear admiral?

Adm. S.: Yes.

I went back in the Yorktown which, for some reason or other, was returning to Pearl.

Q: Was Clark still the skipper?

Adm. S.: No. My classmate and dear friend Ralph Jennings had relieved him by that time. I had a very lazy and pleasant trip back to Pearl Harbor, and I was slated at that time to take command of a group of CVEs that was just being formed, about to be formed, to take out replacement pilots. So I got myself all involved in the planning and the operation of Task Group 100 and so forth -

Q: When you arrived back, before you took over this new command, did you have a session with the commander in chief?

Adm. S.: No. I was about to say that just as I got there and reported to Admiral Towers, he said, "Oh, forget about that. I understand you're going to go to Washington." So that was that and I never had anything, in reality, to do with the replacement business. It fell to - oh, a man from the class of '18, and they did their replacement business for sometime but after the war was over they were primarily concerned with bringing soldiers home.

Anyhow, I had orders to proceed very shortly to Washington to relieve Art Davis on Admiral King's staff as Assistant Chief of Staff for Operations. I also had a month's leave. I was to leave Hawaii on a Monday morning. Sunday afternoon I was taking in the slack on a settee outside Towers' quarters when I heard a dull boom and looked over to the eastward and saw a lot of smoke arising from one of the lochs over there. Shortly, it was obvious that there was a hell of a catastrophe occurring over there. Something big was underway. It turned out that a lot of the amphibious force was over there being prepared for the actual attack on the Mariana Islands. They were preparing for the conquest of them. And that some ammunition had blown up that was being offloaded from an LST, with the result that a lot of gasoline had caught fire, and there had been a real catastrophe.

The next morning I found myself made a member of a Court of Inquiry. Rear Admiral Jack Shafroth was the president of the court and Captain Sam Shumaker was the third member. Several LSTs had been sunk. We had suffered about 1,000 personnel casualties in killed and hospitalized people over there in the loch. It had been a terrible affair. It all started when, as I say, some ammunition was being offloaded from an LST. These were large incendiary shells or bombs and they were being sent down a chute and one of them blew up. This chute was down through the bow opening of the LST and there were quite a number of drums of gasoline on the fo's'sle of this LST, right over the point where the explosion took place. This gasoline ran out and caught fire, other ships caught fire from that one, and so forth.

As I recall it, three LSTs were sunk and several others very badly damaged.

Well, I didn't get my month's leave. I spent that month with this Court of Inquiry. We climbed all over these vessels as they were preparing for this attack on Guam and, golly, the hazards that were being run in the way in which they were being loaded! They were all combat-loaded. In other words, so that the things that the troops ashore would need first were on top and would go ashore first. But it certainly created grave dangers. We went on board one LST where all around the hangar deck at the lowest level they had drums of incendiary material and, sitting on top of these drums all over the place, boxes of 50-caliber ammunition. This sort of thing everywhere.

In the course of this Inquiry I had climbed all over a lot of LSTs and had sort of called upon Shumaker to do the same. This I should never have done for I should have realized Sam had a weak heart. One evening I was to stop by the BOQ where he was quartered, for a drink and to go to dinner; when I was informed he had been found dead on the floor of his room! I have always felt pretty guilty about this. Now Sam was not the kind of man I ever wanted to be, for he was very cynical and, perhaps, a loose liver; but he surely had a razor keen mind.

Let me tell a little story on Sam. When I was first in BuOrd he was there and his teeth were about the most horrible things you ever saw. When I returned to the Bureau a second time, in 1941 about when PanAm was trying to fly the Pacific commercially, he turned up with a nice looking mouth and the little red-headed stenog who had recently joined up (oh, we got Beauty with a capital B in the military during the wars) gaped at him and said, "Oh, Captain Sumaker where did you get those China Clippers?!"

Eventually, we made our report. Frankly, I don't recall what it was, except it said these were the hazards you have to accept in war in order to go ahead, because it had been decided to go ahead with the invasion in spite of these losses, and these were serious losses that the Amphibious Forces incurred.

Then I was released and went back to Washington.

Q: This method of handling ammunition must have had some effect on the crew, did it not, especially after that accident?

Adm. S.: That I don't know. The Amphibious Forces functioned as they were supposed to function in the attack on the Marianas. The only question of morale that I ever heard coming up was that of the big fight between the Marine general and the Army general there.

Q: The Smiths?

Adm. S.: Yes. I never heard of anything else of that sort.

Q: Did you have any brush with the UDTs at that point? They were training out there.

Adm. S.: No, I did not. Of course, I'd heard of them and their exploits by that time, but I had no business with them.

I went back to Washington and checked in, relieved Art Davis, who got a command at sea -

Q: This was quite an assignment you were going to, wasn't it?

Adm. S.: It sounds great. It was a stuffed-shirt job, if there ever was one, because Admiral King and Admiral Edwards and Savvy Cook were quite able to plan in considerable detail all the operations of the U.S. Fleet without any particular assistance from anybody like myself.

Q: Were they inclined to ask for any assistance?

Adm. S.: They were not. They were just inclined to send you a tiny little slip of memorandum paper on which King would write a very terse note saying, "Do this, do that," and that was it. I didn't have to bestir myself because they had Roscoe Good who was running the actual details of all the operations of the ships.

Q: He was your immediate boss?

Adm. S.: No, he was my immediate number two. I was the Assistant Chief of Staff for Operations. He was, in title, the Operations Officer, and that's the way it really functioned. King would issue these very terse instructions, I would pass them on the Good and Good would shortly come up with a dispatch. He had a bunch of the sharpest cookies the Navy had assisting him and the sharpest bunch of WAVEs assisting them that you ever saw in your life, both in looks and capabilities.

Q: Creme de la creme!

Adm. S.: Shortly, he'd come back with either a very short letter or a very well-worded dispatch. I would initial it - I very seldom had any reason to modify any of them in any detail - and pass it up the line. Well, if King didn't like it, it would come back just with a big question mark on it. It was up to you to find out why he didn't like it.

Q: And what means did you have?

Adm. S.: ESP! It was also considered reasonably kosher to go and ask Savvy Cook what was the matter! If something was passed up to King it was generally prepared on the initiative of some staff officer and, if he, King, didn't like it, he'd send it back with a question mark. If he didn't like it very much, he'd send it back with two question marks. If he sent it back with three question marks, you might as well pack your bag and get ready to leave Washington!

Q: By sundown!

Adm. S.: Yes! Even earlier!!!

Q: Tell me a little about the staff. I mean about Cook and Edwards.

Adm. S.: I am about to.

Q: Horne was there, too, wasn't he?

Adm. S.: Admiral Horne was Chief of Naval Operations but he had an entirely separate organization and he ran his organization very quietly and, apparently, very much to the satisfaction of Admiral King.

Speaking of the staff, it's best exemplified by the staff mess at lunch. We had a special room there and King sat at the head of the table, with Edwards on his right,

Cook on his left, and the rest of us in order down the line to the flag lieutenant at the end. When King was there, there was always a very animated and interesting conversation going on between him and Cook and Edwards, and the rest of us just sat and listened. We seldom said anything more than "Please pass the butter," and I know that British officers who were invited into his mess by King were very much struck by the fact that, with the exception of the three at the head of the table, we were just like people who didn't count at all.

Q: And the conversation, what was it on, naval matters?

Adm. S.: Oh, always, matters of operations and policy and so forth, extremely interesting conversations to listen to.
When King wasn't there, Edwards, of course, would sit at the head of the table and the difference was amazing. Everybody chattered like a bunch of magpies. We just carried on like a bunch of plebes!

Q: Perhaps more so than you would normally?

Adm. S.: Yes.

Q: This was a necessary thing, you had to appear there every day?

Adm. S.: Oh, yes. If you were in Washington, that's where you had your lunch, and a very good lunch it always was.

Edwards was a man with a lot of wit. I remember one time towards the end of the war, Mr. Byrnes, who was then Secretary of State, was down in South America and there was something that was under discussion between the Navy Department and the State Department. The Navy wanted something done and the State Department was dragging its feet, and King was talking to Edwards about it. Edwards explained to him this way:

The State Department fiddles while Byrnes roams!"

I remember the time when Edwards was made Deputy Commander in Chief - I forget just what his title was before and he was moved to a nice big office of his own. He and Savvy Cook had previously occupied the same office. He was explaining how he wanted it furnished and he said:

"The only sort of papers that are going to come to me are the kind that I always put in the lower lefthand drawer and I want a bunch of desks around here with nothing but lower lefthand drawers."

Of course, one who was very close to Admiral King was Frog Lowe -

Q: Tenth Fleet.

Adm. S.: Tenth Fleet, yes. Those two, as far as I was concerned, kept their own secrets. In spite of this title

Schoeffel #5 - 243

of mine, I was not let in on any of that at all. I knew nothing about what was going on in the Tenth Fleet. In fact, I had great difficulty in discovering what the hell the Tenth Fleet was.

Q: Yet the jeep carriers in the Atlantic knew about it?

Adm. S.: Oh, yes.

Shortly before I got there, the Joint Chiefs of Staff had decided to set up a committee to consider the possibility of a merger of the armed forces. John Sidney McCain, who was then chief of BuAir was made the senior Navy member, with Art Davis as an assistant member. Admiral Joe Richardson was the senior member of the whole committee for the Joint Chiefs, not as a navy member but as just the senior member. There was an Air Force member, a General George, generally known in the Air Force as Bomber George to differentiate him from another General George, who was Fighter George. I don't remember who the Army member was. He was a very pleasant major general. Then this committee had a whole flock of assistants.

Well, I fell heir to this job, when I relieved Art Davis, and I very soon found out that John Sidney McCain was not in the least bit interested in what was going on in that committee. He attended no meetings, and when I would go around and try to apprise him of what went on, he wasn't the least bit interested. So very soon I just gave up having anything to do with McCain and I became, in effect, the Navy member.

Q: Who was, indeed, back of this idea at that point?

Adm. S.: All the politicians, all the newspaper writers, and so forth. They were all screaming bloody murder, and all the Air Force. The Air Force wanted to get out of the Army and set itself up independently. The Army was very happy to get rid of the Air Force, if they could, and, of course, the Air Force wanted to be set up at least on the same level as the Army and Navy. All the politicians were in favor of this, so this committee was set up and we had a great time. We had a lot of assistants and we'd hold meetings there in the old Munitions Building. Every one of us would have a Webster's Unabridged in front of him, constantly referring to it, to make sure we were all talking the same language.

Q: Looking for subtle nuances in what was being said!

Adm. S.: That's right.
One day, after we broke up, Admiral Richardson said to me:
"Schoeffel, are we getting anywhere?" And I said:
"Well, Admiral, I'm having a wonderful course in semantics."

He chuckled and said, "Semantics, what's that?"

I said, "Well, the science of the meaning of words," and he chuckled again. He was a great fellow. He said:

"That reminds me. I once received a letter from a very lovely lady in which she accused me of being smug. I wrote back to her and said I'd looked up 'smug' and I found that there were two meanings for the word. One was an adjective meaning self-satisfied, complacent, and so forth, and if that was her meaning I indignantly denied her allegation. But there was also a verb, transitive, meaning to dally with amorously, and if that was her meaning, I was her man!"

Q: Was Admiral King interested in this committee?

Adm. S.: He was interested only in what the output might be. The only instruction that he gave me was, "be factual." That was all.

However, I always felt that the Army and the Air Force people were fully instructed by their higher-ups to put the thing across.

Q: It seems like a rather odd study to be under way when the war was being fought.

Adm. S.: Well, we were obviously winning the war by that time.

Q: So this was a luxury?

Adm. S.: Possibly. But, golly, there were innumerable studies of this, that, and the other thing under way in those days, just as there are now, only the studies in those days didn't cost the taxpayer any particular amount of money. This one of ours did before we got through because Richardson said he felt that we should not confine our thinking to Washington, we should go out and see all the commanders in the field of the various services and get their views.

So, we got hold of a great big Air Force airplane, it was one of the presidential stable, no less, with a very splendid pilot, a Lieutenant Colonel Meyers, and we proceeded first over to England. We saw Admiral Stark and various other dignitaries there. Then we went to Paris - this was about a month after the breakout in Normandy, and Eisenhower was established in Paris by that time. When we got through talking business with Eisenhower, he later remarked and surprised us all very much:

"After this war is over, I'm going to be the most unpopular man in the United States." Richardson said:

"General, what makes you say that?"

And Eisenhower said: "Well, you see, there at home they promote them. I get them over here and I have to demote them. When you leave here, as you go out, you will find a major general standing outside the door. When I get through talking to him, he's going to be a major."

We saw this poor fellow standing there as we went out. I never knew who he was or what happened to him or any more about it than that.

Q: You didn't want to either!

Adm. S.: We didn't see Patton. Everybody told us, "You'll have a hell of a good time if you go and see Patton, but you won't learn anything." But we did go up to General Bradley's headquarters. This was very shortly before the Battle of the Bulge and after it broke out I thought, "My God, there we we were and we didn't have a cap pistol, a whole bunch of flag officers and captains and colonels, and there wasn't a cap pistol among us. We could have gotten gathered up by the Nazis in nothing flat."

Q: It sounds a bit like a junket?

Adm. S.: Yes, this was a junket.

We went up there and we talked with Bradley, who talked a lot of sense. After he retired, when I was in BuOrd I became very friendly with Bradley, who was working for one of the watch manufacturers in those days.

Anyway, while we were there an aide came rushing in and said:

"General Eisenhower has very unexpectedly arrived.

He's coming right in."

So we jumped up and went out down a narrow corridor. Eisenhower came in, laughing fit to kill. It seems that, on arrival there, a sentry had stuck a nice great big bayonet right up against his adam's apple and said, "Halt."

Eisenhower said something to the effect, "Don't you recognize me, son?" And the soldier said:

"Well, I've seen pictures of General Eisenhower and you look like him but you don't get in here without a pass."

We went down to Italy and we saw the Army general up in the north there.

Q: Clark?

Adm. S.: Yes. We saw Clark. He was out in the field. His headquarters were in tents, and somehow or another while we were there one of the tents caught fire, and I made myself less than popular by loosening some dogs of General Clark's to get them out of the way. They went tearing off and had to be rounded up later on!

We got down to the Naples area and we saw McNarny down there. In later years, I got quite close to him when he was running Consolidated out in San Diego.

Q: What kind of data were you seeking?

Adm. S.: We were just trying to get views as to whether it

was or was not a desirable and necessary thing to have a closer-knit military organization than we had at that time.

You must remember that, in spite of the great success of the Joint Chiefs in World War II, we had never before had any real cooperation between the military services in any of our previous wars. In World War I, for instance, Josephus Daniels asked the then Secretary of War if it wouldn't be a good idea to set up some joint planning and the Secretary of War told Josephus to go mind his own business. Between the wars, World War I and II, there had been an Army and Navy planning comittee that had done some very good work, but it was far from complete and it had no control over operations at all. It was just a planning outfit. So, many people were very much of the opinion that modern conditions demanded a more integrated military posture than we had had.

Well, to get back to our trip, we went up to Rome. We had a very special audience with the Pope because several of the members of our committee were ardent Catholics.

Q: This was Pius XII?

Adm. S.: I don't recall which one it was, but he was a kindly old gentleman. I was amused by the fact that we arrived and, of course, we were first met by papal guards in their old costumes that they have worn since the 1500s, the Swiss Guards. They were great. Big husky fellows.

Then we went into another room where there was some other group not so well known. They were smaller and were in uniforms of about the time of Napoleon III and carrying very antique-looking rifles. Then we passed into another room where there were even smaller guards - they were getting smaller and smaller as we went on.

Finally, we arrived at the antechamber itself where there were two little gentlemen wearing rapiers, and that was all. Then we went out on the porch where the pope was. He spoke English. He had spent some time in Chicago, I think.

While we were there in Rome I was ennobled by being assigned a room with the bed in which Alfonso XIII had died! That's the closest I ever came to any royalty.

We got down to Casablanca. I don't recall what we were up to down there, but we set out from there to the Azores on our way home. We'd been in the air about eight hours and were about an hour out of the Azores when the Azores told us, "We can't take you. You've got to turn around and go back to Casablanca." It seems that the weather was pretty bad and there was a block of fighters coming in from Newfoundland, and they were giving absolute priority to getting those fighters down, and no bunch of old crocks like us was going to interfere with this. So we had to turn round and go back to Casablanca. That was the longest sixteen-hour flight getting nowhere that I ever made in my life.

Later on we got off and got home all right.

Then we set out for the Pacific and this time we got FDR's own private airplane, no less. Golly, it was nicely fitted up.

Q: The same contingent of men?

Adm. S.: Yes.

It was very nicely fitted up. It had a little sort of a den in there where Uncle Joe Richardson and I played cribbage all the time and he taught me a lot about that game.

We got out to Hawaii first, of course, and we interviewed all the Army and Navy commanders out there. By this time it was obvious that it was practically a 100 per cent arrangement. All the Navy said "no," all the Army said "yes."

From there we went on out to Leyte to see MacArthur. We got out there just about a month after the Battle of Leyte Gulf and, by golly, the airfield there was certainly a disaster waiting to happen.

Q: Tacloban?

Adm. S.: Yes. They had a single strip and it was almost completely surrounded by three rows of airplanes. The innermost bunch were those that were flyable, the second line were those that were repairable, and the third line were only good for cannibalization.

Planes would take off in one direction while planes were landing in the opposite direction. I don't understand why they didn't just smash themselves all up, but they seemed to get away with it.

Tacloban was the muddiest place I've ever seen. At one street intersection there was a big mud puddle where the upper part of the steering wheel of a jeep appeared above the mud. All the rest of the jeep was down there under the mud, in the hole.

We got to MacArthur's headquarters. It was set up in an old warehouse, masonry warehouse, which the Japanese had used an an officers' club while they were there. The fact that this had been an officers' club caused some blankety-blank newspaperman to start a scandalous story about how MacArthur was living in luxury in an officers' club whereas the poor GIs were out in the rain and the mud. Well, the GIs were out in the rain and the mud, all right. MacArthur didn't have the rain coming down on him but it seeped down the walls.

As we went into his quarters, we passed his you might call it bedroom - it was just a part of a very large room in this building - he had a folding cot, there was a very old dresser there. I stopped and I counted what was on that dresser. There was a picture of Mrs. MacArthur, there was a picture of their son, there was his razor, there was his shaving soap, there was his toothbrush, toothpaste, a hairbrush, a hair comb, and a bottle of hair tonic - hair dye, I mean!

He got us out on a little balcony and we had a very interesting conversation with him.

Q: And his point of view was what?

Adm. S.: Oh, he was all for it. He said the recent affair out there showed the utter necessity of the amalgamation of command and so forth. He had us to lunch. It wasn't a bad lunch, it wasn't K-rations but it certainly was nothing very fancy. So whenever I get a chance I try to shout down this newspaperman and his story of MacArthur living in luxury there. He was not living in luxury. He was living a very straitened life, as far as his person was concerned.

From there we went on to Ulithi, where Halsey was in with the Third Fleet.

Q: That was rest and relaxation?

Adm. S.: Yes.

The Army people were very anxious to be very proper in Naval etiquette when we went on board Halsey's flagship, and the upshot of it was that they had me and themselves out in the corridor of this airplane giving them rehearsals, how you went on board and you saluted the quarterdeck and exchanged salutes with the Officer of the Deck. We would not expect any gun salutes but we would expect that there would be side boys and perhaps a Marine guard up there.

We got in to the very small airstrip there at Ulithi, embarked in a boat, and I have the feeling that Halsey was in the Iowa rather than the Missouri at the time. I'm not sure, but anyway we went out to the flagship, and, as we approached, we could see Halsey up there on his forward quarterdeck ahead, pacing back and forth. He could see us coming and he leaned over the side, raised his arms, and shouted, "Hey, Joe!" Richardson leaned out of our boat and shouted back, "Hey, Bill!"

That was all the protocol there was.

Q: After all that preparation!

Adm. S.: Yes. The Army was very disgusted, very disgusted, on a good-natured level.

Halsey had gathered McCain, Mitscher, and various other flag officers who were available there, and we had a discussion with them. He had a lunch there, which put MacArthur's to utter shame, and the Army people said, "Good God, why didn't we join the Navy!" which was my father's attitude when I told him as a small boy that I wanted to join the Navy.

We got back to Washington and we prepared a report, and this report outlined a very simple and straightforward form of organization for a unified military service of the

United States. I signed the report and at the very last moment Richardson said, "No, I won't sign. I will submit a minority report."

Well, this threw a big monkey wrench into the works but we put in our report and I have felt ever since that, had an organization such as we recommended been put into effect, we might very well have avoided this terrific multiplication of bureaucracy that has occurred in the Department of Defense.

Q: What was the nature of your proposal?

Adm. S.: It was a very straightforward proposal for an over-all Chief of Staff and a staff formed of the various services, and just spreading out from that. It was a simple and straightforward one.

Admiral King was, naturally, not in the least pleased with this report, but he never loosed his terrors on me!

Q: And Richardson's report, the minority report, what did that say?

Adm. S.: I don't recall just what Uncle Joe said.

By that time, there were already bills in Congress to form some kind of amalgamation of the services. Admiral King took me to Mr. Forrestal, who didn't like our report any better than Admiral King did. I must say I made a very poor witness in attempting to defend our report. I was very much dissatisfied with myself. They questioned me -

Q: Forrestal and King together?

Adm. S.: Yes. They didn't grill me. They weren't unpleasant in any way, but it was obvious that they did not like it at all.

The upshot of it was that Mr. Forrestal got hold of a chap whose name I can't remember - all I do is go through this thing saying "whose name I can't remember" - but in whom Mr. Forrestal had a great deal of confidence, and I remember his making the comment that he thought that our committee had been much sounder in consideration of the military aspects of such a merger than it had of its civil aspects. He was undoubtedly right.

Q: Well, it was an entirely military committee, wasn't it?

Adm. S.: Yes.

He and Mr. Forrestal eventually put together the arrangement that was first entered into. The original Department of Defense was a policy-making outfit. They did not attempt to run all the details of everything like the Department of Defense after McNamara got through with it has to do.

In the summer of '46 my year on Admiral King's staff was

up. Practically all of us were there just on one-year tours.

Q: I hope you're going to tell me a little bit about Admiral King himself and your contacts with him.

Adm. S.: My contacts with him were largely at these lunches I spoke of. I never made any trips with him, so I didn't have that opportunity. He was in his office and my office was some distance away. I had very seldom to go into his office. I didn't see much of him. He was a hard taskmaster but he was the sort of a man the Navy needed in that job in time of war. I have the greatest respect and admiration for him.

Q: Will you say sometting about Savvy Cook?

Adm. S.: Oh, he was a very pleasant fellow to work with and for. I can't remember any particular incident about him.

Coming back to an incident in the messroom, I remember one time either Cook or Edwards told Admiral King that Admiral Dickie Byrd was on his way east and would shortly be in Washington. Well, King blew up. He pounded the table and said:

"Look here, you two, I am perfectly willing to be in the same latitude with Byrd or in the same longitude, but not in both at once. Either you've got to think up something for me to go and do outside of Washington when he gets here or for him to go and do."

I only spoke up once in that mess. It was very near the end of the war and the big subject was rolling up the bases that were no longer needed. Edwards was holding forth very persuasively to King, saying, "To do a proper job, we've just got to tell these people that none of them get home until they've got all the material moved out and everything accounted for."

At this point, I spoke up. I said:

"I'm sorry to say that the experience of the United States in all its past wars is that as soon as a war is over there is going to be such a big public shout for bringing the boys home that you won't be able to give a thought to the material we're going to have to abandon out there."

For once in my life I was right.

Q: Oh, very.

Adm. S.: Those at the head of the table listened to me and they didn't pipe me down. They didn't say aye, yes, or no. That was that.

Q: Did you have anything to do with Bill Sebald at that time?

Adm. S.: No. I never knew him until after we moved -

Q: You never knew him on the staff then?

Adm. S.: No.

There was a classmate of mine there, Matt B. Gardner, generaly known as Mary Gardner. He was Assistant Chief of Staff for Plans. He had a very hard-working job and one that was a real job. He had to attend all the JCS meetings and things of that nature. He was right in the know-and-do, but, as I said, earlier, my job was really very much of a stuffed-shirt job.

Q: That's rather surprising because I thought of the staff as a streamlined one that didn't permit the luxuries.

Adm. S.: They didn't need an Assistant Chief of Staff for Operations. They had a splendid Operations Officer in Roscoe Good and everything would have gone just as well if it had gone directly from them to Good rather than going through me. In fact, much of the time I was away, enough of the time, on these junkets, as you call them! So much of the time the business did go directly to Good and from the top.

Q: Let me ask now, in terms of the report that was submitted and was discussed by King and Forrestal, was it useful in any sense when they ultimately drew up the plan - ?

Schoeffel #5 - 260

Adm. S.: I think not.

I want to tell you one little incident about Admiral King that impressed me very much, with his basic and ultimate fairness.

It was at the time of the Potsdam Conference and he was over there. The war in the Pacific was not yet over. He called on the telephone one day and wanted Walter Dulany and me to come to the telephone. Dulany was Assistant Chief of Staff for Readiness. He had all the logistic angles. Well, I went in the phone booth with him, but Dulany did all the talking from our end and the listening. I just got the secondhand from him.

King called and said that General MacArthur and the Army were demanding that we construct artificial harbors for the invasion of Honshu, which was due to come off in the spring of 1947.

Q: Similar to the ones we used in Normandy?

Adm. S.: Of that nature.

Well, the U.S. Navy had always thought that the artificial harbor off Normandy was a lot of malarky and had taken a great deal more effort than it proved to be worth. The U.S. Navy in general wanted none of this artificial harbor business. Dulany expressed such views and Admiral King said:

"Look here, now. General MacArthur is about to have

to lead the greatest amphibious operation in all history, far greater than the landings in Normandy, and it ill behooves us to put any snags in his way, to upset his thinking in any way. If he wants artificial harbors and it is possible for us to give him artificial harbors, we are going to do it. Can it be done? That is the question. I will call back in about two hours and get your answer."

So we went off, and it was entirely up to Dulany. I had no special information. He called back and he said:

"It can be done provided the job is given the same priority as the Manhattan Project."

Well, to show you what a stuffed-shirt I was in that operation, I didn't know what the Manhattan Project was. I'd never heard of it. So, I don't know what King did with this information but he said, "We will do everything we possibly can to support General MacArthur's operations. It's not a question of whether we think it's worthwhile or good, it's a question, can we do it?"

And when you consider how so many people think that MacArthur and King, for instance, were absolutely at swords' points, I think this shows what a basically fair man Admiral King was.

Speaking of the Manhattan Project, as we left I asked Dulany what it was and he gave me some very cursory remarks which told me nothing. I initialed the orders to the Indianapolis to pick up some very highly secret material and deliver it out in Guam.

I had been called in by a fellow - one of the nice old gentlemen in the Navy who was on duty down in Admiral Horne's outfit - and had had a conversation with him and with Deke Parsons in which they had given me a very thumbnail explanation of an atom bomb, which was not completed at that time. What they wanted from me was my recommendation as to a good, snappy naval aviator who had enough sense to understand atomic matters and would go in as Deke Parson's assistant on the job. I was able to recommend such a man, whom they took - again, I can't think of his name, but it's immaterial. But when I initialed these orders for the Indianapolis I thought to myself, I wonder if this has anything to do with the fly-by-night atom business that they were telling me about.

Q: And how much prior to that had it been?

Adm. S.: Had what been? My conversation?

Q: Yes.

Adm. S.: Oh, some months. I don't recall how long.

The first I ever heard of any atom business was when I was in the Research Division in the Bureau of Ordnance. I was in a conversation one day with Sam Shumaker who was then the number two man in the Research Division. We were talking about the very considerable improvements that were then under way in explosives by adding powder and metals to the TNT, and he made some remark, "Well, I think that this will be about as far as we will ever be able to go, unless something comes of this uranium business."

I said, "What's the uranium business?"

And he said: "Well, there is a possibility that uranium may be made into an explosive of vastly greater strength than anything we've ever had before."

I think I heard of the test down in the southwest, the ground test of the atom bomb about the time it happened. I'm not sure.

Anyway, back in the summer of '46, my year being up, I received orders to report to Nimitz's staff as Forrest Sherman's relief as Assistant Chief of Staff for Plans. Just before I was due to be detached, I got bursitis in my right shoulder. Although I have never been at all muscular, I have almost always enjoyed the best of health. In fact, recently, not having been so healthy, I said I didn't really enjoy it, I just took it for granted. But I got bursitis in my right shoulder, and bursitis can give you hell. I went down to the sick bay in the Navy Department and they said: "This requires x-ray treatment, but they've got all kinds of x-ray machines out there in Guam. You just go ahead and report in and they'll take care of you."

So I got out there. By this time, my arm was really practically strapped to my side. If I tried to initial a paper, I had to do it with my left hand and that's terrible.

I got out there on the very day of the surrender ceremony up in Tokyo, so I was not at the ceremony. I was in Guam, sitting in Sherman's office. He came back and I relieved him.

One afternoon I was there in that office when a scarecrow of a man came in, came up to the desk and held out his hand, and he was a very dear friend of mine who'd been taken prisoner on Wake. He'd just been released and I never would have recognized that man, because he was as well built as you are when I knew him and by the time he came out he was like one of those candles.

Well, here I was, Assistant Chief of Staff for Plans, but what was one going to plan. That was the big question. Shortly, it became obvious that "bring the boys home" -

Q: The Magic Carpet was your plan!

Adm. S.: Magic Carpet went into effect. I remember talking to one enlisted man who was on his way home. I said:

"Oh, you're going back by the Magic Carpet?" And he said:

"Well, Sir, it ain't my idea of no magic carpet, but I sure am glad to be on it."

Q: This was a considerable operation to plan?

Adm. S.: I wasn't called upon to do any planning for it.

Q: As a matter of fact, I think much of that had been done before the war was over, wasn't it?

Adm. S.: I don't know. It was mainly improvisation, the scheduling of the vessels - oh, the man who had taken over these jeep carriers and was going to take out the replacement pilots was Ezra Kendall. He still had command of them when the war was over and he was the one who did the planning and the operation of very much of the Magic Carpet plan.

There we were on Guam, and I went to the medicos and they said:

"Oh, dear me. We've got all kinds of x-rays for finding bullets and looking at fractures, but we haven't got anything of the kind that will do yoru shoulder any good."

So the upshot of it was that I got sent out to one of the hospitals there on Guam. They put me on an operating table and they took a couple of syringes, each about a foot or two long, about the kind you would use for giving a shot of something to an elephant, and under proper sedation they put one into each side of my shoulder and they pumped back and forth. They got a lot of sediment out of my shoulder and it was much better. Over the next few months, with the light exercise they gave me, it cleared up completely and I've never had any trouble since.

A year or so later, I began to have similar twinges in my left sholder and I was scared to death. I went down to the sick bay and told the doctor what had happened and asked him if they were going to do this to me again. He said, "Well, there'd been a great advance" - I forget the name of the medicine they had developed since then - but he gave me a couple of pills and said:

"It'll be all right in three days or else you'll be in a hell of a shape."

Well, I was all right in three days.

Q: Buthazoladine.

Adm. S.: Oh, is that it?

Q: Yes.

Adm. S.: Okay. Do you know it? I'm rather glad I'd had bursitis because when I got home a woman said:

"Oh, my, I know that's terrible. You know, it's worse than childbirth."

Ever since then I've said, "You women can give me no more guff!"

Q: We're going to lap back to Washington for just a moment. You recalled one or two things about Admiral King that you wanted to put on.

Adm. S.: The reaction of Admiral King and Cook and Edwards to the battles of the Philippine Sea and of Leyte Gulf was in both cases a feeling of distinct disappointment.

Q: Oh, really?

Adm. S.: Yes.

Q: Of course, they watched them with great detail.

Adm. S.: No. We got dispatches. We intercepted dispatches, but there wasn't much that we had that you could piece together to get a picture of what was under way.

Q: It's true what Admiral Burke says, when a battle's under way, you really don't have time to send detailed dispatches to the commander in chief.

Adm. S.: No.
Well, as I say, there was a feeling of disappointment, particularly after the Philippine Sea, because it had been hoped that Halsey would be able to - I mean Spruance - annihilate the Japanese fleet, which did not occur. I believe it was following that that Admiral King put into his instructions to be passed on through Nimitz to the Fleet Commanders that "when an opportunity is found, or can be made, to destroy," as I recall it, "major enemy combatant units, that becomes the paramount objective of the operation." There were apparently no such instructions at the time of

the Philippine Sea battle. This instruction had a lot to do with Halsey's setting up the Live Bait Operation after the first raid on Formosa. This was the one when a couple of torpedoed ships were being slowly towed out to safety and were covered by a couple of CVL's while the weight of the Third Fleet lurked in ambush not far away, in hopes the Jap fleet would come out. I understand they sniffed at the bait but got cold feet. One of the CVL's was my old Cabot (no longer under my command) and she covered herself with glory. Her fighters broke up several Japanese raids which were made up of 70 or 80 planes. It was about this time the Cabot earned her nickname of the Iron Woman.

Q: Was Admiral King aware of Spruance's point of view? I mean protecting the landing forces for Guam.

Adm. S.: I doubt it. I don't know, but I doubt it. I never heard any discussion on the subject.

We knew a good deal more about what was going on at the Battle of Leyte Gulf than we did in the Philippine Sea battle.

Like everybody else, we took it for granted that Halsey had formed that task force, whatever the number of it was, and stationed it off San Bernardino Strait before he headed north. We received his dispatch saying that he was "going north with three groups." Oh, in retrospect, it's so easy to criticize. It would have been so fine if he'd said, "I'm going north with three groups" - he meanwhile had started one over toward Ulithi to resupply or something of that sort - so we took it for granted that the strait was guarded.

We were just as surprised as anybody else to find out that it wasn't.

After the battle was over and Halsey's report came in, Cook gave me the job of making an analysis of that report. This was the first intimation that any of us had about this "all the world wonders" business, because the dispatches - the dispatch from Nimitz to Halsey that caused Halsey to blow up had had that padding eliminated, at least as we saw it.

So, here, Halsey sent in his report and he quotes this dispatch and, here, for the first time, appear the words italicized, underlined, and in red ink, "all the world wonders." Well, we certainly wondered at that. We didn't know what the hell it was all about.

Then Halsey came in and reported himself, and he went in and had a pow-wow with Admiral King. I haven't the faintest notion of what was said and so forth, but they didn't shoot each other. There were no noticeable explosions, windows were not blown out, so I guess it was reasonably amicable. Somewhere around that time Halsey ran into his typhoons at sea in the course of which several ships were lost. A Court of Inquiry was convened, as required by the Navy Regulations, and it recommended he be relieved. It is well known he wasn't relieved for the higher-ups evidently thought of him as Lincoln did of Grant when Old Abe asked what brand of whiskey Ulysses drank. "He fights."

Another case of casualties being forgiven to fighters was the retention of Kelly Turner as ComPhibsPac after the disaster to the LST's in Pearl Harbor that I have already mentioned. This brings to mind a story about Turner, for the truth of which I cannot vouch, but which is quite characteristic.

When he went to sea he manned his bridge wing and ran everything by TBS, constantly ordering, constantly bawling out the laggards. On the way to Okinawa one destroyer had much trouble with reception on its TBS and was always having to ask "Say again all after - " which infuriated Turner. At Okinawa however he sent this boat to conduct a bombardment which it did to the Queen's Taste - something really right for once. But the Japs shot back and damaged her so badly that Turner decided to send her back for repairs. He grabbed his transmitter and said, "Proceed Ulithi for repairs. Good bye and God Bless You." And the acknowledgement came back "Say again all after God."

In my analysis of Leyte Gulf I was much struck by an analogy to what sometimes happened in land warfare in the old days but of which I had never heard in sea battles; that is, one force breaks through the center of the other, whereupon some hero on the threatened side gathers up the cooks and bakers and with this motley crew repels the attack.

I believe, though I'm not sure, that Halsey knew Ozawa

had resumed an easterly course very shortly after 9 p.m. when the change was made, for he said he figured the Jap Center Force was so badly damaged as not to be much of a threat. But Kinkaid did not know of Ozawa's action until about 1 or 2 a.m. and he was understandably worried. He queried Halsey about whether TF? was no station off San Bernardino but Halsey never saw those dispatches until after day break at about the time the Japs were chasing our CVE's (cooks and bakers) around.

I believe it was a mercy for our side that Kincaid did not know that was going on farther north. Had he known he would have been in a truely terrible quandry and might well have drawn his forces in from Surigao to Leyte Gulf itself. Then there would probably have ensued a whale of a day surface action which might have proved to be, in Wellington's words "a very close-run thing."

As I recall it our never-formed Task Force That-Did-Not-Guard-the-Strait was to have our three most modern battleships, cruisers, destroyers and a carrier or two. I think Oazwa originally had the two super-battleships, of which one (Musashi?) had been sunk in the Cibuyan Sea leaving him only one battleship (Yamato?), cruisers and destroyers. The super BB was obviously stronger than any single one of ours and, had there been a surface fight off the straits, we might have suffered some pretty heavy casualties. But again we might not for the gunnery of Ozawa's force the next day can only be ranked as mediocre to poor.

Admiral Ching Lee who would have commanded our force was a true gunnery expert but I do not know what chance his ships had had to train their main batteries.

I think some of the torpedo plane pilots of the CVE's should have gotten Medals of Honor for if ever men acted "beyond the call of duty" it was some of them. They fired their torpedoes, then backed off out of sight and came in again <u>without</u> torpedoes, but the Japs <u>didn't know that</u> and maneuvered wildly. This contributed considerably to the great confusion in his force that was a factor causing Ozawa to limp away.

Q: Perhaps you can answer a question that I posed one time and have never received an answer to. I asked if Halsey was aware of the Sho Plan and its contents before he went north.

Adm. S.: I do not know. We were aware of it. We had translations in Magic, but it was in such guarded language that I doubt that anybody in our headquarters took in the idea that this northern force was a decoy.

Q: And Ozawa had the main force coming up?

Adm. S.: Yes.

Q: Which was clear in the Sho Plan.

Adm. S.:   Yes.

I don't know whether Halsey ever knew anything about it, but I certainly, in reading the Sho Plan, as it appeared in our Magic, never gathered any such idea. Maybe more subtle minds than mine did, but I didn't hear anybody saying anything about it.

Q: In other words, it wasn't that clear?

Adm. S.:   No, it wasn't. It was by no means clear. I suppose the clarification of it was made plain to the Japanese commanders by messengers sent around and telling them orally just what they were trying to do within this framework.

By that time, we were reading a great deal of Japanese communications, Magic was filled every day with translations of Japanese, German, Italian, French, English communications, but never in my year there did I see one single word of Russian.

I have been given to understand since that the Russians use what is known as a single-copy form of encoding, which means that there is never any repetition, I'm told. Well, I know very little on that subject, but I should think this would require a vast library of books to encode and decode and be able to pick out the particular one you wanted and have the fellow at the other end be able to match it, because if you've got something that's unique, absolutely unique, and you're asking somebody else far away to match it, that's a tough job.

I don't know whether we've ever broken any Russian stuff since, but if we did during World War II it did not appear in Magic. It was kept at a much higher level of secrecy than I was open to. I told you I didn't know anything about the Manhattan Project and I knew so little about the Tenth Fleet. There were an awful lot of things going on around there that I was not privy to.

Q: I rather think it was something in that area, too, that was going on.

Adm. S.: Admiral King was a great believer in the need to know and he applied it and applied it plenty. If you didn't need to know, you didn't get to know.

Q: Consequently, it nullified things.

Adm. S.: Admiral King came in very mad one day to the lunch room and when he was mad the veins really stood out on his forehead. He had been on a flight to New York, I think the day before, and had arrived over the airport in New York in bad weather and had had to wait while six or seven airplanes landed ahead of the one he was in. He felt that he was on business of extreme importance for the United States - I don't recall just what it was - and he was very mad about this.

The result was that shortly afterwards a five-star priority was set up to be used at airports, meaning that if General Marshall or Admiral King arrived over the airport, the air controllers would push everything else aside and let them in.

Q: I can see where that might result in some danger, too.

Adm. S.: Yes.

Going back to Halsey, he has maintained that he never heard himself called "Bull" Halsey until the end of the war or after it was over. I think this means that the doctors didn't examine his hearing very well when he was a lieutenant, because he was a lieutenant duty officer at the Naval Academy when I was a plebe, and I'm quite sure we all called him "Bull" in those days. We liked him very much, but I'm sure we called him "the Bull."

Q: It's interesting, in talking with various naval officers who knew him in lesser and greater degrees of intimacy, some of them will say "Bull" and some will say "Bill." Most of them say Bill, but I've noticed this and wonder if it wasn't just a matter of habit with some of them that they called him Bull.

Adm. S.: Well, probably those who were very much his juniors, such as I was, on the level of midshipman: it was "The Bull" with us.

Jonas Ingram. He was down in Brazil and his dispatches and attitude caused a great deal of amusement between King, Edwards, and Cook, at their end of the table. They were always getting a big laugh out of what Jonas Ingram was up to.

Ingram wanted a fine yacht down there. He had a lot of entertaining of Brazilians to do and he wanted a fine craft to entertain on. Have you ever heard of the Big Pebble?

Q: No.

Adm. S.: Well, the Big Pebble was a very commodious and very palatial houseboat.

Q: Slow-moving, too?

Adm. S.: Yes.

Roscoe Good really got the jitters moving the Big Pebble down the Atlantic coast, across the Caribbean, and farther down the Atlantic coast to wherever Jonas wanted her. But apparently it filled his bill all right.

Q: He wasn't disappointed?

Adm. S.: Apparently not.

Jonas was one of those who didn't need a long-distance telephone. He leaned out of the window and called New York direct!

Enough of these vignettes.

As I say, I flew out to Guam and I was on Admiral Nimitz's staff at the time.

Q: Did you have conversation with Nimitz when you arrived?

Adm. S.: After I arrived, yes. Nothing very much. I didn't see much of him. The one I saw most of was his chief of staff - oh, my, a fellow with the most unhandsome face in the world. What the devil was his name?

Shortly we laid back to Hawaii and it was amazing. I always thought of Hawaii as very hot and humid, but after Guam it was football weather. We got established back there and I found that I was in another one of these stuffed-shirt jobs, because there wasn't any planning to do.

Q: No, but you have to maintain the organizational chart, don't you?

Adm. S.: Yes, but what to do to keep them busy? Of course, those who were good at it could go and pitch horseshoes with Admiral Nimitz after lunch, but we couldn't all do that.

Then Nimitz got relieved by Towers, and what a house-cleaning there was in the Nimitz headquarters. I mean personal quarters, living quarters, because Nimitz's ideas of furnishing a place were on the Victorian side, and Mrs. Towers, Peggy, had very mod ideas. They moved everything out, including a stuffed seagull and things like that and fixed it all over.

Things went along for a little while and then Towers was relieved by Spruance. I don't recall whether Spruance cleaned the Towers's furniture out or not. Of course, Spruance could be just as quiet as anybody in the world. After a while, he took me on an expedition to Tokyo to see MacArthur. It was some question of getting Chinese armies up into Manchuria in an attempt to forestall the communists up there.

We arrived in Tokyo and here the city was all gone except for in almost every block there was a chimney sticking up where the old bathhouse had been and the great big beautiful hotel was quite undamaged and was doing business.

Q: The imperial palace was there?

Adm. S.: The emperor's palace was okay and the American embassy was untouched. I'm not sure about the other embassies, but the American embassy was untouched.

Q: That was because of the fire-bombing and for the most part those other buildings withstood it?

Adm. S.: Yes.

MacArthur invited the two of us out to the American embassy which he had made his quarters. Mrs. MacArthur and their young son had joined him out there by that time and they were ensconced in the old embassy. We had a most delightful lunch there served by great big Japanese men, every one of them well over six feet tall, and all attired in ancient Japanese costumes. It was quite a sight.

Q: Were they wrestlers or something!

Adm. S.: No, they weren't these huge-bellied things that go in for Japanese wrestling. They were just big men. It's become apparent in the last generation that if you feed a Japanese right, he can grow up as well as anybody else. The only reason they were small was they didn't eat the right stuff.

Well, as I say, we had a delightful lunch. Nothing really fancy with regard to food, and Mrs. MacArthur said it was most amazing. Then the word got out that MacArthur was coming there and was going to be quartered in the old embassy, all the old embassy employees just came flocking back of their own accord. They all walked in, one after the other, and everyone took up his or her old duties. They had laid away all the crockery, all the linen, all the silverware. They knew where everything was. They just went there, opened the drawer, and went to work, as though there had never been a war.

Q: And they were about to eat again, too!

Adm. S.: We came to the conclusion that, although we were having great difficulty at that time maintaining the crews in any of our American amphibious craft, we could pour large numbers of Chinese troops from south China into Manchuria, provided the Chinese armies would arrive at the ports of embarkation at the right dates.

Then we turned around and went off, went back to Hawaii.

I don't know whatever came of that. I don't know whether any of them were ever embarked or not. It wasn't long afterwards that I was detached, returned to Washington, and got immersed in other things.

Q: We certainly had a contingent up there in that area.

Adm. S.: Oh, yes, but whether we were able to - if we did get any considerable number of Chiang Kai-shek's troops up there they just turned in their suits and gear to the communists and were so much to their aggrandizement rather than stopping them.

Q: There was no line of demarcation between the two elements, was there? Was there any question at that point, or was it at a later time, of getting the Russians to release the Japanese they held prisoner?

Adm. S.: I don't know whether the pressure on that had started or not. I really don't know. It has always been a great mystery to me as to how and why the Japanese Manchurian army collapsed as rapidly and completely as it did. They had apparently been pretty successful in their various campaigns against the Chinese and they certainly had the reputation they built up in the Russo-Japanese War to build upon. Up to the time of Okinawa, their troops in all cases fought and died on the spot. The only prisoners we ever took before Okinawa were men who were unconscious or completely unable to defend themselves. None of them ever surrendered voluntarily. At Okinawa there began to be some signs of deterioration in morale, because we took about 10 per cent prisoner there. Prior to that time, we had never had any more than 1 to 2 per cent prisoners in any contact with the Japanese, and then, here, suddenly, the whole presumably proud Manchurian army just gives up almost immediately to the Russians: and I doubt very much that the Russians were that much better than the Japanese in their tactics and their material.

Q: The end result, was it not, was that very few of those men ever got back to Japan?

Adm. S.: Very few of them. I had that from Turner Joy, who

had to sit opposite the North Koreans a long, long time.

Later on, whenever our people tried to raise the question of these Japanese prisoners, the Russians just refused to talk. They would not talk about it in any way, shape, or fashion. I imagine that the only ones they released were the ones who they had indoctrinated with communism.

Q: We did send, as I recall, Admiral Settle up into that part of the world to deal with that whole situation.

Adm. S.: Yes. Well, I don't know how much he had to deal with that one. I know he was out there.

Q: I don't mean the prisoners. I mean the Chinese situation.

Adm. S.: Yes, he was out there. He, by the way, is a very dear friend of mine.

Q: Tell me what your job was when you were in Pearl with Towers and then with Spruance.

Adm. S.: It was still Assistant Chief of Staff for Planning. Then, in Spruance's time, it was decided that they were just going to have to make it possible for the wives to come out to Hawaii. So I started looking around Honolulu for a place to put up my family and was having very little success when, to my surprise, in came a dispatch detaching me and sending me to Washington as Deputy Chief of the Bureau of Ordnance. That solved the housing problem right away! Because my family was already well ensconced in Washington and had been there all during the war.

Q: And you were going back to a job that really had some activity to it?

Adm. S.: Yes.

I got to Washington and reported in. George Hussey was the Chief. George had not particularly wanted me as his Deputy, but he was told that he had to have an aviator. I don't know whether he then picked me directly or whether I was offered and accepted. That's immaterial.

Q: Did that rule pertain to the bureaus as well as the ships?

Adm. S.: Yes, it did. Well, I don't know whether it applied to the Bureau of Ships, for instance.

Q: No, I mean as to fleet commands. It applied to the bureaus as well as fleet commands?

Adm. S.: It applied certainly to the Bureau of Ordnance but I don't know about the other bureaus. I rather doubt that it had much application. I don't believe that a non-aviator was demanded in the Bureau of Aeronautics.

We were very happy to be associated with the Husseys because they had been at Dahlgren when we were there and we were very good friends, and everything was very pleasant.

One of the chief jobs at that time, of course, was closing down a very large part of the huge ordnance establishment that had built up during the war, and it was really huge. In many cases, disposing of the real estate and so forth, and we had to be very careful to see that that was done with as much concern for the public's interest as was possible.

I remember, though I can't remember the details, some cases that were pretty darned complex and where any missteps could be very much misunderstood as getting away with murder. There was one case, the details of which I can't recall, some somewhere down in Kentucky. It involved real estate that had been used as a proving ground for the firing of 20-mm and 40-mm guns and ammunition, and the ground was all full of unexploded projectiles here and there. Nobody knew just where. It was pretty dangerous stuff.

Well, the upshot of it was that, in order to get rid of the place and get rid of the responsibilities involved for keeping people out of there, we actually paid a man to take over the real estate. He got the real estate and we paid him to take it, but he took over responsibilities.

Q: For clearing it out, too?

Adm. S.: Yes. If he could clear it out safely, why, he had something worthwhile. If he couldn't, he certainly had a white elephant on his hands.

The news of this got out and a bunch of newspapers down there in Kentucky got together and sent their best muckraker hotfoot to Washington. When we got through talking to him, he was the most abashed and retiring man you can imagine. He went back and he wrote a very fine article. He said:

"I went storming to Washington intending to shout all kinds of "malfeasance in office," and I expected to find admirals cringing to right and left. Instead of that, I found what I think was a good business deal for the United States."

Interview #6 with Rear Admiral Malcolm F. Schoeffel,
U.S. Navy (Retired)

Place: His son's residence in Alexandria, Virginia

Date: Thursday morning, 7 June 1979

Subject: Biography

By: John T. Mason, Jr.

Q: This morning, Sir, I think we go back to April 1, 1946 when you became Deputy Chief and Assistant Chief of the Bureau of Ordnance.

Adm. S.: The duplication I cannot explain. I had forgotten that there was such. I have no recollection of it at all.

Now, Doctor, you said the other day that you wanted much detail.

Q: Yes.

Adm. S.: I will have to ask you to ask me questions because I don't really understand what it is you want.

Q: Well, some detail as to your function there in the Bureau of Ordnance and some of the projects that you were specifically interested in and worked on.

Adm. S.: Well, my function right at the start was not an easy one because the chief, Vice Admiral George Hussey, had gone off to Bikini for the atomic tests out there and left me holding the bag on congressional budgetary hearings!

Q: That was something of a task, was it not? But you were something of an old hand in the Bureau of Ordnance, so you knew your way around.

Adm. S.: Yes.

One thing that I had to do was appear before the House committee that was headed by Carl Vinson. In the request for funds that the Bureau had submitted was a request for a modest amount to permit the delivery to the British of an antiaircraft fire-control system, in which they were interested. The original wording of this request as sent in by the Bureau was, I think, reasonably clear, but somebody up the line somewhere in the Navy Department changed the wording around in such a way that it became very unclear.

Well, I had to defend that unclear wording and, at that time, Congress had just decreed that there should be no more lend-lease. It had been cut off. This wording was such that many congressmen feared that this was an attempt to evade their cutoff and to extend lend-lease.

Q: What sum of money was involved?

Adm. S.: $100,000, maybe, something like that. I don't remember exactly.

I was called up and, here, Mr. Vinson had the entire Armed Services Committee at the table. They started firing questions at me and very soon had me completely bowled over, completely out of my depth.

Q: That's hard to imagine!

Adm. S.: Well, I was. Mr. Vinson took pity on me and cut the Gordian knot by saying:

"Gentlemen, it becomes very evident that this witness cannot testify adequately on the policy questions involved. Let us table the matter."

So it was tabled and I was off the hook.

Having a full committee there - there must have been twenty of them - was very different from any budgetary hearings that I ever attended because they had a Naval Appropriations Committee and the Naval Appropriations Committee was broken down into subcommittees that might have three, four, or five members, by Bureaus, and it was seldom that you saw more than three of these members at once. Usually, after about ten minutes, two of them would get up and disappear and the chairman of the subcommittee would carry on the entire hearing all by himself.

Q: So it was almost a man-to-man thing?

Adm. S.: Yes, and one time the higher-ups in the House of Representatives tried to get everybody together for something or other and word was coming in to the subcommittee chairman "for God's sake, hurry up and get your business over with and get out here where we need some votes," or something of that sort. He kept putting them off and putting them off and, finally, to speed up the proposition, he just went along and said: "Isn't this so?" My answer would be "Yes." a little more reading on his part, and "Isn't this so?" "Yes." And that was the hearing.

However, these subcommittee chairmen were by no means stupid or fools in any sense of the word. In general, they knew a very great deal about the business in hand, what it might cost, and so forth. They were a very sharp bunch of cookies.

Q: That's why they were chairmen of subcommittees!
But in this instance you had the full committee?

Adm. S.: Yes.

Q: And they were determined not to be circumvented?

Adm. S.: Yes, they were determined not to be circumvented.
George got back shortly from Bikini and told us all about it. This was just after the end of World War II, and the Bureau of Ordnance had grown tremendously in that war.

I have said earlier that back in the period '36 to '38, when I was first in the Bureau, there were, all told, about thirty or forty people in it, officers and civilians. And the annual appropriation of Ordnance and Ordnance Stores ran about 30 or 40 million. By the time I got back there in '46, the total number of personnel in the bureau itself there in the old Navy Building was running about 1,100. The annual appropriation for Ordnance and Ordnance Stores for which I was appearing before the committee was a request for 800 million. We had acquired a great number of ammunition depots and ordnance-manufacturing plants throughout the country. Total employment in these depots and plants ran, I think, about 30,000. We had become a railroad owner with more track than all but two or three other railroads. We had over 10,000 miles of track.

Q: Why was this necessary?

Adm. S.: In the ammunition depots. This track was by no means laid end-to-end. It was just switchyards running to the innumerable magazines, is what it amounted to, but we had some 10,000 miles of track. The longest single one was probably in the ammunition depot in New Jersey, not far from Monmouth. I disremember the name of it, but it was about fifteen or twenty miles inland and I think we had some - well we had tracks running from there down to a very long pier at which ammunition ships could be loaded. That was our longest bit of track.

Shortly after I got to the Bureau I had to fight, bleed, and die on the subject of a railroad order that we had given. We were shipping a great deal of ammunition by railroad, and ammunition has to be tightly wedged and held in a car. In an ordinary boxcar, this means doing it by cutting up lumber and using it to wedge the ammunition. The Bureau had requisitioned somewhat over - the construction of somewhat over 900 special ammunition freight cars and had specified a certain form of ammunition stowage in there. However, this was challenged for a long time by the Pullman Company, whose representative was Steve Early who had been one of FDR's righthand men in the White House in Washington.

Q: And had clout!

Adm. S.: Yes, and he moved heaven and earth to make us accept a form of stowage arrangement that we considered to be very much inferior to the one that was specified. Oh, gosh, how we fought over that, and eventually conducted quite a number of tests which showed very conclusively that the one Early was fighting for would not stand up. So we were able to get our 900 freight cars, and that was the largest order for freight cars that any railroad in the United States had given for years.

So I was really in the railroad business for a while!

Schoeffel #6 - 292

Now I remember this affair of the ammunition cars didn't occur until 1951 when I returned to the Bureau as Chief.

Q: What about the railroad's personnel? Were they civil servants?

Adm. S.: Oh, yes.

After Hussey got back, I went out and visited as many of the depots and plants as I could, and I soon found that the way to see an ammunition depot was to climb in one of their engines with the engineer or the skipper of the station and the Public Works officer and a few others like that and see it from the railroad angle. That was the way in which you saw the slums, if any, of the station. If you took the highways, you saw the best parts of the station. If you took the railroad, you saw the things that weren't so good.

Q: That's frequently the case today, too.

Adm. S.: Yes.

I remember very vividly one visit to the ammunition depot in Indiana. They had what they called an inspection car of which they were very proud. It was a very small passenger car mounted on a Ford chassis and equipped with flanged wheels. I was sitting up next to the boss engineer, the railroad engineer, of the station, who was driving this thing and he was saying, "Over here, we need this and over here we need that," and so forth, when we approached a switch and he failed to notice that it wasn't set right. The next thing we knew we were off the track! Well, everybody said, "Think nothing of it because we have a jack built into this car of which we are very proud, so we will now demonstrate the jack." And, of course, the jack wouldn't work.

At this point, I made myself extremely unpopular with all those present by saying:

"Only about a quarter or half a mile back, I noticed a telephone stand. Why doesn't somebody go back there and call in for some help?"

Somebody else whispered in my ear, "If he did that, the boss engineer would never hear the end of this because he would fire any one of his men who did what he's just done."

Well, they proceeded to find some ties that were stacked up alongside the tracks, and they all got to work and they jacked that car back on the track and we went on. The subject was never mentioned again in Indiana!

Then I went out and visited what is now known as China Lake; it was then Inyokern. I was flown in there by Jack Hayward, later a vice admiral and his last duty was President of the Naval War College. I was shocked by the aridity of the place and I thought to myself, "My Lord, they're talking about trying to make this a permanent station. How will they ever get anybody to live in this place?"

Q: In a desert, isn't it?

Adm. S.: It was. It wasn't really a desert. It was next door to it, though. Years before, probably in the 1890s or early 1900s, there had been sizeable orchards out there. If you flew in, you could see the outline of where these orchards had been. Then the city of Los Angeles set up their Owens River Valley water project and they took all the water that had been used for irrigation in the Owens River and sent it down to Los Angeles, and that dried up the valley.

But, as I say, I was shocked at the aridity of the place, but in the course of this visit I went on up to the older ammunition depot at Hawthorne, Nevada, which is out in the real desert. Hawthorne had been set up near the end of World War I and was therefore twenty or twenty-five years old at the time I was there. In their quarters area, they had some very fine trees which I was told had been first planted when the station was set up. So I thought to myself, "Well, if they can do that in twenty or twenty-five years in that desert, they certainly can do as well down at Inyokern:" and they have, because nowadays the station itself is pretty well treed and pretty leafy and pleasant.

Not too long after he returned from the Bikini tests, Hussey called me in one day and said he'd just had very, very bad news. He had had to have a special physical examination and they had told him he had heart murmurs and would have to be retired physically. That was very bad news. He was retired and here, thirty-three years later, he's still living and in fairly good shape!

Q: So the heart murmurs - ?

Adm. S.: Yes.

Apparently, it was a matter of policy on the part of the Secretary at that time to try to weed out some of the older flag officers -

Q: By physical examination?

Adm. S.: Yes.

Then Admiral Noble came as his relief.

Q: Which Noble was that?

Adm. S.: Chuck Noble - oh, golly, my memory!

Q: Well, Charles.

Adm. S.: I know it so well and I can't think of it. Albert Gallatin Noble. He was an old ordnance man with a great deal of experience in the Bureau. He had been in amphibious work during the war out in the southern Pacific, MacArthur's theater.

Well, shortly, the results of my appearance before the

appropriation committee came back and I felt that I had made an utter failure of it because we asked for $800 million and we got $400 million. I don't know how this was arrived at nor do I really understand how we made out with the money, with that amount of money.

Q: It was indeed a time of retrenchment in government, wasn't it?

Adm. S.: Yes. I really expected that with that sort of a cutback, I would be thrown out of the job, but I was not.

Q: Was there some effort to reduce the functions of the Bureau of Ordnance at that point?

Adm. S.: No. That's one great fault of our system, at least as it was run in those days. I do not recall any case of reducing the functions in order to save money. It was just reducing the money, so that it became an extremely difficult thing to do.

Q: Was it the intention of the Bureau to continue with all the development process for various ordnance that was under way?

Adm. S.: Yes. I do not recall that we discontinued any

development programs. These programs were directed by the Chief of Naval Operations. I will come to the question of the relationship between the Chief of the Bureau and the office of the Chief of Naval Operations when I talk about my tour as chief.

One of the main things that was completed during my tour as Deputy was the Naval Ordnance Laboratory out at White Oak. At the time World War II broke out, the Naval Ordnance Laboratory was quite a small operation down in the old Naval Gun Factory in the Navy Yard and primarily concerned with the design of fuses for projectiles. Somehow or another, in the course of the war, it became very much interested in mines and in countermining and had become a very large, hard-working, and effective organization.

With the move out to White Oak, they expanded their field of operation and before very long we found that we had two very capable laboratories working for us. One of them being the operation at White Oak and the other was the one that was being built out at Inyokern. We were able to keep these two from being in any form of bad competition. They competed for certain things, but I do not recall ever running into any acrimony on the subject. There might well have been later on. After I retired, I was with an organization that had a somewhat similar problem, where competing laboratories were very acrimonious about each other.

Q: Wasn't there an attempt at a division of duties between

these two places?

Adm. S.: Oh, yes, and it was effective. Inyokern was primarily concerned with air weapons. That was why it got started, and with rockets. The Naval Ordnance Laboratory was primarily concerned with underwater weapons.

One of the interesting places that I visited in those days was a water tunnel at Penn State University. I don't remember the name of the man who ran that operation, but he was certainly a most interesting individual and he had a very interesting operation up there. It was a tunnel like a wind tunnel, except that the fluid in it was not air, it was water, and he was testing underwater weapons there, torpedoes particularly. I got a great deal of pleasure out of visiting that place.

Q: When you mentioned White Oak, you said they had done a lot of work during the war on mines and mine warfare.

Adm. S.: Yes.

Q: Let me ask why this whole area seems to be neglected in peacetime?

Adm. S.: I wish I could answer that question effectively. I cannot. It is, I imagine, primarily because there is so little glamour in it. Your weapon is put out somewhere and it's very seldom you know whether it functioned effectively unless you happen to capture a prisoner and find out from him.

Another form of warfare that is much neglected in peacetime is nets and booms. This had been built up into a big thing in the course of World War II. We had miles of steel nets in storage at various stations and, although I never saw any netting at work with my own eyes, I've seen some movies of torpedoes caught in nets, which are very spectacular things. The way in which the torpedo thrashes around and endeavors to clear itself reminds you exactly of a rattlesnake in a period of great excitement.

Q: I asked that question about mines and mine warfare because we're perfectly cognizant of the fact that our potential enemy, Russia, doesn't succumb to this lack of glamour. She continues to improve in this area.

Adm. S.: They certainly have. I hope that the Naval Ordnance Laboratory has continued to work on mine material. I know that by the time we got into the Korean War we had practically no minesweeping capability left and one had to be improvised again. I really cannot answer your question at all satisfactorily. It is a question of the priorities set by higher authority. The Bureau, by the time of the end of World War II, no longer had the power to proceed in its own way. Anything it wished to initiate had to be approved and directed by the Chief of Naval Operations. I do not consider this situation to be of itself bad. It had been instituted in the Forrestal-King regime and was intended to insure that the Bureaus did not waste effort hither and yon, but concentrated on what the fighting forces needed to win a war.

But a situation of this sort demands that the CNO's office show imagination and judgment; and I must say that in the later '40s and the early '50s I think there was a lack of both. In those days everyone was hypnotized by the aircraft and atom threats almost to the exclusion of all else. As a result any attempt to improve submarine weapons, particularly torpedoes, was met by the derisive question, "And what targets will you use this against?" - for in those days Russia had almost no merchant marine.

This resulted in a situation such that, a year or so before I retired and when the first atomic submarine was nearing completion, Hyman Rickover could say, "We're going to have a ship that can outrun any of the weapons if carries." Most people took this as a slur on BuOrd and my boys were furious; but I said, "It's absolutely true; only much of the fault lies upstairs. Our error has been not to pound the table hard enough." The upshot of it was I formed a very small and informal committee of submariners in the Bureau whose job was to dream up weapons compatible with an atomic sub. I don't believe they were the very first to conceive of an atomic rocket - I believe someone in Consolidated

Aircraft did so first - but, soon after I retired, they had worked out a feasible outline for the weapon that was eventually built under the name "Polaris". That was my whole part in this very successful program, just "the gleam in papa's eye."

We were at that time, naturally, much interested in rocketry, and in the first beginnings of guided-missilry, particularly antiaircraft guided missiles, but we hadn't gotten very far.

Q: But you were borrowing heavily on the experiments of Dr. Goddard, were you not?

Adm. S.: Well, yes. Of course, Dr. Goddard was the pioneer of it all in the United States, but things had gone far past that, past his work, by that time, by 1946.

There was another laboratory out in Maryland, the Applied Physics Laboratory of Johns Hopkins, run by Dr. Ned Gibson, and he was a most effective, splendid leader, also an extremely witty chap and a wonderful toastmaster at a dinner. They were working at that time on the beginnings of the Terrier missile and the very beginnings of the Talos missile. They were primarily interested in the ramjet form of propulsion, which they had first proved only a short time before, but it had a long, long way to go, and the Talos missile was just emerging into its first operational stage when I finally retired in 1955, also the Terrier was just getting into operation at that time.

Well, they had that one there.

We got involved in the atomic business to the extent of the Atomic Energy Commission - well, it hadn't been set up yet - but the atomic people set up an operation down at our mine depot in Yorktown, Virginia. I was sent out to Los Alamos and given, along with several others, a short course in atoms, about a ten-day course. So I knew something about it, no very vast amount, some of the bombs. The original one that was dropped on Hiroshima had a type of firing device that had been designed by certain civil personnel who had been lent to General Groves's operation by the Bureau of Ordnance, and the Bureau had cooperated importantly in the design of the type of bomb that was dropped on Nagasaki, which was the implosion type.

Q: Much smaller in size, was it not?

Adm. S.: No. The implosion bomb was called the Fat Boy, the other type was smaller and it was known as the gun-type of firing mechanism because the mechanism consisted essentially of a small gun inside the bomb which brought the two chunks of uranium close together very rapidly so that they formed a critical mass and went off. I don't think that the gun type was used thereafter. I think it was the implosion type that was more often used.

Most of my time was spent really on administrative

problems such as getting rid of the real estate that we no longer wanted. I have spoken of the case of a place down in Kentucky where we actually paid a fellow to take the real estate away from us because it was so full of unexploded small-arms projectiles.

I had one unusual assignment. George Hussey called me in one day and said he'd just had a call on the telephone from the wife of the man who was in command of the Naval Ordnance Plant just outside of Detroit, one that had been used for manufacturing Oerlikon guns, and she thought her husband was going crazy. George sent me out there to look into the situation and, sure enough, that man was off his rocker. He was just scared of everything. He was convinced that his place was going to blow up or that there would be a big fire just outside and everything would be burned down. So, with his wife's collaboration, I got in touch with the District Commandant over in Chicago and he sent some doctors over in an ambulance, and our man seemed to be just as gentle and as willing to cooperate as you could wish for. He didn't put any snags in the way of the doctors, and they picked him up shortly, put him in the ambulance, and drove him away. I never knew what became of that one. His executive officer, naturally, had to take over.

Q: This was an era when some top-flight scientists were still contributing to government efforts?

Adm. S.: Oh, yes, and they did for some years afterwards. In the course of that period I had the pleasure of visiting Dr. Urey in his laboratories outside of Chicago. He had a great big laboratory there which looked just like what the movies would expect a top-flight chemist's laboratory should be. He had glass jars and tubes and retorts all over the place, all connected up, with liquids in them and bubbling away.

Well, he told me that what he was trying to do was to measure what the temperature of the water of Lake Michigan had been quite a number of thousands of years ago. How did this come about? Well, he was there on the beach one day, picked up a shell, looked at it, and thought, well, this thing wouldn't grow here now, so I wonder what the temperature was when it did grow here. So he proceeded to sail into this and it involved isotopes, and that was Urey's great contribution to atom radiology, a thorough knowledge of isotopes.

I really don't remember very much more about that period. I was snooping around, trying to get to sea and finally was successful just about the end of 1948.

Q: Before that, let me ask - did you get involved in the second Bikini tests?

Adm. S.: No.

Q: I'm sorry to have interrupted you.

Adm. S.: I finally got away about Christmastime in 1948 and went as Commander, Carrier Division 6. In that division was the Kearsarge and I'll be darned if I can remember the name of the other carrier because we never did have the division together as a division.

The most interesting part of my job was that I was also ex officio Commander, Task Force 28, of the Second Fleet. The Second Fleet being the outfit that ran training operations on the Atlantic coast, and most every time we went to sea it was at the direction of the Commander, Second Fleet. Task Force 28 was the air element of the Second Fleet. The very first operation it had was to proceed with two carriers and a number of destroyers from Norfolk up to Narragansett Bay against submarine opposition.

Well, I got hold of all the submariners I could find who were not actively involved in this operation. They assured me that any submarine captain would be an idiot who took his boat inside the 20-fathom curve. so I based my operation entirely upon the idea that they would operate outside of that. We went up by a very circuitous route and then swung into the entrance to Narragansett Bay, and those blankety-blank submarines had just gone up there and put themselves down on the bottom and waited there quite quiescent until we came past the Beaver Tail buoy and headed up the final channel

in depths of about 10 fathoms. I considered this to be
damned foolishness of the worst variety, but Jimmy Fife was
then Commander, Submarines, and his boys went around throwing their chests out about how they had torpedoed us right
and left, but I still maintained that had it been war they
wouldn't have been there. They wouldn't have dared be there.
One German submarine got up in that region and he was chivvied
and hunted for three or four days and finally got hit.

In that job I relieved Admiral Ziggy Sprague, who had
had the misfortune to get chased all over the waters outside Leyte Gulf by the big Japanese force. I took over his
staff and a very excellent staff it was. I then began a
year at sea that was just full of fun for me. The best thing
about being an admiral is to be a comparatively junior rear
admiral and going to sea with ships to maneuver around and
really have yourself a great time. That's what I did all
year!

Q: When were you selected for admiral?

Adm. S.: Back in '43 while I was still in the Cabot. They
didn't have any selection boards at that time. They had
panels, as they called then. I never knew how one of those
panels operated, but there being a war on, we did not go
through such an arduous form of selection.

Well, as I say, then began a year that was just pure
delight to me.

My operations officer was a fellow by the name of Sam Brown and he was one of the most competent officers I have ever run into. He was terrific, a very excellent pilot and very sharp in the operations of ships.

Shortly, we took a training operation down into the Caribbean and went in to Guantanamo. Sol Phillips, a commodore, was in command at Guantanamo at that time, and he came out and called on me as soon as we came to anchor and asked me which I liked, golf or fishing. I wasn't a golfer in those days, so I said fishing. "Well," he said, "that's great." His wife was a great fisherwoman and he said, "She will be out tomorrow morning in my barge and she'll come alongside and pick you up. She knows all the places to go fishing."

The next day was a Sunday and we were having a big church service on board at the time Mrs. Phillips - her first name was Cherry and she was a cute little thing - came alongside in the barge, causing much craning of sailors' necks as to what was going on. As soon as the church service was over I ran below and changed, went down to the boat, and she took me up the Guantanamo River. Shortly, I hooked on to what I thought was a rubber boot, it had about that much life in it, and pulled in a nice big fish, which she called a snook. Down in Florida nowadays snook are considered game fish, an excellent fish. I tell people about this snook I took in the Guantanamo River and hell, I thought it was a rubber boot and they won't believe me, and I don't believe their stories about how gamey the Florida snook are.

Q: Maybe this was an old guy!

Adm. S.: Well, we fished up and down the Guantanamo River for several hours and we got no more bites. Meanwhile, all my staff, who were great fishermen from way back, embarked and they came up the Guantanamo River. We would pass each other about every half or three-quarters of an hour, one going in one direction and the other, and at that point I would break out my snook and hold it up in a different position. So they didn't know how many snook I had, but apparently I had half a dozen nice big ones.

But, my, oh my, how Guantanamo had changed. By this time in 1949, it was really a lovely place and the people down there wanted to stay. They didn't want to get ordered out. They'd say, "Oh, golly, I've only got eighteen more months here," living like this because they'd get good servants for not very much, Cubans who came in to work there. The men liked it because there was plenty of interest. There was available there on that station every form of decent recreation for a ship's crew that you can think of. So Guantanamo was a very, very different place from what it was when I was first there in the summer of 1916, coaling ship.

While we were there I got a dispatch from the Navy Department telling us that a private airplane on its way from Bermuda to Jamaica had failed to arrive in Jamaica and we were to go out and search for it. So we got under way at break of drawn, stood out, went up to the islands just to the north of Cuba, and spread out over this region. We spent two days searching in rather heavy weather. We didn't find anything and in most of the books about the Bermuda Triangle you will find reference to the loss of that airplane and the fact that the Navy ran a big-scale search for it without result. I am no believer whatever in the myth of the Bermuda Triangle being a place where evil things cause airplanes and ships to disappear. Sure, airplanes and ships disappear there, but they do all over the world.

Well, we didn't find anything there.

We went on several other operations and finally along about midsummer I was sent in the Coral Sea, which was not a ship of my division, to the Mediterranean to operate under Forrest Sherman in the Sixth Fleet.

Q: This was a six-month tour?

Adm. S.: It wasn't quite six, but it was close to it.

I went over there. I had a rather odd accident en route. My white uniforms had gotten in pretty poor shape so I had ordered some more and they didn't arrive. I got down to Norfolk about ready to shove off for the Mediterranean and I had no new white uniforms, so I sent them out to be washed, and in a day or so the ship's service officer came up to the flag plot and you have never seen a ship's service officer in a worse state in your life than he was. It seems that for no reason that anybody could understand, just as they got to washing my white uniforms, a shower of fuel oil came down the pipe and they were all over fuel oil. He said:

"We'll do what we can. We'll bleach them out, but we can't guarantee anything."

So, immediately on arriving at Gibraltar I had to go ashore and try to get something there that would do, and I eventually got fixed up, but it was an embarrassing situation.

At that time Commander, Naval Forces, Europe, had his headquarters in London and he had a cruiser as a flagship. When there was a relief in the Sixth Fleet, he would come down from London and the relief would take place in Gibraltar. This occurred. I think it was Jock Clark I relieved but I'm not sure of that.

Anyway, we went into the Mediterranean and had a very interesting and pleasant cruise there. We spent a fair amount of time in Naples, of course; we went over to Crete and spent a fair amount of time around that bay at the western end and conducted amphibious operations there.

Q: Suda Bay?

Adm. S.: Yes. While I was there I went one weekend over to the capital city of Crete, Candia, at the east end of the island. We had two destroyers with us. It was the time of the year when the Etesian winds, so-called, were blowing very strongly. The Coral Sea was much too large a ship to go into the bay of Candia, we had to anchor out. The destroyers could get in alongside the mole there and get out of this very heavy sea, but we were anchored. It was so bad that we had to say "no liberty," but got an official invitation from the mayor of Candia, so we picked up some of the staff, got into a helicopter and went ashore in that. It was the only contact we had with the beach.

Wehil I was ashore there, I was given a most interesting trip to Cnossos and was shown around that by the curator of the big Greek museum there in Candia. That was a great privilege to see that place with him showing me around and pointing out all the matters of interest.

Then we went up to Piraeus, outside of Athens. While we were there we went on an expedition to see the Acropolis and happened to get a guide who spoke pretty good English. At one point, he said:

"You know, I was in the American army in World War I."

"You were? Where were you on duty?"

"Oh, I was at West Point."

"What were you doing there?"

"I was a waiter in the messhall. I waited on the football training table. Did you ever hear of a Mr. Oliphant?"

Well, when I was a midshipman, Olly was the big, bad wolf of the Army football team and when we had our snake dances around Bancroft Hall, the great thing was to shout. Well, Oliphant and McEwan were the two big, bad wolves. We used to shout, "Get Ollie, get McEwan, get the whole damned team." We never did!

I believe the word "etesian" means seasonal and there is a season of the year when the wind blows very freshly out of the north; and back in the days of Homer and Odysseus it must have made traveling by sea very difficult in the Aegean.

From there we went up to Lemnos and had the anchor just in the mouth of the great big marvelous bay of Lemnos. In World War I this bay was used as the main naval base by the British and the French in their campaign against Gallipoli, but we couldn't get in because the Germans had put a net across the mouth of the bay and this had not yet been removed. With the exception of the British-French expedition that had used Lemnos, practically nothing had happened on that island since Jason and the Argonauts were by there. According to Robert Graves, Jason and his Argonauts just raised cain in Lemnos. That was the place where the women had arisen and killed off or exiled all the men.

Q: The Amazons?

Adm. S.: No, they were over in Asia Minor or the Black Sea coast.

I got the staff together, we all climbed in the barge,

and we went up and explored this beautiful big bay. On the way back, we were feeling a little on the thirsty side and we sighted a dock just off a little hamlet near the mouth of the bay that had a Greek flag up. We put in there and we were met by a most amazing welcoming committee. All the chief people of this little hamlet were down on the dock to welcome us, the postmaster and the policeman and the this and the that. They took us over to a little inn and they certainly gave us of their very best because they broke out wine that they had had buried all during the German occupation and they fed us this wine. They thought it was great. I thought it tasted like turpentine and didn't like it but had to drink it just the same to be decent.

Well, they were just filled with love for America at that time. I don't know what they think about Americans nowadays but this was about a year after the so-called Truman Plan for aid to Greece had been put into effect, and they said that from the Truman Plan they had gotten fishing boats. They said they had been fishermen for generations and the Germans took away or destroyed all their fishing boats. They said, "They just pulled our means of livelihood right away from us. You've come along and you've given us fishing boats and you have not insisted upon giving us American-type fishing boats. You have given us the same type of fishing boat that we used before hand and that we think is best adapted to our waters."

So it was really a love feast, and it exemplified what we found all over Greece at that time. You'd go into some little port and a Greek-American would almost always bob up and all the ones I met were people who were a credit to both nations. He was usually somebody who had owned a shoe-shine stand in Trenton or had been running a newspaper stand in Seattle, or something like that. He would act as our interpreter and we would just have the swellest time imaginable.

Then we went on up to Constantinople, and I certainly was amazed at the Gallipoli Peninsula. I had been very much shocked by the arid appearance of most of the Greek islands out in the Aegean Sea. We got up to the Dardanelles and I'd read so much about the extremely arid condition of Gallopoli that I expected to see a true desert there. As a matter of fact, if was a great deal greener and much better wooded than the Greek islands were. It reminded me very much of much land in Oklahoma, dotted around with live oak trees and things like that.

We got up to the Narrows, which was as far as the British and French were able to get back in 1915. I don't wonder they had a hard time because the current was boiling through those Narrows at a great rate and the Narrows are very narrow, and the forts were so placed that they could just shoot like the deuce right down those narrows. The forts were obviously very old things. You could see some of the guns up there poking over the barbettes and they looked as though they dated from about the time of our Civil War.

We crossed the Sea of Marmora and appeared off the mouth of the Bosporus about sunrise, and a lovelier scene ahead you can hardly imagine, the minarets and the sky lightening up and the cumulus clouds, all very Maxfield Parrish. I ran below and wrote my wife:

"We are approaching a city of the greatest beauty."

Two or three days later, after I'd been ashore there, I wrote her:

"Belay that. It's different."

Q: It was a mirage!

Adm. S.: It's different. Have you ever been there?

Q: No. Adm. S.: Sherman had learned some Turkish and I went with him to a review of some Turkish troops. I just stood off in the distance while he went down the line of the troops, and he was able to lead off by making a remark that's the equivalent of "Glorious soldiers," or something like that. It made a big hit with the Turks, naturally.

We had quite a time there. We went down and looked over a Turkish ammunition depot at a naval base not far away, and it was obvious that the Turks had a great problem, because I doubt if they had made any guns of their own or ammunition of their own for two or three hundred years.

They bought everything from anybody, all over the world, and they had to keep the ammunition for all these different forms of ordnance sorted out. I don't know how well they did that. That was their problem.

Q: Had we sent in that team of naval experts to help them build up their navy at that point?

Adm. S.: I think that came a little later.

We had a very pleasant time in Constan. I went around and visited lots of museums, mosques, and suchlike things, and somehow or other got the reputation of being an intellectual because I liked to go and look at museums. This caused an amusing situation when we got back to France.

We pulled out of there and I don't recall exactly where we went but we had various gunnery exercises, aircraft exercises, and amphibious exercises along the way. We got out to the western Mediterranean. Sherman had reason to stay in Naples, so he sent me out with the Coral Sea and some destroyers and the submarine that was attached to the Sixth Fleet at that time, with just instructions to go somewhere and conduct some air and submarine operations. So we laid out a circle of fifty miles' radius and we told the submarine captain to proceed there and we would for the next two days stay somewhere in that circle. He was to make as many attacks on us as he could.

So we got down there and the first night engaged in

fueling the destroyers. We had a tanker with us, and the tanker on one side was fueling the Coral Sea and a destroyer on the other, which was fueling from us, when this operations officer of mine called me and said:

"We've got a disappearing radar blip about ten miles away up here which we think is the submarine."

I was very loath to stop this oiling, so I called the skippers of the two ships alongside and said:

"If we make a turn here, just a degree at a time, with me calling the changes, do you think that you can hold on and continue the oiling so that we can avoid casting off."

They said, well, let's try it.

Q: It was a calm sea, I take it?

Adm. S.: It was very calm. So we tried it and it worked like a charm, and I went and turned in, leaving word to be called somewhat before sunrise, but I wasn't called. I woke up and it was sunshine, went on the flag bridge demanding to know why not and the Chief of Staff, Captain Leper, was there and he said:

"Well, something has happened over here and I thought that you'd just as soon sleep. Along about two o'clock we got a radio message from the submarine saying, 'A single submarine cannot possibly catch an outfit as agile as yours. May we surrender and join your side?'"

This submarine was fitted with a CIC for the control of aircraft. So we sent them some airplanes and let them play on our side for the rest of the operation. I was always amused by that.

Then we went up to Portofino and the Italian Riviera, and we were challenged to a golf match by a local golf club. I think they wanted eighteen players on a side and, believe it or not, the Americans had to draft me to make the final player. I hadn't played golf in ten years, didn't have any clubs, or anything of the sort. We got over to this course and I found I was matched against two Genoese ladies, both of whom were hot shots. They had handicaps of about five or six, and I was terrible, but we had a pleasant afternoon, just the same. Then at a dinner given at the golf club that night - the golf club had suggested playing for a cup, well they presented themselves with the cup and they had another cup for the Coral Sea, anyhow, although they had beaten us hands down.

We got over to Genoa and saw what was reputed to be the home, the boyhood home, of Christopher Columbus. And we went to Nice. There, I had dinner one night with the Duke and Duchess of Windsor (but so did about two thousand other people at the same time!) They were having a movie gala and everybody who had two dimes to rub together was there at the dinner. I was there as the guest of the mayor of Nice but I could only see the duke and duchess two or three tables away.

Off on the Italian Riviera I was presented with a beautiful watercolor painting of the <u>Coral Sea</u> by the Italian Naval Academy, which I had visited. They had an official painter there, and they made it a practice, when foreign ships came in, to give the flag officer a painting of his flagship from the bow and they would give the captain of the flagship a painting from the quarter. This painting was done from a photograph of the ship lying at anchor in the calmest water you can imagine, but the painter put a great deal of life in it, roaring winds, all wild, the ship barging through the seas. It's a splendid painting. The painter was an old rip - I never did meet him - but he had been an Austrian naval officer during World War I. Following that war, he was hanging around Venice and I know various of our ships that went up to the Venice-Trieste area would have him come on board and cadge lunches. Then he would pay for these lunches by painting a picture of the ship on the wardroom door. Back in the twenties there was a fair number of our destroyers that had themselves all painted on the wardroom door. He was painting in oils in those days.

By the time he became the official painter of the I Italian naval academy in '49, they said he had a tendency to go AWOL every now and then and for a couple of weeks they wouldn't know where he was. Then they would get a collect cable maybe from New York, maybe from Tokyo, maybe from Capetown, saying "Send me a ticket and I'll come home," and they would send him a ticket. Home he would come and he would be confined to the station for three or four months, he would be a good boy, and then he would go on another bender!

Q: This was an interesting time in the Mediterranean and a leisurely time -

Adm. S.: Yes. There were no Russians down there yet.

Q: Was the Royal Navy much in evidence?

Adm. S.: No, not much. We ran an operation against Malta. We were supposed to make an air attack on Malta. The Maltese had some jets over there - we didn't have any jets yet. Our fighters were all either F4-Us or F8-Fs, and the F8-F was the most delightful little airplane, very small, and it was about the last of our piston-engine fighters.

As I say, we ran an operation against the British on the island there and they came boiling out with their jets. We had probably the biggest combat air patrol in all history up overhead. We had every fighter we carried up there before the British got out to us. They came diving down on us and you never saw so many angry-looking airplanes chasing after somebody else in all your life. The F4-Us could just about keep up with the jets.

Well, as I say, we got up to Nice and I saw my first girl in a bikini at that time. A couple of Americans who ran a museum, the Picasso Museum, over at Cap d'Antibes came out and, as I say, I had gotten a reputation for being an intellectual. They wanted to take me up into the country and introduce me to Picasso and this I viewed with a great deal of dubiety because Picasso was being a very prominent communist in those days. I managed to get out of it without hurting their feelings too much by saying I was sure that Picasso would be bored to death with meeting me. So I declined to go but I went with them over to their museum and I'm afraid I rather shocked them by shaking my head and saying, I couldn't see it at all. As far as I was concerned, with the exception of one thing there in their museum, Picasso was a cartoonist, not an artist. They accepted that without getting too mad. There was one thing that was in there, however, that was a real work of genius. It was a big jar made of red material and the cover was the head of a vulture; and you never in your life saw anything that looked more evil and vulturine than that jar did. Maybe it was my admiration for the work that went into that thing that kept them from getting mad at me.

Then we set out for the United States. We returned home. We passed through the straits in most beautiful weather, oh, it was terrific. The land was down to the eastward, when the lookout made a very surprising report, "Iceberg dead ahead." I naturally broke out the strongest glasses possible to check up on this and it turned out to be the Italian training ship Cristoforo Colombo standing into the straits under full sail, and a very beautiful sight, the only time that I ever saw a square-rigged ship at sea under full sail.

We stood over rather close to it and passed the word to all ships that here was a sight that few of us had ever seen or would ever see again at sea and anybody who had a camera had better lay up topside and get some pictures. So I hope a lot of people took pictures of this ship as we went by.

After we got back to the States, we went off on a big amphibious and antisubmarine operation down in the Caribbean. We were opposed by about a dozen submarines, all of them snorkel boats, and the snorkel submarine was brand new at that time. However, these submarines were equipped with normal American submarine torpedoes, I think it was the Mark 11, whose characteristics we knew well, and, by doing a little plotting-board work, I was able to work out a maneuver that would be quite effective in avoiding torpedoes, provided the submarine was picked up before it got through our destroyer screen. I got my staff well instructed in the use of this method, which was to make a radical turn of at least 80 degrees from the bearing on which the submarine was reported and at speeds of 20 knots or more. If that was done very quickly, it was physically impossible for a torpedo from the submarine to reach us.

My staff got to be very adept at this, but I was really very, very much concerned at that time by the troubles we were having with our sonar. The sonar operators were forever picking up false sounds and they seemed quite unable to differentiate between the false and the real. This had been a problem all during this year that I was at sea, and I had conducted many operations just for training the sonar operators and had seen to it that when we were up around Quonset they were sent regularly over to the sonar school that was maintained somewhere around there.

It was really a joy to watch the staff operate on this basis because a report would come in from a destroyer in the screen and probably about five seconds later an order to make the necessary turn and to build up to speed would be out, another five seconds and the whole outfit would be turning to get away from the submarine. I kept a personal diary of our submarine contacts, reported contacts, during that cruise. We had some fifty-three reported contacts and I was able to boast that they never laid a glove on us.

After the operation was all over, I went to New London and attended Jimmy Fife's critique on the operation. I believe that of those fifty-three reported contacts three were actual and real. The others were all spurious. This was a situation I really could never understand.

Q: Was this a new sonar, a post-World War II sonar?

Adm. S.: I don't believe so. During World War II we had excellent results with sonar, and I saw no reason to believe, except lack of training of the operators, that we shouldn't have equally good results in '49, but we were certainly getting all kinds of spurious reports.

Q: Catching sounds from fish and things like that?

Adm. S.: Possibly. I don't know. I know that in some cases, a destroyer would report a submarine and then be told off to do something about it, and they would undoubtedly give later reports of knuckles in their own wake. They would get an echo from their own wake and would report that as another contact.

We went on down to the Caribbean and I had exercises against these submarines on the way down, then when we finally got down there, they all went off about their business somewhere and we made a start for the eastern end of the Caribbean. The operation would take us clear across the sea to near its western end. In an attempt to possibly lure submarines away from us, I sent a destroyer with a noisemaker clear around the north of Haiti. The way the operation was laid out it was obvious that our force could either go through the Caribbean or go north around Haiti to our objective. There weren't any submarines up there north of Haiti, as it turned out, as I learned later, and this attempt at deception got nowhere.

Admiral Wu Duncan was along on this expedition in a cruiser, but he was not exercising any tactical control. He was Commander, Second Fleet, at that time. And John Ballentine, whose exact position I don't remember, was also along. When the operation was over, we were due to stand in to the harbor of Port of Spain, down in Trinidad. Duncan said that, of course, he was going to be the number one man and he turned all social activities over to Ballentine, and my job was to be the officer in tactical command and get this force into the harbor of Port of Spain. I was always very proud of that situation because we had a very large force indeed. We had two or three battleships, five or six heavy cruisers and some light, we had a total of five carriers, three large and two CVLs, and thirty or forty destroyers - the amphibious craft didn't go down there with us. We just took the real fighting ships in.

Q: Were all these component parts of the Second Fleet?

Adm. S.: Yes. It was the whole Atlantic Fleet turned over to the Second Fleet for this operation.

Horatio Nelson took a fleet through there but didn't stop. "Fighting Bob" Evans took his Battle Fleet in there but the fleet that I took in there made "Fighting Bob" Evans's fleet look like small potatoes because I took about half a million tons of warships in there. This shows that being a comparatively junior rear admiral at sea and being given the tactical command meant you had a lot of fun.

We were there for a while then we set out to the north and had more antisubmarine exercises on the way. Whenever we sighted a merchant vessel, we'd ask them if they'd seen any submarines and, if so, where and so forth. Finally we were about in the latitude of Norfolk and we sighted a vessel that looked like a warship but it was very slow in answering this question, when suddenly one of the lookouts said, "He's got a submarine alongside." So we did the world's fastest turn to the right to get out of there, and I can remember one of the battleships turning so rapidly it almost looked as though it were spinning on its stern, because they were getting pretty damned close to this vessel with a submarine alongside.

Q: What nationality was it?

Adm. S.: It was U.S. and it turned out that they were out from Norfolk on a research problem of some sort and the submarine that they had alongside was not in our operation at all, it was something quite separate and distinct.

In the course of this whole operation from start to finish, we had one very successful aspect of it. The Atlantic Fleet was much interested in the subject of counter - oh, radar, I've forgotten the proper term for that - at that time and we had some gear in the Coral Sea that was supposed to be effective but we never could get anything much out of it, and I don't think any of the other surface ships were getting very much.

Sam Brown pointed out that our attack airplanes, ADs, had a counterradar device and we would send them out at night looking for submarines that had their radar turned on, and they had outstanding success with this. Our planes would fly very low, pick up the radar of a submarine, and then home in on it, and before the submarine could get our airplane on its radar, our planes were passing right over their periscopes. In fact, had it been war, we would have reduced the submarines almost to the situation of World War I, as far as picking up anything is concerned, because we soon taught them that they didn't dare use their radar, and they would be back entirely upon such sonar as they had and their eyes.

We were very successful at that.

We stopped in to Guantanamo on the way north, and along about there a Canadian carrier joined us and stayed with us for a while, and as we passed I think it was the Bahamas a bunch of British land-based fighters came out and conducted an operation against us. Golly, they would come in low. They were prop airplanes but they were so low that their propellers were throwing up spray. However, we had with us an airplane that carried a very special radar whereby it could look down and see these low flyers silhouetted against the sea, then this could be automatically transferred onto our radar in our flag plot. As long as we knew where that airplane was, we knew very exactly what was going on.

We also had another strange thing happen on the way north. The antisubmarine exercise was over and we were going along. It was Sunday afternoon, beautiful weather, when a merchant vessel appeared over on our port bow on a course that was cutting right through our formation. Well, lots of people would maneuver in such a case but I had indoctrinated all my captains that the rules of the road either gave us the right of way or they did not. If they did not, we maneuvered. If they did, we held our course and speed. This vessel came along, went right through our destroyer screen, and one of the destroyers zigged a little, apparently to let him get by without colliding, and he kept coming right for my flagship, absolute dead collision course. The captain of the flagship was down there on his bridge looking up at me and I was looking down at him. It got to the point where I said:

"Bowser, I think you'd better fire your saluting gun."

Just about that time we saw somebody go running up a ladder in the merchant ship, run over to the middle of the bridge, and he changed course and passed by on our port side.

Evidently, these people had been running on an iron mike and had nobody on watch.

Q: What nationality was that?

Adm. S.: Mexican. You wouldn't have thought they had money enough to own an iron mike! I can't imagine any other reason for this strange situation.

Anyhow, we got back to Quonset and I went over to New Haven and listened to the submariners' critique. As I say, we figured that our surface vessels might have made three contacts, although we had fifty-three in my diary.

Then I was detached and sent to duty as Commander, Naval Air Test Center, down at Patuxent.

Q: I can see, as you recount the story of that task force in the Mediterranean and elsewhere, that it was just a fun cruise.

Adm. S.: Oh, it was great.

Then, as I say, I went to Patuxent.

Q: Was this something you wanted to do?

Adm. S.: No. I would much have preferred to stay at sea but there was no chance of that, so Patuxent was very fine duty.

Q: Tell me the state of Patuxent at that time, when you took over.

Adm. S.: It was a very flourishing and going concern. It

was involved in aircraft testing of practically every variety you can think of. One thinks of a test pilot as being somebody who takes an airplane up and does all kinds of loops and rolls with it, wrings it out, and there was some of that done down there, but mostly it was much quieter work.

There was the Flight Test Division and if there was any wringing out to be done, they did it but most of their time was spent in very careful, accurate, engineering tests, flight tests of airplanes. There was the Electronics Test Division, which tested all the electronics. There was the Armament Test Division, which tested out all the guns and the fire control, and airplanes were beginning to acquire electronic fire control at that time, just beginning. There was the Service Test Division, and they operated in a rather unusual way. They did not try to get any hotshot pilots in that division. They tried to get run-of-the-mill pilots and then they just took airplanes and flew them and flew them and flew them to see what errors the run-of-the-mill pilots could make, so that they could find ways and means of correcting them.

Q: Oh, I see, whereas the hotshot -

Adm. S.: They were in the Flight Test Division, primarily.

We had a fifth division, what the devil was that?

We had these divisions, we had a very large and fine runway, one of the longest in the United States at that time, a 10,000-footer, and we had a place for setting up and testing catapults, we tested blind-landing devices, all kinds of things. We had a lot of helicopters down there. I started taking helicopter instruction and got as far as making one solo hop, and I was due to go out again that afternoon but I was called from the hangar and told - of course, they were very tactful - that unfortunately somebody had overspeeded the engine and it required a little work. Well, I knew perfectly well who had overspeeded the engine. It was I.

Q: Was this a Sikorsky model?

Adm. S.: Yes. They would have it all ready for me tomorrow. Well, tomorrow came and it got like a Spanish manana. It went on and on and on until finally they found so much trouble with the engine that they had to send it back to the manufacturer. The engine was a peculiar one. And I got detached before I finished my helicopter instruction!

Q: So you never qualified?

Adm. S.: I never qualified.

Q: Did you have any relations with other testing centers in the country?

Adm. S.: Oh, yes, with Edwards. We had some Air Force test people on duty with us. We sent some of our own people out to Edwards. We had some British test people there and so forth, and we had the test pilots' school.

Q: Yes, tell me about that.

Adm. S.: That was run by Tom Connolly and it was a most successful operation. Tom was a great leader of it.

In the course of writing fitness reports there were two officers on whom I had made very terse statements when they were commanders - "This man is flag-rank caliber." One was Sam Brown, my operations officer in CarDiv 6, and the other was Tom Connolly.

Q: Well, Tom Connolly made it. Did Brown?

Adm. S.: Oh, yes, Brown made it. Unfortunately in some way which I have never understood he got into a big technical argument with some of the people in the office of the Secretary of the Navy, or SecDef - I think that's who it was, SecDef people, and he was shuffled off into duty that somebody had to do, president of the Board of Medals and Awards.

Well, to get back to Patuxent. I had a great time down there. My wife and I had the most lovely quarters.

Q: That big, white, frame house?

Adm. S.: It's not white frame, it's brick colonial, named Mattaponi. I spent a fair amount of time trying to discover the origin of the word. Obviously it's Indian. Most of the people down there would dismiss that question and say:

"Well, there's a Mattaponi River over in Virginia that's formed by the junction of the Matta, the Po, and the Ni."

This didn't satisfy me very much because I knew that part of this Mattaponi house we were in was built in 1668, or something like that, as a summer place for Lady Baltimore.

Q: The Calvert family?

Adm. S.: Way back then, and most of the house was built in Georgian days. Nobody knew exactly when because all the county records had burned up. In the old counties, it was always the county records that they burned up. Well, getting back to the origin of the name Mattaponi. It seems to me that the Calverts wouldn't have given it that name because back in their days they were carrying on a war with Virginia. Anyhow, it seemed more probable that the Matta, the Po, and the Ni got their names because they diverged from the Mattaponi than the other way.

Finally, somebody gave me a copy of a paper put out by the Maryland Historical Society way back in the 1870s. The chap had studied the languages of the Indians of the

Chesapeake and, since the Ojibwas out in Michigan were closely allied to those people, he had gone out and lived with the Ojibwas for some time, and, in the Ojibwa tongue, Madda meant a swampy place and poni meant the end of the trail through the woods. Well, in very early days there was a trail leading from where St. Mary's City was, through the woods, over to a swampy place that was just down the hill from this Mattaponi house. In fact, there still is a very lovely little road called Mattaponi Street that runs from St. Mary's City to where this swampy place used to be, because the swampy place is now all taken up with hangars. So I am sure that that is the origin of the name - it means a swampy place at the end of the trail through the woods.

It was a lovely old house. It was falling apart when the Navy went down there to set up the station in 1940. It had been purchased by a wealthy man in Washington who was going to return it to its original colonial state. Well, the Navy wasn't interested in the original colonial state and wanted to make quarters out of it so they fixed the place up with hardwood floors, which really riled the old ladies of the county because they wanted nice broadwood floors in there instead of modern things. We had electricity, hot water, steam heat, and things like that. It was far the finest house I have ever lived in in my life, and it had a beautiful location.

A lot of the very best people in naval aviation were on duty down there. My memory again - I have forgotten the name of the number one test pilot. He was a very tall and very handsome fellow who had a great name. Bob Dixon was there. He was in the Flight Test Division. And a fellow with a French-Canadian name was also in that division. They were very outstanding pilots.

We had an amusing incident once. This was a time when there was a great deal of public interest in, now they call them UFOs, but they called them flying saucers in those days, and an article had appeared in Reader's Digest saying, "Oh, yes, indeed, there are flying saucers and they aren't all from outer space, the Navy is experimenting with them at the Naval Test Center at Patuxent." I knew damned well we didn't have any flying scauers, but we did have one thing that at night could look more like a flying saucer than any flying saucer anybody else had dreamed up. One of our jobs was to try out navigational lighting for helicopters and one of the ideas was to put short neon tubes out at the tips of the rotor blades. Well, when that thing got spinning up with these neon tubes on, it certainly looked exactly like all the descriptions you ever read of a flying saucer.

Q: Maybe that's the origin of the flying saucer?

Adm. S.: Well, flying saucers were first sighted apparently out in Washington state and by day, so I guess it wasn't quite the origin.

Anyway, when we first got this thing fitted out and

turning up on the ground, I shouted for my flag lieutenant and sent him to the telephone to call up all the sheriffs and all the telephone operators for miles around and tell them that if anybody reported any flying saucers overhead that night it was nothing but a test job on a helicopter. We heard no -

Q: Rumors?

Adm. S.: Apparently, they were able to scotch all rumors.

At that time we were heavily engaged in the Korean War and it was an open question as to whether we might get engaged with Russia. I thought that there was grave danger of doing so and I had a lot of the people down there preparing plans for what sort of a naval air test center we would require in case of a war with Russia. I don't know whether anything ever came of this or not because it was way too soon.

In later years, I heard many juniors beefing about, oh - they don't get orders out soon enough, "They ought to be able to let us know earlier where we're going next." At that point I am prone to pat them on their heads and say:

"Now calm down. Listen to a real tale of woe."

Along in the fall of 1950 some most flattering rumors started running around the station saying that I was about to be ordered out and I might go either as Chief of the Bureau or Ordnance or Chief of the Bureau of Aeronautics. This was very, very flattering indeed to be considered for two such -

Q: Yes.

Adm. S.: The story was that Dorsey Foster, who was then Chief of Naval Material, was about to retire and either Noble from BuOrd or Pride from BuAer would relieve him and that I was told off to relieve whoever got stepped up.

I could get no information. Then, about Christmas, Foster happened to come through Patuxent and naturally I ran out to meet him. I asked him about these rumors and he said:

"Forget them. It's all decided and you aren't in it any more."

So I went back and told my wife that everything was fine, we were going to stay there, hoped to have another year, and so forth -

Q: Just settle back down in Lady Baltimore's house!

Adm. S.: Yes. Then came New Year's Eve. It was a work day. About 4:29 in the afternoon, I was just pushing my pencils up in the pencil rack and getting ready to go home, when the telephone rang and it was the then chief of Naval Personnel, Johnny Roper, a classmate of mine, and he was quite to the point. He said:

"Red, I don't want any backtalk out of you, no argument whatever. It's all been decided at the highest level. You get up here tomorrow and relieve Chuck Noble."

I said:

"My God, Johnny, tomorrow's New Year's." He said:

"Make it the day after."

That was the advance notice that I got.

Well, I got up to Washington -

Q: The day after New Year's?

Adm. S.: Yes, relieved Noble, and, since he was fleeting up to be in charge of the Naval Material Office, he was getting quarters down in the Navy Yard. At that time, no quarters went with the office of chief of BuOrd, for which I was, in the long run, very thankful.

We owned a house over in Belle Haven, south of Alexandria.

Q: Jimmy Hall lives over there, doesn't he?

Adm. S.: Right next door to Jimmy Hall.

We had it rented. The lease ran for another year and two or three months, but just about that time our tenant wrote in and asked to be released from this lease because -

Q: Was he a service man?

Adm. S.: No, he was with one of the big companies and he was being ordered somewhere else.

This just fitted in beautifully, so we let him break the lease and go. I was not relieved by a flag officer at Patuxent. The number one man in flight test just took over from me. He already had quarters down there and did not want to move into Mattaponi, so I was able to get permission for my wife to remain in Mattaponi until such time as either a relief was ordered or our tenant got out of our house. The latter way was the way it happened. Then we moved into our own house in Belle Haven and remained in that house until we moved to Florida.

I would much have preferred to be ordered as Pride's relief in the way in turned out.

Q: In the Bureau of Aeronautics?

Adm. S.: Yes, but there's no reason to get upset or to beef about that.

By the time I got to BuOrd, the big thing was to get the guided-missile program under way, really get it going. Noble had convinced the authorities that we should be able to go into production situation very shortly on the Terrier missile. At this time, the President had appointed - what the devil was the old man's name, he had been president of Chrysler Automobile and he was a most forceful self-made man who came up from a machine shop?

Q: Engine Charlie Wilson?

Adm. S.: No, this was a different man. The President had appointed him as coordinator, if that's the proper word, of the various guided-missile programs. He was a great man on problems in production. He was by no means strong on problems of research and so forth, but when it came to turning out large quantities of material of a known and frozen design, he was the peer of anybody.

Well, I found that I had fallen heir to a fight left over from Noble's day between the Coordinator and the Bureau in regard to a certain plant we wanted to put up for the production of Terrier missiles. He wanted us to put up a one-million-square-foot plant, put the whole program in a single building. I found that all the people in the Bureau, and I agreed with them, thought that this was biting off more as a start than we ought to try to chew, that it would be better to put up a plant a half or a third of that size and then, as things came along, put up additional plants, if they were necessary.

Q: It wasn't a question of money, then?

Adm. S.: It was not a question of money, no. It was a question of pure engineering judgment.

This Coordinator was strongly in favor of the big plant and he insisted upon it. After interviewing him several times and getting into pretty hot-mouthed arguments, I came to the conclusion that he knew a hell of a lot more about engineering production than I did or, in fact, than any of the people in my Bureau really did, so I eventually acceeded, and this plant was put up thirty or forty miles east of Los Angeles. I can't remember the name of it, but it was a beautiful big plant. One of his arguments was that in production you've got to think big and if you don't think big you find yourself always running back to the toolroom to get the design changed and so forth. I perforce adopted his philosophy on this.

We had a very difficult time actually getting that missile into production and it was just beginning to be produced to any degree when I finally retired in 1955. The development had been contracted to Consolidated Aircraft down in San Diego, with the Applied Physics Laboratory supposedly giving them guidance. Well, I regret to say that things got to the point where they were fighting with each other and innumerable changes were being introduced into the missile. Things just weren't getting done. They were particularly having difficulty with the devices that were supposed to check out the missile - as though you were trying to measure something accurately and you didn't have a good ruler. However, the Coordinator pounded the desk at me and so forth and said:

"You've got to make one man the czar of this job."

So I picked out a submariner in the Bureau by the name of Boyle, who was in the guided-missile division, and sent him out to the plant. In a matter of three or four months, he managed to get things fairly well straightened out.

In the meantime, one of the things that the Coordinator had insisted upon was that we have some sort of a guarantee from Consolidated. So, after some thought, I directed the Contracting Division to insert a requirement that the company would guarantee the missiles to the point of their checking out at the launcher. They were not responsible for the launcher, they were not responsible for the radar that guided the missile on once it was launched, and not responsible for the rocket angle of it. I felt that they could not be called upon to guarantee anything more than that their work, the missile, could check out when it was put on the launcher. I know there were people around who said, "Oh, you ought to get a guarantee that it will work against a target in the air."

Well, I just had to reply that the way the thing was contracted out, that was quite impossible.

However, apparently this had a very helpful effect because I'm told that when the word got around out in San Diego, and at this plant of ours outside of Los Angeles, that the company had accepted a guarantee, everybody turned to and started working like hell, whereas a lot of them had been apparently loafing on the job beforehand, and we began to get some results.

At that time retired Air Force General McNarney was President of Consolidated and we were about to have one of the early test shots out at Inyokern. I went out to view this and McNarney came up from San Diego and we were taken out and ensconced in bleachers to watch this thing. The

Terrier took off and headed in the direction of the drone airplane that was coming in, and then the Terrier didn't seem to quite follow the scent and the next thing we knew the thing was way up in the zenith and then we saw it turn around and start down, and it looked as though it were headed right for the high school. Well, it didn't come within half a mile of the high school, but it failed to get anywhere near its target, its proper target. Everybody started to laugh and say that the trouble was that "You two old buzzards up there in the first-base bleachers scared the devil out of it!"

Not long afterwards we began to get sucesses and they went on and built up to a very fine figure. I know eventually that Terrier was put in quite a number of ships.

Q: But the bugs were not out of it, were they, because Eli Reich ttld me about his project in the sixties with Admiral P. D. Stroop, the Terrier and the other two?

Adm. S.: Stroop was skipper there at Inyokern at the time this happened, and he had a charming young daughter. Well, after this episode out on the field, the Stroops took McNarney and me over to the club for dinner, and this young daughter so worked upon McNarney that she even got him out on the dance floor. He probably hadn't danced in fifty years, but she got him out there and had him hopping around in great style!

Q: He was McNarney of the "nuts" fame, was he not?

Adm. S.: No, no, this was an Air Force man. He had been in command of the Army Air Forces down in Italy in the last of World War II.

Then we had the Talos, which was a more ambitious guided missile than the Terrier. It was able to reach out maybe 100 miles. It was being worked up at South Bend, Indiana. I forget the name of the company that had the contract for construction, but again it was under the technical directions of the Johns Hopkins Applied Physics Laboratory. It had never gotten to the actual test in the air stage when I retired.

We had an unusual experience with regard to that. One day some Air Force officers came to see me and said they wanted to know whether we could produce some Taloses for the Air Force. They wanted to rig antiaircraft protection for some of their bases and they were not at all satisfied with what the Army could promise. They thought the Talos would be much more satisfactory from the viewpoint of its expected performance. The result was we got some Air Force people over in the Bureau where they were working on Talos at the time I retired.

I don't know what ever came of that. I rather imagine that it eventually died, but I don't know.

Q: What about Tartar? Did that come up, too?

Adm. S.: That was just in the gleam-in-papa's-eye stage when I retired.

Q: And what about Sidewinder?

Adm. S.: Sidewinder? Oh, that's something of a story. During my time as Deputy Chief and when I came in as Chief, various people were trying to do things with infrared, but practically everything that came to the stage of actual service or field test fell flat on its face, so infrared had acquired a very bad reputation. You couldn't get any research or development money for any form of infrared guidance.

Q: You mean the Navy turned thumbs down on it?

Adm. S.: Absolutely.

We had an arrangement with our chief laboratories, such as out at White Oak and out at Inyokern, whereby a certain amount of their annual budget, 5 per cent or some such figure, would be set aside for basic research to be chosen by the station itself. The technical directors would get up their programs and let some of the boys who - well, they never let anybody figure "why is grass green," but they permitted the boys to have some money to fool around with some far-out ideas.

What was the name of the engineer who later became Technical Director at Inyokern? A marvelous little fellow, who had the idea for the Sidewinder.

Q: Dr. McLean.

Adm. S.: I don't recall.

Well, he had the idea for the Sidewinder but the only money he could get was some of this off-the-cuff stuff, some of this elective, and it wasn't very much. But he plugged along under cover, in spite of strong disapproval from up top. At that time, the Navy went completely overboard for the - oh, a little dart rocket. Everybody had the idea that the only way to shoot down other airplanes was to use the equivalent of a shotgun armament instead of a rifle, so Inyokern had worked up a small - Mighty Mouse - rocket and a rocket dispenser. We bought Mighty Mouses by the million. They were all tested out and went through our Naval Ordnance Plant at Shoemaker, Arkansas. I don't think any Mighty Mouses were ever used against another airplane. If it was, it was after I retired. But I know that they have been used, they were used, in Vietnam as an antipersonnel weapon. I doubt if they were used to any very great extent, but some of them were used, anyhow.

Well, as I was saying, Mighty Mouse had official backing. Sidewinder had none. I always felt Sidewinder was the better weapon and it eventually broke through. It began to get higher-up official recognition and then I retired, but I know that it was used with much success in later years.

I have spoken of the necessity of getting the approval of higher-ups. When I went as Deputy Chief, it was very apparent that the old position of the chief of a material bureau in the Navy Department was crumbling rapidly, and by the time I became chief of bureau it had collapsed completely. The chief of a bureau was no longer a person of any real power whatever.

Q: What caused this?

Adm. S.: The formation of a bureaucracy in the Department of Defense. They said, "We will do all the thinking and all you people do is just as we tell you." They just took over lock, stock, and barrel.

As I say, you no longer had any real power. Now, here were these sizable organizations that had to have somebody act as top man, true. But the old days when, for instance, the Chief of the Bureau of Ordnance practically decided what armament and what armor a ship would carry were long, long past. We had to get the approval and the direction of the Chief of Naval Operations before any new program could be initiated or continue to be carried on. He, in turn, eventually had to get the okay of the bureaucracy of the Department of Defense before anything could be carried further. That was the sort of a situation I refer to.

I did not have the authority to decide which contractor would be awarded a contract. This was decided by the application of a set of Procurement Regulations which had been worked out by Mr. Koehler when he was Assistant SecNav, and the decision was further checked by the Office of the Chief of Naval Material. These Regulations were excellent and I have no fault to find with them. I merely cite this to show that I, as a Bureau Chief, had little or no power.

In regard to the Sidewinder, the people in DOD, and they had some of the best technical brains in the country up there, there's no doubt about it, thought that infrared was a rogue that would just lead one astray, so they would not for a long time authorize anything in that area.

Shortly before I retired, the navy had outfitted a ship on the West Coast for the testing of guided missiles, and throughout my time as Chief of Bureau I did my best to hold together two organizations that had grown up during the war, organizations of civil contractors. One of them was the Ordnance Committee - I mean the Guided-Missile Committee - of the American Ordnance Association, and there was a very similar civil organization of manufacturers. The Naval Ordnance Advisory Committee. I used to sponsor about every six months a meeting of these organizations at or near one of our stations to get together and discuss various ordnance problems. We would propose various questions to them, asking for their advice as to how to get certain things done, and sometimes they came in with some very excellent and worthwhile advice. Some of these problems were things that never could be adequately solved, such as this one.

We were shipping out great amounts of ammunition for the Korean War and much of the shipping was being sent out from Mobile Bay, a place over on the west side of Mobile Bay. I went down there to visit this place and, here, for two or three miles along the railroad track that led up to the pier were great stacks of lumber that had been used for shoring up the ammunition in the railroad cars. This had been just wrenched out of the cars and thrown out alongside the railroad tracks. Well, it hurt the puritan in my innards to see such waste. Practically all the time I was there in the Bureau, I was trying to find somebody who could suggest a good way to make use of that lumber again, and nobody ever came up with anything really worthwhile. The only thing to do was burn it. It was full of nails, very difficult to get the nails out. At the Ordnance Station in Indiana they decided to get generous with it and they would put it out beside the road and anybody in the countryside round about who wanted some firewood could come and pick it up. Well, that sounded great until a bunch of racketeers over in Indianapolis heard about it and decided to come out in big trucks and scoop it all up and take it away from the local farmers. I don't know what they did with it but they found some way to dispose of it to their advantage.

Q: You can be sure of that!

Was Dan Gallery involved in any way with the program when you were there?

Schoeffel #6 - 350

Adm. S.: Dan relieved me when I left the Bureau of Ordnance in 1938. He was there for two years and he evidently had a very successful two years because he made a great impression on everybody around there. When I went back everybody around there was talking about what a hell of a fine fellow Dan was. He left a number of cartoons and a number of jingles around.

Q: But he did get involved with missiles, didn't he?

Adm. S.: I don't recall that Dan was particularly in the missile business, except that of course he was the officer in tactical command of that particular operation when they stood a big missile up on the flight deck of a carrier and shot it off.

Q: And it almost came back as a boomerang!

Adm. S.: Yes, but I don't remember Dan as particularly engaged in the missile business in any other way. I may have a lapse of memory there. One of his brothers was the skipper down at Indian Head at that time, and I used to go over there to Indian Head quite frequently because they had some vacant cottages over there and I'd go over and spend the weekend in one of them. They also had probably the most dangerous golf course in the United States. It was a nine-hole golf course and almost all, but not quite all, of the fairways ran right across one central point. If you got out there to that central point, a ball was likely to come at you from any direction.

Q: Did Ed Hooper work for you in the bureau?

Adm. S.: Yes, he was there.

Q: What was he working on? Asroc or something like that?

Adm. S.: I don't remember just what. I thought he was in the atomic business?

Q: He had been, yes.

Adm. S.: When I first went as Bureau Chief, the Deputy was Jack Snackenberg, a little, very handsome chap, sharp as a tack, and very able. He was with me for a year or so and then he was detached and went over I think it was to Norway on one of these liaison missions.

Q: With MAAG?

Adm. S.: Yes.
Then Deke Parsons came as my Deputy. Deke, of course, was a big atomic authority in those days and he was a ball of fire. I never will forget the horrible shock it was one morning to get down there to the office and find that this man who seemed so healthy the afternoon before was dead.

The story is that his wife woke up in the middle of the night and found him awake with a copy of the encyclopedia on his lap and he said:

"Well, it isn't so and so."

He had a pain in the upper thorax. She went back to sleep and the next thing she knew he was groaning and so forth. She got him to the hospital, and they started him from the ambulance to one of the laboratories and en route he died. Then Fred Withington came to take Parson's place and filled it until I retired.

We had a very ambitious program on computer mechanisms at that time. By the end of World War I, we had established at Dahlgren a very large computer for handling ballistic computations. Prior to that time, the Bureau had not had any machinery for this purpose. In fact, so far as I know, the only machinery for ballistic computations that existed was a computer of an early variety up at Aberdeen. Well, during the war, the bureau set up a big computer down there and, by the time I was Deputy Chief, a violent controversy was raging among the computer folk. The really far-out fellows looked upon our computer there as being something too crude to be mentionable because it was run by electric relays instead of by electronics. It had been devised by a fellow up at Harvard University, who ran an applied mathematics section up there. I went up to visit tim and he took me over and showed me around his place and he said he had a very difficult time with the "ivory tower" mathematicians up there. They looked upon applied mathematics as being nothing more than adding up a grocery list! He said:

"I have invited them all to come over and look at the place, and half of them won't even come over here."

He was a great exponent of the electric relay because, at that time, it was much more reliable than anything else, and his machines would grind out stuff very rapidly and in great quantity but they occupied a not-too-large building, about twice the size of this room, I guess. They operated on the basis that one machine would work a problem on the plus side and the other machine would simultaneously work the problem on the minus side, and then at the end they were supposed to meet and come to zero. If they didn't come to zero, you knew something was wrong.

Q: Soundslike an accountant, having to keep things in balance!

Adm. S.: Yes!

The Naval Ordnance Laboratory had a very splendid technical director - what the devil was his name, a great, big handsome chap - and his boys had dreamed up an extremely advanced computer that would be able to handle problems that the one down at Dahlgren couldn't think of touching. The Bureau had contracted for them with IBM to build this thing.

Well, first off, we ran into quite an argument with IBM because in those days they had a policy that they didn't sell their machinery to anybody, they just built it and rented it out.

Q: Yes.

Adm. S.: Eventually, we were able to overcome them on this one because there were obviously going to be few, if any, repeats of this machine.

I know many of the mathematical brains of the country looked rather askance at our machine because they thought it was too advanced. One of them, I know, told Parsons it was "a very challenging notion." Parsons was very palsy-walsy with the big physicist brains of the country. He knew them all on a first-name basis.

Things went along and IBM was doing pretty well in getting ready to deliver the machine, and they wanted to know just where to deliver it. Well, at that point, the Technical Director down at Dahlgren walked in and started pounding my desk and saying that we should set up Dahlgren as the "military computer center for the United States."

Q: Who was this, Ruckner?

Adm. S.: No, his first name was Cliff. He had been an instructor in mathematics at the PG school when I was a student there in '23, a little bit of a fellow, very, very able.

This left me a little aghast because the people out at NOL were the ones who had given birth to this notion, not Dahlgren, and I was further somewhat biased against Dahlgren because if this meant more personnel down there we had to provide housing for them, whereas NOL was just on the outskirts of Washington and you could tell people to go find themselves a place to live.

It got to be somewhat "smoke and flame" but finally I did a rather craven thing. I called in Parsons and said:

"Now look here, Deke, this problem is one that requires a great deal more technical knowledge than I shall ever have and I think you have it so you come to a decision as to which one of these places gets this thing, and I will stand by it."

I had hoped that he would decide in favor of the NOL but he finally decided in favor of Dahlgren. The computer had not yet been delivered when I retired, but I suppose it went down there because I understand that the place is now hardly a Naval Proving Ground any more but a Naval Computer Center.

Q: Did you have any considerable problems with the Congress and the budget in your term as chief of the bureau?

Adm. S.: Oh, we had our problems, yes, but they were not disabling in any way.

Q: Had your budget been increased again?

Adm. S.: I can't recall. Wait a minute. There was one problem. About my last year, we were pretty much scraping the bottom of the barrel for funds and were yelling for this and that and the other thing, and Congress passed an additional appropriatton. What do they call those additional ones? A supplementary appropriation. We were given $300 million, if I recall correctly, with the proviso that it had to be all contracted out by the end of the final year which was only three months away. This put a big strain on our machinery but the boys and girls got it done and done well. It was mainly for ammunition for the Korean War.

Q: I would think that it might result in some waste, too?

Adm. S.: I don't believe that there was any waste in it. I think it was a matter of -

Q: Such hasty -

Adm. S.: Very largely of bolstering up programs that needed money, and it was almost entirely production money. I don't think that there was much, if any, research money in that.

Q: Was that the reason for the stipulation? It was production money and they wanted to give a spurt to industry, or what?

Adm. S.: I don't know. I only know that manna fell from heaven and I didn't go around asking too much about how the manna got started!

Aside from facing them in the hearings, I almost never saw Congress, almost never. I had no social contacts with any of them.

A question arose about getting more Terrier missiles at sea than had previously been programed for.

Q: They were to be on cruisers, were they?

Adm. S.: Yes, this was the whole point. I attended a briefing over in the office of the CNO, largely by our people and some people from the Bureau of Ships, as to how much it would cost to modify one of the heavy cruisers to be a guided-missile ship, and it came to a figure that was almost the figure of building a brand-new cruiser. At that point, with no preparation on the subject, I stood up and argued against it. I said:

"This is god-damned foolishness, to spend all that money just to get one ship capable of firing missiles. What you seem to want to do is to have a great big magazine forward and a great big magazine aft and have just one spot out there in the ocean from which you can send out any missiles."

Our missile-test ship out on the West Coast had a Terrier setup which was comparatively modest, and I argued as well as I could for putting that sort of an arrangement on a good many ships. I felt sure that that could be done for the same amount of money that they were talking about for this one cruiser. However, I think the attitude of the meeting was, "Well, the old man is getting a little old and it's a good thing he's about to retire!" Because I know that my view did not prevail.

Q: No, they reconditioned what, the Chicago and one other, wasn't it?

Adm. S.: I don't recall just which ships, but I always thought that what we needed was a modest number of Terriers on the maximum number of ships, instead of a whole lot of Terriers in a very few ships.

Q: All the eggs in one basket, so to speak?

Adm. S.: Yes, and were you going to have the basket handy when the eggs were laid?

It eventually, about this time, became apparent that I was not going to be promoted. Quite a number of my juniors had already snapped up all the jobs that I would have liked to have. I would particularly have liked to be sent either as Commander, Second Fleet, or Commander, First Fleet. I think I would have been well qualified for either of those positions. Wu Duncan had said to me:

"The Secretary is looking for younger blood."

Q: The secretary at that point being Thomas?

Adm. S.: Yes, I think that's who it was.

So I applied for retirement having had by that time some thirty-six years of commissioned service. I had over the years seen certain admirals who stuck around and stuck around until they were of mandatory retirement age, and everybody had gotten to be a bit contemptuous of them, and they had just clogged up the promotion list for younger people. Furthermore, at that time, I felt that what I called "My index of employability" was at a maximum. So I retired and went with the General Precision Corporation.

Q: What job did you occupy there?

Adm. S.: They gave me the high-sounding title of Director of Weapons Planning.

Q: Where was this located?

Adm. S.: Their headquarters were in New York. They had a very large number of subsidiaries. They had no Washington office at that time, and I first established an office in Washington.

Q: How long did you stay with them?

Adm. S.: I was with them for about seven years.

Q: That's a nice way to end a business career, isn't it?

Adm. S.: Yes.

I spoke earlier, way back in my days in the Bureau of Aeronautics, of meeting a Mr. Reichel, of Russian descent. Well, at the time I retired, it was he very largely who got me my job. He was at that time chief engineer for the General Precision Corporation. Right after the end of the war, he went with a small outfit in New Jersey by the name of Kearfott. During the war the Kearfott company manufactured a lot of radio compasses for aircraft and were very successful at it, but primarily, they were a very small company engaged in a very restricted business, making airport frames for ships, round ones for oceangoing ships, square ones for ferry boats!

Q: A specialized business.

Adm. S.: Yes, and they had been in that business for many years. Right after the end of the war, Mr. Reichel got completely fed up with the tantrums of Mr. Bendix over in the Bendix Corporation, so he left there and went with Kearfott, and he built Kearfott up from a tiny little company into a company doing well over $100 million worth of business a year, largely in gyroscopes and fire control and many forms of electronics.

Schoeffel #6 - 361

The Kearfott Company amalgamated itself with General Precision and, as part of that amalgamation, Reichel became the chief engineer of General Precision. The Kearfott Company had been a sort of family company run by a splendid old gentleman, Mr. Herbert. I can remember a couple of years before I retired Mr. Herbert came down to see me and wanted my advice as to whether he should sell out to General Precision or not. I advised him to try to stay on his own feet. He and his family saw otherwise and I think they did well out of it.

General Precision no longer exists. It's now a part of the Singer Corporation.

Q: Oh, that huge combine?

Adm. S.: Yes.

Q: And you during that time served as anchor man in Washington, did you?

Adm. S.: Yes.

During my tour as Bureau Chief I had a very interesting contact in Canada with the Simard organization up there. While I was Deputy Chief, I got sent up to Canada with a delegation of our engineering talent to look over the Canadian ordnance organization with an idea of working with them. The invitation for the U.S. Bureau of Ordnance to go up there came, of all things, from the Canadian Air Force.

I arrived in Ottawa with my delegation and we were met by the Air Force people, only to discover that the Canadian Army and the Canadian Navy were both looking at this operation with a great deal of jaundice! They didn't know what the hell was up. Well, I guess we got the affair somewhat calmed down because we were taken off and we viewed all the Canadian ordnance operations at least in the eastern part of the country, from Toronto east, and they had a very considerable manufacturing capacity for small arms, but they had really no research capability whatever.

On the way back to the United States, we flew over the city of Sorel, which is on the St. Lawrence, at the mouth of the Richelieu River, and looked down and saw a great mass of what looked like modest-sized warships down there, cruisers, destroyers, and things like that. We asked what this was all about and somebody said that we were passing over the plant of the Simard organization, that they had large steel works there, and that they had bought up some two hundred warships of various varieties intending to scrap them and use them in their steel works.

Q: Largely Canadian ships, I suppose?

Adm. S.: Yes.

Q: Their World War II escort ships?

Adm. S.: Yes.

Then, when I went back as Chief of Bureau, I found that we had entered into a contract with the Simard organization for the manufacture of a large number, for that time, of very advanced 3-inch antiaircraft gunmounts of a more or less automatic design. I then became acquainted with Mr. Edouard Simard, who was the member of the family in charge of the Sorel operation, and they certainly had an operation there. They had a shipyard in which they had built twenty or thirty ships during World War II. They could work on ten ships at a time but they only had one launching way. They'd start a ship way out among the trees and the cows and then they would move it widewise to another spot, work some more on it, then move it sidewise farther. They had about ten stages before they finally got to the one launching way.

Q: The sort of thing they do at Ingalls now, isn't it?

Adm. S.: Do they?

Q: They've got more than one launching place, but they start a ship in one shipyard and move it over to another.

Adm. S.: I didn't know about that.

Well, this great navy of theirs had disappeared and naturally I wanted to know what happened to that, and Edouard said that when the Korean business broke out they sold most of these vessels back to the Canadian government, and he maintained that they sold them absolutely at cost price and the company did not make a nickel on the transaction.

Q: A patriotic gesture.

Adm. S.: Yes, and I think that he was telling me the truth because he was very much the gentleman. He had quite a history. He came from a family that had settled on the Saguenay about 1630 and he said, "My forbears were all either farmers or fishermen. My father was one step up. He had a small cargo-passenger boat that went out from Quebec and up the Saguenay, and," Edouard said, "when I came along everybody expected me to follow in the family footsteps." But he had, as a boy, saved up all his money and once a month he would go and spend a quarter for a copy of Popular Mechanics, then he'd spend all month reading every last word in it and soon he had it practically memorized.

Well, by the time he got to be in his late teens, the family realized that he was not going to follow in their footsteps, so they heard about some sort of a clerical job down in Sorel. He went down there and took that job and, after a year or two - this was back before World War I - he went in with a number of others and they bought out a very small shipyard there in Sorel. This shipyard just repaired canal boats because, he said, a lot of canal boats ran up the Richelieu River to Lake Champlain and then cut down the

Erie Canal and either went to New York or out to Buffalo. They would all go back to Sorel come winter to get repaired, and his little shipyard worked on them.

He said they had great difficulty scraping together enough money to buy the shipyard, about a dozen of them as partners, and he said:

"One of them had a rich wife. She put in $500," so they got the shipyard for, I think, $2,500.

Q: That was her total dowry, I suppose!

Adm. S.: They certainly had a hard time that first winter because they had to work on these canal boats and the canal boat owners didn't have any money and wouldn't have any until the next summer when they got going again. So he said:

"Every Saturday night we would have a meeting of the partners and decide how we were going to divide up such assets as we had. There's Joseph over there, he will get fifty cents, and Michel here he has a bushel of potatoes so he doesn't need anything," and that sort of thing.

Well, they got going. I don't know just what year this was but it was before World War I because in World War I they got into the business of making shells for the Canadian army and they made a lot more shells in World War II. I'd seen their factory at a distance and it was a rather respectable-looking operation.

They were having considerable difficulty in the manufacture of these gun mounts for us but they eventually achieved success and they had the first one ready for delivery. Some of these were for the Canadian navy but the majority were for the U.S. Navy.

Well, Simard invited me up there to be on hand for the ceremony he was going to put on, and what a ceremony! There were two special trains coming down from Ottawa. There was considerably more than a quorum of the Canadian parliament on hand, formed of both the Senate and of the House of Commons. The premier of Canada was there, St. Laurent, and the Simards put on a lunch in three great big circus tents. Everybody for miles around was there with their whole family, and French-Canadian families being what they are there were plenty.

Mr. St. Laurent wanted to go around and look the crowd over, being a politician, and I was invited to be among those who went trotting after him; and I could understand why he was a very good politician because he recognized people all over the place and he called them by their first names and he always spoke to them in the right language. He never made any errors. It was either English or French and he got it right every time.

Then, of course, came time for the speeches and up there every speech had to be in two languages. The speaker would carry on for a short paragraph and then the translator of the other language would repeat it, back and forth, back and forth.

Q: And he had to be adept himself in the second language.

Adm. S.: Yes. They really put on a great party, but after it was over and I returned to Washington, Mr. Simard unwittingly put me in a most embarrassing situation because he insisted that he must present me with a fine silver service. I fought, bled, and died trying to convince him that in the United States we just didn't do business that way, and he was all set to be completely insulted. Well, I didn't want to insult this fine fellow, so eventually I found a way out that I think worked. I said:

"Very well" - he insisted that my name be on the tray - "you engrave on there that this silver service is presented to the U.S. Navy's Bureau of Ordnance in the person of Rear Admiral Malcolm Schoeffel."

It was so engraved and, as of four or five years ago, just after my son had moved here, I was down in the new offices in Washington and my very dear secretary, Jean Child (oh, how she loved to trot out this silver service and serve tea) she brought it out!

Q: So it does belong to the U.S. Navy and it bears your name? That was a very sagacious solution and he accepted it?

Adm. S.: Yes, he accepted it. I presume - I'm not sure, I can't remember for sure, whether I did the proper thing and reported it to the Secretary of the Navy and got authority for receiving this thing, but if I didn't I was an idiot and I don't think I was quite that idiotic. I know that my dear friend and classmate, Harold Martin, was presented with a couple of Arab steeds by one of the Arabian emirs and had great difficulty in getting authority to hold onto them somehow.

Index to

Series of taped interviews

with

Rear Admiral Malcolm F. Schoeffel
U. S. Navy (Retired)

APPLIED PHYSICS LABORATORY - JOHNS HOPKINS: p. 301;

ARMORED CRUISERS: Schoeffel comments on the squadron of armored cruisers - their purpose and usefulness, p. 116-8;

USS AROOSTOOK (tender): p. 72; p. 79;

ARTIFICIAL HARBORS - for invasion of Honshu, p. 260;

ASW (Anti-Submarine Warfare): see entries under Car Div 6.

BAINTER, Fay: Actress - her romance with Comdr. Reggie Venable, p. 51-2; p. 54;

USS BATTLE FORCE - PACIFIC: Adm. Reeves becomes commander - asks for Schoeffel on staff, p. 147; the able staff assembled, p. 151-2; methods and plans for improving recovery of BB and CA planes, p. 153 ff; Schoeffel improves upon the net idea and it works successfully, p. 153 ff;

BLANDY, Capt. W. H. P.: Knox makes him Chief of BuOrd, p. 185; Schoeffel asked to come back as Aviation Assistant to the Director of Research, p. 186;

BOMB SIGHTS: early use, p. 125;

BRADLEY, Gen. Omar: p. 247;

USS BROOME: new DD commissioned in Philadelphia, p. 51; her romantic trip down the East River, p. 51 ff;

BROWN, Adm. C. R. (Cat.): p. 135-6;

BU AIR: Schoeffel assigned there to aircraft instruments desk, p. 99-100; the new air speed meter, p. 102;

BU ORD (Bureau of Ordnance): Schoeffel relieves Forrest Sherman on Aviation Desk, p. 168-70; interest in improved bombs, p. 170; p. 172-3; Adm. Stark is head of Bureau, p. 169; efforts to purchase Bofors and other guns - subject of proper guns not resolved, p. 173; Schoeffel again in BuOrd (1941) when Blandy comes in and reorganizes Bureau - this time Schoeffel is Aviation Assistant to Director of Research - chief job to find personnel to handle aviation ordnance matters, p. 186-7; Schoeffel serves as U. S. Navy rep on International Bomb Board, p. 189; torpedoes, p. 193-7; Schoeffel ordered back to Bureau (Apr. 1, 1946) as Deputy under Adm. Hussey, p. 283 ff; immediately confronted with budgetary hearings, p. 287-8; the item for AA fir control system wanted by the British, p. 287-8; the growth of the Bureau in WW II, p. 290; struggle with the Pullman

Company over special ammunition freight cars, p. 291; Schoeffel's tour of depots and plants, p. 292-4; Bureau appropriation is cut in half, p. 295-6; completion of ROL at White Oak, p. 297; Schoeffel's comments on mines, nets and booms, p. 298-9; early developments in rockets and guided missiles, p. 300 ff; the major project when Schoeffel took over as Chief was to get the guided missile program under way, p. 339 ff; Schoeffel named a czar for the TERRIOR missile production, p. 341 ff; the story of SIDEWINDER, p. 346 ff; Schoeffel comments on the loss of authority by the Bureau Chiefs to the Department of Defense, p. 347 ff; Schoeffel held frequent meetings with members of guided missile committee of the American Ordnance Association and the Naval Ordinance Advisory Committee, p. 348; the Bureau and computers, p. 352 ff; contracts with IBM to build an advanced computer, p. 353-4; the question of its location, p. 355; a supplementary appropriation has its problems, p. 356; Schoeffel argues against the conversion of a cruiser to a guided missile ship, p. 357;

BURROUGHS, Capt. Sherman E.: Assistant to Schoeffel in BuOrd (1936), p. 168;

BUTLER, VADM Henry B. Jr.: Commander - Aircraft, p. 159;

USS CABOT (light carrier): Schoeffel becomes first skipper (1943), p. 198 ff; shake down and training, p. 199-209; the Marshall Islands, p. 215-7; attack on Truck, p. 223-6; other operations, p. 227 ff; second attack on Truk, p. 231-3; Schoeffel detached, p. 233; p. 268;

CAR DIV 6: Schoeffel becomes Commander (late 1948), p. 305 ff; takes CORAL SEA to Mediterranean to operate under Adm. Sherman, p. 309 ff; account of visit to Greek Islands, Turkey, etc. p. 310 ff; ASW operations, p. 316-7; Amphibious operations, p. 316-7; Amphibious Operations (and ASW) in the Caribbean, p. 322;

CLARK, Admiral J. J. (Jocko): p. 214-5;

CNO - SHIP'S MOVEMENTS SECTION: Schoeffel (1940) ordered to section, p. 179; effort to get PBY's flown east from San Diego, p. 183-4;

COMINCH Staff: Schoeffel named as Assistant Chief of Staff for Operations, p. 235; a "stuffed shirt" job, p. 238;

CONNOLLY, Vice Admiral Tom: ran the Test Pilot's School at Patuxent, p. 332;

COOK, Admiral Charles (Savvy): p. 238; p. 240

USS CORAL SEA: Schoeffel takes her to the Mediterranean for short period under Adm. Sherman and the 6th fleet, p. 309; p. 311; p. 326;

CRETE: Schoeffel visits island in the CORAL SEA, p. 310-11;

CRISTOFORO COLOMBO - Italian training-sailing ship, p. 322;

DAHLGREN PROVING GROUND: Schoeffel, as naval aviator, on duty there (1931), p. 139; his main job - evaluation of the Norden Bomb Sight, p. 140 ff; experiments with bombs, p. 146-7; the computer for handling ballistic computations, p. 352-3; finally gets the advanced computer manufactured by IBM, p. 355-6;

DANIELS, The Hon. Josephus: p. 48; p. 54;

DAVIS, VADM Arthur: Schoeffel leaves VT-2 and becomes assistant to Lt. Comdr. Davis on Adm. Reeves' staff, p. 134 ff; p. 139; p. 235; p. 243;

DeLANY, VADM Walter S.: Assistant Chief of Staff for Readiness to Admiral King, p. 260-1;

DEMOBILIZATION - WW I; p. 48-9; navy efforts at recruitment to offset, p. 49-51;

DOOLITTLE, Lt. Gen. James H.: student at M.I.T. with Schoeffel, p. 91; his experiment with a Jenny off the Boston Lightship - with Schoeffel, p. 92-3;

DUNCAN, Admiral Donald: p. 358;

EARLY, Steven: Washington representative of Pullman Co., p. 291;

EDWARDS, Adm. Richard S.: p. 238; p. 240-2; p. 258;

EISENHOWER, Gen. Dwight D.: p. 246-8;

FLEET CAMERA PARTY: p. 166-8;

FLEET TRAINING: Schoeffel reports to Washington in June, 1935, p. 164; duties, p. 165-6; the Fleet Camera Party, p. 166-7;

FORD, Lt. Percival H. (Henry): leading Chief at Dahlgren when Schoeffel was there, p. 142; story of how he tamed an insane man who was on the rampage, p. 148 ff;

FORRESTAL, The Hon. James: Secretary of the Navy - Schoeffel briefs him and Adm. King on the report submitted by the special committee on unification - neither one was pleased with the proposals, p. 255-6; Forrestal works with an expert on a proposal to set up a Defense Department as a policy making outfit, p. 256;

FURLONG, RADM Wm. Rea: succeeds Adm. Stark as Chief of BuOrd - later dismissed by Secretary Knox, p. 170-2; p. 185;

GALLERY, Rear Admiral Daniel; p. 350;

GENERAL PRECISION CORPORATION: Schoeffel retires and goes with them to open a Washington Office, p. 358-9; p. 361;

GLASSFORD, RADM Wm.: skipper of the DD SHAW when she collides with AQUITANIA (1918), p. 36-8; p. 151;

GREER, VADM Marshall R.: p. 63; p. 73 ff;

GUANTANAMO: Schoeffel comments on great change in the base from earlier days, p. 307-8;

HALSEY, Fleet Admiral Wm.: visited by special committee investigating subject of unification, p. 254; the Battle of Leyte Gulf, p. 267-8; calls on Adm. King in Washington to report on Leyte, p. 269-70; Halsey 'the Bull', p. 275;

HAWAII: marine disaster involving explosion of ammunition on LST, p. 235; Schoeffel named to Court of Inquiry, p. 235-6;

HUSSEY, Admiral George: Chief of the Bureau of Ordnance, p. 283-4; p. 286; p. 289; he retires on physical disability, p. 294-5; p. 303;

INGRAM, Admiral Jonas H.: p. 276-7;

INTERNATIONAL BOMB BOARD: set up by JCS to develop designs for standardized bombs to be used by British and U. S. planes, p. 188; Schoeffel serves as Navy Rep., p. 189-91;

INYOKERN (China Lake): Schoeffel visits there, p. 293-4; p. 297-8; p. 342-3;

JAPANESE ARMY - in Manchuria: p. 280-1;

USS KIMBERLY: flush deck DD - Schoeffel assigned to her from Queenstown, p. 34; escorting the AQUITANIA, p. 35-7; the Battle of Bull Rock - an account of WW I listening gear, p. 40-41; state of torpedoes, p. 44; experiences with a vast storm, p. 46-7; put in reserve, p. 51;

KING, Fleet Admiral Ernest J.: p. 235; his manner of operating as COMINCH, p. 238-40; the staff mess at noon, p. 240-2; p. 255; p. 257-8; he telephones from Potsdam - about MacArthur's wishes for artificial harbors for use in invasion of Japan, p. 260 ff; his reactions to battles of the Philippine Sea and Leyte Gulf, p. 266-9; p. 274;

USS LANGLEY: p. 120; p. 125; p. 152

SS LAPLAND: British troop carrier, p. 29-31;

LEE, VADM Willis A.: on battleship desk in Fleet Training (June, 1935), p. 164-5;

SS LEVIATHAN: first duty after graduation - trip on transport to Brest (1918), p. 22 f; the coaling operation, p. 26-28;

USS LEXINGTON: joins the fleet, p. 128; the fleet problem - attack and defense of the Panama Canal, p. 128-9; King as skipper of the LEX, p. 137-8; p. 161-3;

LEYTE GULF: p. 267-9; Adm. Cook has Schoeffel make an analysis of the Halsey report on Leyte, p. 269-71;

LISTENING GEAR: WW I vintage, p. 39-40;

MacARTHUR, General Douglas: visited by special committee investigating wisdom of unification of armed forces, p. 252; he wanted artificial harbors for the proposed invasion of Honshu, p. 260-1; Schoeffel - With Adm. spruance - calls on the General - lunch at the Embassy, p. 278-9;

McCAIN, Admiral John Sydney: As Chief of BuAir he was senior navy member on JCS committee to study merger question of armed forces, p. 243 ff;

McNARNEY, Major Gen. Jos. T.: President of Consolidated Aircraft - present with Schoeffel at Inyokern for TERRIOR missile test, p. 342-3;

MAGIC - CODE BREAKING: p. 272-4;

MAGIC CARPET: p. 264 ff;

MAJURO: p. 220-2;

MORALE - in WW II: contrasted with WW I, p. 210-212;

MOULTON, Capt. Bobby: succeeds Read as skipper of the SARATOGA, p. 174-7; dies suddenly while ship anchored off Honolulu, p. 178;

U. S. NAVAL ACADEMY: appointment, p. 6-7; p. 12-13; summer cruises, p. 14-15; scholarship, p. 19; demerits and on the report for mutiny, p. 20-22; Schoeffel ordered back to Academy after M.I.T. to instruct in aerodynamics, p. 96-8;

NAVAL AIR TEST CENTER: Patuxent, Md. - Schoeffel takes over as Commander, p. 329-30 ff;

NAVIGATION: Celestial navigation for planes, p. 104 ff; Schoeffel tries some navigational experiments in flight to Norfolk - the results, p. 109-110;

NIMITZ, Fl. Admiral Chester W.: Schoeffel becomes (1946) his Assistant Chief of Staff for Plans and becomes involved with the MAGIC CARPET, p. 264-5; p. 277;

NOL (Naval Ordnance Laboratory) White Oak: p. 297;

NORDEN BOMB SLIGHT: p. 140-3; used experimentally in bombing tests on cruiser PITTSBURG, p. 145-6;

NORTH ISLAND: Schoeffel and others get more training - land planes on North Island, p. 73 ff;

USS OKLAHOMA: the newest of the battleships (1919), p. 16;

OZAWA, Vice Admiral J.: p. 271-2;

PARSONS, RADM Wm. S. (Deke): Deputy in BuOrd for Schoeffel - his sudden death, p. 351; p. 354-5;

PBY: efforts in 1940 to fly PBYs from San Diego to East Coast, p. 183-4;

PENSACOLA: Schoeffel ordered there (July, 1921) for flight training, p. 61; state of training in 1921, p. 63 ff; physical requirements for enrollment - illustrations of the tests given, p. 69-70; p. 145-6;

PG SCHOOL (1923): Schoeffel takes course in aeronautical engineering, p. 84 ff; the second year at M.I.T. p. 86-7;

PILOT TRAINING: example of inadequate training - reasons for, p. 227-30;

PIONEER INSTRUMENT CO. (Brooklyn), p. 100; company later merged with Russian inventors in Philadelphia, p. 103;

USS PITTSBURGH: Schoeffel transferred from BROOME to the flagship, p. 55; her trip to the Baltic - she runs aground, p. 56-7; the court of inquiry, p. 58-9; and the "fortunate" event that saved the skipper, p. 60; target practice in the Mediterranean, p. 60; p. 116; p. 118-9;

POLARIS: the first "gleam in papa's eye", p. 300-301;

QUEENSTOWN (Cobh), Ireland: in WW I, p. 33-4;

USS RANGER: Schoeffel becomes scouting commander, VS#1 on the new RANGER, p. 158; p. 159;

READ, Adm. Albert C.: skipper of the USS SARATOGA (1938), p. 174;

REEVES, Admiral Jos. Mason: As Commander Aircraft takes carriers south, p. 128; launches a night operation with dawn attack, p. 129; becomes commander of Fleet (1930) with Capt. A. B. Cook as Chief of Staff, p. 139; takes command of Battle Force p. 147; his outstanding staff, p. 151-2; succeeds Adm. Sellers as Cinc U. S. Fleet, p. 157;

REICHEL: Russian inventor - supplies air instruments to BuAir, p. 101 ff; becomes Chief engineer of General Precision Corporation - employs Schoeffel when he retired from the Navy, p. 360-1;

RICHARDSON, Admiral J. O.: senior member of JCS Committee to study subject of Unification of Armed Forces, p. 243 ff; trip to talk with commanders in the field, p. 246-51; to MacArthur in the Pacific, p. 251-55; Richardson files a minority report - Schoeffel signs regular report, p. 255;

USS SARATOGA: p. 128; p. 132-4; p. 158; Schoeffel (1938) becomes navigator, p. 173; FLEET EXERCISES IN Hawaii (1940), p. 175-8;

SCHOEFFEL, Rear Admiral Malcolm F.: background information, p. 1-2; early desire for naval service, p. 5; meets his future wife, p. 86; marriage while a student at M.I.T., p. 90; p. 104; p. 115; p. 139-40; his promotion to LCDR, p. 147-8; a family flight to Chicago, p. 179-80; promoted to Rear Admiral, p. 233; a serious attack of bursitis, p. 263-5; named as head of BuOrd (1951) p. 337; Schoeffel retires, p. 358-9; with General Precision Corp. for seven years, p. 359-60; Schoeffel describes a Canadian trip to view ordnance efforts, p. 361 ff;

SELLERS, Admiral David Foote: Cinc US Fleet, p. 156;

USS SHAW: DD cut in two by collision with SS AQUITANIA (1918), p. 36-8;

USS SHENANDOAH: lighter-than-air craft, p. 107;

SHERMAN, Admiral Forrest: Schoeffel relieves him as Assistant Chief of Staff for Plans on Nimitz' staff (1946), p. 263; in Command, 6th Fleet in Mediterranean - Schoeffel goes over in CORAL SEA to operate under him, p. 309 p. 315;

SHO PLAN: p. 271;

SHUMAKER, Capt. Samuel Robert: on Board of Inquiry with Schoeffel - dies of heart attack, p. 236-7; p. 262;

SIDEWINDER: the story of Sidewinder missile, p. 346 ff;

SIMARD, Edouard: head of Sorel, Canada branch of the family business, p. 361-3; the story of the Simard empire, p. 364-8;

SPRAGUE, Admiral Thomas L.: skipper of USS INTREPID, p. 232;

STARK, Admiral Harold R.: Chief of BuOrd, p. 169; succeeded by Adm. Furlong, p. 170-2;

STRAUSS, RADM Louis: his first appearance in BuOrd, p. 187-8;

STROOP, Adm. P.D.: in charge of bombing efforts on the cruiser PITTSBURG, p. 145-6;

SUBMARINES: their use as escorts for Battleships in exercises off San Diego, p. 122-3;

TALOS - missile: p. 344;

TERRIER - missile: p. 340 ff; the testing at Inyokern, p. 342; p. 357-8;

TOMLINSON, Capt. Daniel Webb IV (Injun Joe): Chief trainer at North Island, p. 74-5; p. 77-9; p. 125;

TOWERS, Admiral John: relieves Nimitz as CincPac, p. 277-8;

TOWNSEND, Lt. Comdr. Guy D.: takes 2nd year of PG school at M.I.T. with Schoeffel, p. 86 ff;

TORPEDOES: Schoeffel discusses the torpedo problem of the U. S. Navy at outset of WWII, p. 194 ff; also efforts to develop a flying bomb, p. 197-8;

TRUK: attack on, p. 223-4; p. 231-3;

TURNER, Admiral R. Kelly: becomes Chief of Staff to Adm. Butler, p. 158; criticizes Schoeffel and then apologizes, p. 16; p. 270;

UNIFICATION: JCS sets up special committee to consider post war (WW II) merger of Armed Forces - Schoeffel serves as a navy member, p. 243 ff;

UREY, Dr. Harold C.: p. 304;

VENABLE, Lt. Comdr. Reginald S. H. (Reggie): p. 51-5;

VINSON, The Hon. Carl: Chairman, Armed Services Committee, House of Representatives, p. 288;

VO-1: squadron to which Schoeffel reported on the AROOSTOOK, p. 79; exhibition flight to San Francisco, p. 79-81;

VS-1: Schoeffel becomes squadron commander - based on the RANGER, p. 158; practice carrier-type landings at night on the beach and then shipboard, p. 159-63;

VT-2: Schoeffel becomes flight officer attached to LANGLEY (1927), p. 120-2; the development of dive bombing, p. 124; plane types, p. 127; the fleet exercise involving the Panama Canal, p. 128 ff; the smoke screen laid by the "enemy fleet" - kudos for Schoeffel, p. 132-3;

WEEMS, Capt. Philip: his work in navigation, p. 105-6;

WRIGHT, Admiral Jerauld: p. 169;